The Intervention

ANITA HEISS is the author of non-fiction, historical fiction, commercial women's fiction, poetry, social commentary and travel articles. Anita has won four Deadly Awards for Outstanding Achievement in Literature, for her novels including *Manhattan Dreaming* and *Paris Dreaming* and for the Macquarie PEN Anthology of Aboriginal Literature. Anita is an Indigenous Literacy Day Ambassador and a proud member of the Wiradjuri nation of central New South Wales. She was a finalist in both the 2012 Human Rights Awards and the 2013 Australian of the Year Awards (Local Hero). Her latest novel is *Tiddas* (Simon & Schuster).

ROSIE SCOTT is an internationally published award-winning writer who has published six novels, a collection each of short stories, poems and essays and edited two anthologies. Her award-winning play *Say Thank You to the Lady* was the basis for the film *Redheads*, which received several international prizes. She is a permanent member of the Council of Australian Society of Authors, received the Sydney PEN Award, and she and Tom Keneally were nominated for the Human Rights Medal. She was a co-founder of Women for Wik. She was nominated for the education section of 100 most influential people in Sydney for her work in mentoring and teaching asylum seekers. Her last novel *Faith Singer* was on the international list of 50 Essential Reads by Contemporary Writers compiled by the Orange committee, the *Guardian* and Hay Festival. Her latest book is *A Country Too Far*, an anthology on asylum seekers co-edited with Tom Keneally. In 2016 she was awarded the Special Prize at the NSW Premier's Literary Awards.

The Intervention
An Anthology

Edited By
Rosie Scott & Anita Heiss

A NewSouth book

Published by
NewSouth Publishing
University of New South Wales Press Ltd
University of New South Wales
Sydney NSW 2052
AUSTRALIA
newsouthpublishing.com

© Anita Heiss and Rosie Scott 2016
First edition published by 'concerned Australians' in 2015. This edition published 2016.

10 9 8 7 6 5 4 3 2 1

This book is copyright. While copyright of the work as a whole is vested in University of New South Wales Press Ltd, copyright of individual chapters is retained by the chapter authors. Apart from any fair dealing for the purpose of private study, research, criticism or review, as permitted under the Copyright Act, no part of this book may be reproduced by any process without written permission. Inquiries should be addressed to the publisher.

National Library of Australia
Cataloguing-in-Publication entry
Title: The intervention: an anthology / Rosie Scott and Anita Heiss (editors).
Edition: 2nd edition
ISBN: 9781742235127 (paperback)
      9781742242460 (ebook)
      9781742247861 (ePDF)
Notes: Includes bibliographical references.
Subjects: Intervention (Federal government)—Northern Territory.
Aboriginal Australians—Northern Territory—Government relations.
Aboriginal Australians—Northern Territory—Social conditions.
Human rights—Australia.
Other Creators/Contributors:
Scott, Rosie, 1948–, editor.
Heiss, Anita, 1968–, editor.
Dewey Number: 362.849915

Design Josephine Pajor-Markus
Cover design Xou Creative
Cover images FRONT COVER: 'Customised NT Intervention sign', entrance to Daguragu community, May 2011. Photography copyright/courtesy Brenda L. Croft; customised protest artwork by John Leeman referencing Aboriginal Flag (copyright Harold Thomas, 1971).
BACK COVER: 'Fight racism' sign, entrance to Kalkarindji community, May 2011. Photograph copyright/courtesy Brenda L. Croft. INSIDE FRONT COVER: 'We know where we stand', 45th Gurindji Freedom Day Anniversary banner, 2011. Photography credit copyright/courtesy Brian T. Manning, artwork copyright/courtesy Chips Mackinolty. INSIDE BACK COVER: 'Trespassers keep out', screenprint 1982 (detail), copyright/courtesy Avril Quaill.

All reasonable efforts were taken to obtain permission to use copyright material reproduced in this book, but in some cases copyright could not be traced. The author welcomes information in this regard.

CONTENTS

ANITA HEISS & GEORGINA GARTLAND
Preface to new edition ... ix

ROSIE SCOTT Introduction ... 1

ANITA HEISS We Are Many Nations But We Are One People ... 7

ROSALIE KUNOTH-MONKS Reflections on the Intervention – Quotes Made between 2011 and 2014 ... 14

PAT ANDERSON The Intervention: Personal Reflections ... 26

RACHEL WILLIKA A Statement, 2 October 2007 ... 40

DJINIYINI GONDARRA Quotes from Speeches on the Intervention ... 43

P.M. NEWTON 567,000 km Driven ... 48

CHRISTINE OLSEN Crossing the Gap ... 53

YINGIYA MARK GUYULA A Statement, June 2011 ... 57

LARISSA BEHRENDT The Dialogue of Intervention ... 61

NATALIE HARKIN Intervention: A Poem ... 71

DJINIYINI GONDARRA Response to the Prime Minister – Julia Gillard's Announcement of a Second Intervention in the Northern Territory, 26 June 2011 ... 72

DEBRA ADELAIDE Welcome to Country ... 74

NICOLE WATSON From the Northern Territory Emergency Response to Stronger Futures – Where is the Evidence that Aboriginal Women are Leading Self-Determining Lives? ... 82

JOHN LEEMANS Media Release from the Gurindji, 28 July 2011   96

MELISSA LUCASHENKO What I Have Heard About the Intervention – Trigger Warning: Rape. Paedophilia. Racist Violence   99

LIONEL FOGARTY Philosophies Exterminated   104

DJINIYINI GONDARRA A spokesperson for the independently established Yolŋuw Makarr Dhuni (Yolngu Nations Assembly), Statement 2011   106

JEFF McMULLEN Rolling Thunder: Voices Against Oppression   107

NORTHERN TERRITORY ELDERS AND COMMUNITY REPRESENTATIVES Press Conference Statement, Melbourne, 4 November 2011   128

BRUCE PASCOE Bread   132

ALI COBBY ECKERMANN Four poems

    Intervention Payback   141

    Unearth   144

    A Parable   145

    40-Year Leases   146

JOHN LEEMANS Stronger Futures, 11 June 2012   147

BRENDA L. CROFT Signs of the Times   149

RODNEY HALL The Constitutional Connection   165

YOLNGU STATEMENT 24 June 2012   174

SAMUEL WAGAN WATSON Intervention Rouge – A Poem   177

DJINIYINI GONDARRA AND ROSALIE KUNOTH-MONKS
Yolngu Nations Assembly and the Alywaar Nation Media
Release, 27 June 2012 — 179

EVA COX The Intervention: Bad Policy and Bad Politics — 181

DENI LANGMAN Traditional Owner of Uluru – A Letter to
the Politicians of Australia Who Will Debate the Stronger
Futures Legislation, June 2012 — 197

ARNOLD ZABLE Here is Where We Meet — 199

YALMAY YUNUPINGU Human Rights and Social Justice
Award – Excerpts from her Keynote Speech,
24 June 2014 — 212

ALEXIS WRIGHT Be Careful About Playing With the Path
of Least Resistance — 215

YOLNGUW MAKARR DHUNI Stronger Futures,
October 2013 — 228

CONTRIBUTORS — 230

ACKNOWLEDGMENTS — 244

NOTES AND SOURCES — 248

ANITA HEISS & GEORGINA GARTLAND

PREFACE TO NEW EDITION

The Intervention began in 2007. The first edition of this Anthology was published in 2015 where we tried to tell the story of this unprecedented policy and give voice to the opposition to it. This collection remains relevant and in demand and this new edition will ensure that it remains in print.

There is demand for this book in classrooms where human rights issues, especially relating to Indigenous Australians, are highlighted. The demand for ways to use the Anthology further has led to the development of teacher's notes, available through the publisher's website. Education of the general Australian public to the 'facts' of what has happened under Australian legislation was one of the main purposes of this Anthology.

The book has clearly made a significant contribution to understanding the impact of the extraordinarily extensive intrusion into the lives of Indigenous people in the Northern Territory (NT). This is very gratifying for me, my co-editor Rosie Scott and all the contributors. But the legislation still stands, so the struggle continues.

So much time has passed since Prime Minister John Howard and his Indigenous Affairs Minister Mal Brough announced the Northern Territory National Emergency Response in June 2007 that it is worth reflecting on the chain of events.

On 15 May 2006, ABC's *Lateline* aired a program about alleged widespread sexual abuse and domestic violence in Aboriginal communities. The program spoke to Nanette Rogers, the Crown Prosecutor in Alice Springs, who had three years of experience as a public defender in the NT. And so the call for an intervention began.

On 8 August the NT government established a Board of Inquiry into the Protection of Aboriginal Children from Sexual Abuse. This inquiry was co-chaired by Pat Anderson, who appears in this book, and Rex Wild QC. The purpose of the Inquiry was to find better ways of protecting Aboriginal children from sexual abuse. After extensive consultation with Indigenous people, they produced the 2007 'Little Children are Sacred' report.

This report identified measures that its authors believed were central to addressing the allegations of child sexual and other abuse: dialogue, community empowerment, ownership, awareness, healing, reconciliation, strong family, safe communities, culturally relevant programs, law. In short Anderson and Wild wanted 'both [the NT and Federal] governments [to] commit to genuine engagement and consultation with Aboriginal people'.[1]

This consultation never happened. On 15 June 2007, the 'Little Children are Sacred' report was made public. But before due consideration could be given to the report, only six days later on 21 June Howard and Brough announced their plan to introduce the Northern Territory Emergency Response (NTER), which became known as 'the Intervention'.[2] At the time the report was misquoted and government leaders misrepresented the facts, statistics and NT Aboriginal communities – and spoke of paedophile rings. In 2009 such claims were disproved by the Australian Crime Commission (ACC) – yet there has been no apology.[3]

The measures they unveiled were unprecedented. They necessitated the suspension of the *Racial Discrimination Act 1975* (RDA) and included deployment of military personnel to Aboriginal towns and communities across the NT; bans on pornography and alcohol; prohibition of considering customary law in bail and sentencing; quarantining of welfare payments; compulsory acquisition of seventy-three remote communities,[4] associated outstations and ten town camp regions, of townships held under provisions of the *Native Title Act*; the phasing out and scrapping of the successful Community Development Employment Projects (CDEP) scheme; and the transfer of workers onto income support for other agendas – including the control of their income and expenditure behaviour.⁵

Anderson and Wild were anguished that their 2007 report was misused for these purposes and all its recommendations dumped.

On 6 August 2007, the *Northern Territory National Emergency Response Act* (NTNERA) – which as we will see in this book was bipartisan policy – was rushed through the Senate and passed. The NTNERA did not once mention the words 'child protection'.

Kevin Rudd became Prime Minister in November 2007 with Jenny Macklin as the Indigenous Affairs Minister. The Rudd government ordered a review of the Intervention,⁶ which was released in October 2008 amid controversy. Significant recommendations were ignored, including the need to engage and reset relationships with Aboriginal people and to reinstate the RDA. It found the NTNERA was discriminatory and yet controversial aspects like compulsory income management were retained, despite advice to the contrary.

Two senior officials from the UN Commission on Human Rights visited Aboriginal communities in 2009. They reported the Intervention was racially discriminatory, took control away from Aboriginal communities and stigmatised Aboriginal people. They noted that the special measures were not compliant with United Nations (UN) guidelines and the Intervention was inherently flawed. They found the NTNERA was not benefitting the people, infringed basic human rights and breached Australia's international obligations. UN officials requested that the government redesign the Intervention in partnership with Aboriginal people and called for a holistic approach.⁷ These recommendations were quickly dismissed by Minister Jenny Macklin.⁸

In 2009 John Lawler of the ACC determined, after an 18-month multimillion-dollar investigation, that there was no 'organised paedophilia in indigenous communities'.⁹

A year later in 2010 the UN Committee on the Elimination of Racial Discrimination (CERD) confirmed its serious ongoing concerns with discrimination under the NT Intervention and recommended that 'special measures' in Australian law be made compliant with the Committee's 2009 guidelines,[10] and that the RDA be reinstated and prevail over other legislation.[11] On 31 December 2010 the RDA was reinstated, yet only superficially.[12] As noted in *Walk With Us*, published by 'concerned Australians' in 2011:

> During the Senate Inquiry that preceded this legislation there had been numerous calls for a *'not withstanding'* clause to accompany the reinstatement of the RDA in order for it to be able to override any other discriminatory legislation. This did not happen. The result is that the RDA is unable to protect Aboriginal people in the Northern Territory from measures entrenched in law that discriminate against them.[13]

As we write in 2016 the special measures remain non-compliant and they still have not been consented to.[14]

Against the will of NT Aboriginal people, the Intervention was rebadged in 2012 and extended for another 10 years.[15] There was a clear decision by government to discriminate at almost every level in the process of transferring Intervention legislation across to (the ironically named) *Stronger Futures in the Northern Territory Act 2012*.[16] Deni Langman, a tradional owner of Uluru, calls this legislation 'Stolen Futures' in her letter on page 197 of this Anthology.[17]

The legislation passed through the Senate in the early hours of 29 June 2012. Again, little public attention was given to it. A major component related to income management. While some changes had been made in 2010 to include a new form of *voluntary* income management, blanket and *compulsory* income management could also still be imposed under set conditions. These changes were rolled out in 2010 to other welfare recipients in the NT and then later to other trial areas outside of the NT in an attempt to make this major social welfare reform agenda appear non-discriminatory.[18] However, compulsory income management continues to impact mostly

PREFACE TO NEW EDITION

on Aboriginal people and has recently been shown to remain discriminatory and ineffective.[19] Other paternalistic, punitive and controlling measures have similarly proved unhelpful.

One of these is the School Enrolment and Attendance through Welfare Reform Measure (SEAM) program whereby parents' income support can be suspended if their children consistently fail to attend school. SEAM has been proven to not be effective and there are other serious misgivings as shown in a recent 2016 review.[20] However, the Parliamentary Joint Committee on Human Rights (PJCHR) has not looked at Aboriginal solutions or priorities and instead recommended more social workers and the need to improve SEAM.[21]

It's only a year since the 2015 release of the first edition of this Anthology yet there have been many changes in Australian politics. Here are those most relevant to this book:

> Mal Brough, the architect of the Intervention has become implicated in the Peter Slipper affair for reasons far removed from this policy. He announced in February 2016 that he wouldn't seek pre-selection for his seat when it was revealed that he was being investigated by the Australian Federal Police. Yet he leaves behind a toxic policy that continues to deny the human rights of those it impacts on. Mal Brough's grossly inflammatory comments and other distortions allowed the easy roll out of the Intervention.[22] This has been overlooked by most.[23]

> The NT Intervention has been shown to have failed.[24] Professor Jon Altman's unrelenting voice of concern and critique of the Intervention and subsequent polices throughout has remained steadfast but sidelined by government.[25] In addition, a March 2016 report by the Castan Centre for Human Rights identified failures in human rights and found that most gaps that were being addressed are in fact widening.[26] The Intervention has not benefitted Aboriginal people. The rate of Aboriginal self-

harm, violence and incarceration has skyrocketed in the NT. Incarceration rates are not even included in Closing the Gap statistics – in fact they are denied, despite ongoing and more recent calls for including them.[27]

In March 2016, the Commonwealth Government handed alcohol management powers of Aboriginal communities back to the NT Government. The Stronger Futures review of this measure was damning and recommendations made that these powers revert to go back to Aboriginal communities.[28] Communities such as Elliott, 750 kilometres south of Darwin, are hoping to introduce their own alcohol management plan. It's often forgotten that prior to the Intervention 80 per cent of remote communities were dry.

The Royal Commission into Institutional Responses to Child Sexual Abuse has reminded us that sexual abuse is everywhere, not just in remote communities in the NT. Indeed statistics at the onset of the NTNERA seem to have been grossly distorted by our nation's leaders.[29]

There is a growing pool of evidence – including information contained in this and other books and reports – of the escalating rates of Indigenous self-harm, suicide and violence.[30] And, there remains a lack of transparency and accountability in the implementation of the Stronger Futures measures.[31]

In February 2016 the Australian Greens fought to retain the independent review into Stronger Futures. The Turnbull government, supported by the Labor Party, had in October 2015 looked at removing section 117 of the *Stronger Futures in the Northern Territory Act*, which required an independent review of the Act's first three years. The review was originally due in June 2015. Clearly the government does not want its flawed legislation to come under any scrutiny.

PREFACE TO NEW EDITION

In March 2016, long-awaited and overdue, the PJCHR released its second review, 'Review of Stronger Futures'. The review failed to address the recommendations of the previous committee's concern regarding flawed government consultations and their failure to abide by the 'Features of a Meaningful and Effective Consultation Process'.[32] While this review also examined for the first time land reform measures in community living areas, again it overlooked serious concerns. It is beyond the scope of this Preface to address this report in detail, but we urge interested readers to seek out the book, *In the Absence of Treaty*, that backgrounds serious concerns on loss of land control and the removal of the onus on the government to consult with the people.[33]

The PJCHR review was damning of measures like SEAM and compulsory income management, which were seen to be race based, ineffective, and limiting of other rights – including the right to social security and to an adequate standard of living. But, as Stronger Futures is approved government (and bi-partisan) policy, it recommended a continuation of the measures with few modifications. There is no onus on the government to respond.

Again, Aboriginal priorities such as housing, health, quality education, culturally relevant services, affordability of food, land control, the right to live and work on country, the right to be consulted and included in decisions from the outset of policy formation, and the right to self-determination and sovereignty have been overlooked.

Consultations over land reform issues are no longer guaranteed.[34] Food security is an increasing concern and there are have been dystopic reports of starvation at Homelands in the Utopia region made by remote community leader and Anthology contributor, Rosalie Kunoth-Monks, as recently as

April 2016, nearly nine years after the initial Intervention.[35] Rosalie has also spoken of profound disempowerment and despair – the worst in decades – within her community.

In March 2016, a Senate Finance and Public Administration Committee tabled its final report into the Indigenous Advancement Strategy (IAS) – introduced by the now-deposed Prime Minister Tony Abbott. The IAS was labelled chaotic and deeply flawed.[36] And because $534 million had been cut from the Indigenous Affairs portfolio many Aboriginal organisations missed out on funding and have ceased. There has also been a mainstreaming of Aboriginal services, so that community members are required to use mainstream services as opposed to community controlled and focused providers. (When services are 'mainstreamed' they do not incorporate the cultural values or practices of Aboriginal groups and they are often not attended by Aboriginal people for those reasons.) The Committee recommended a full internal review of the IAS to be undertaken of the Department of Prime Minister and Cabinet (DPM&C). The Australian National Audit Office 'has an audit underway to assess whether the department of PM&C has effectively established and implemented the IAS. The report is due to be tabled in spring 2016.'[37] In the meantime Jon Altman, following the 2016 budget, has called a radical shake-up in the next parliament and for a 'Stand alone Indigenous Specific Agency' to take over the functions that sit currently under the DPM&C.[38]

As this book goes to print an election has been called by Prime Minister Turnbull. Pat Dodson, former Chair of the Council for Aboriginal Reconciliation, has entered the Australian Senate as a replacement on a casual vacancy for Western Australia. He is opposed to the Intervention, as is the departing Labor Party senator for the NT Nova Peris, and the Australian Greens. Pat

PREFACE TO NEW EDITION

Dodson's frustration with Malcolm Turnbull and the continued policy of exclusion was palpable. Earlier this year Dodson added:

> So unless Mr Turnbull and his Government has some other methodology, they need to put it on the table so that Indigenous participation can take place. Without that, the ideas around improving the quality of life for Indigenous peoples are going to be fraught with difficulty.[39]

While no-one assumes that this Anthology will influence policy making, it is hoped that the words within will bring these serious concerns to the fore and onto the national agenda and have more people talking about the failures, discrimination and denial of rights of Australia's First Nations people. The people who hold the solutions are ignored and denied the right of participation. Indigenous affairs is in 'deep, deep crisis'.[40]

Increasingly we have heard calls from Aboriginal people to walk with them and for a restoration of their fundamental human rights, human dignity and for the right to determine their futures.

This Anthology is a plea, a call to action for all who read it. We need you to continue to listen to the people, read beyond the bombardment of negative stereotypes, or government rhetoric, and to pressure the Australian Government to repeal the Stronger Futures legislation.

ROSIE SCOTT
INTRODUCTION

Anita Heiss and I decided to publish an anthology gathering together some of Australia's best writers and thinkers to analyse and illuminate one of the most invasive, puzzling and unprecedented actions by a government in Australian history – the 2007 Intervention by the Howard government.

We think that these writers and Indigenous leaders will bring a new perspective and urgency to an issue that has remained largely outside the public radar.

We believe that the basic premises of this intervention are deeply flawed, resulting in a serious breach of human rights. It has never been fully debated nationally nor has there been significant consultation with the Indigenous communities most affected.

In June 2007 Prime Minister John Howard announced after the tabling of the 'Little Children are Sacred' report, 'It is a disgrace that a section of the Australian population, those little children, should be the subject of serious sexual abuse.'

A week or so later the Howard government staged a massive military and police Emergency Response costing $587 million, as outlined in the *NT National Emergency Response Act 2007*.

This Act prescribed a number of drastic measures which appeared strangely irrelevant to their stated aim of combating child abuse. Some of these measures contravened the *Racial Discrimination Act 1975* and several revolved around land use. Nowhere in this very extensive legislation was there a significant mention of a child or children.

Since then there has been little or no change in the figures of child sexual offending in the Northern Territory.

This extraordinary, costly and largely unexplained action has had immense and long-reaching effects on the very cornerstones of Indigenous community and identity. There has now been substantial evidence gathered that much of this change has been negative.

As the Intervention has morphed into Stronger Futures for another ten years in a disgraceful bipartisan agreement, many commentators have been asking what the justification for this continuation is, given the alarming figures of increasing suicide rates, child health problems and unemployment.

The fact is the real motives of this Intervention have never been fully explained or justified and in spite of constant opposition by Indigenous communities, most significant Elders, peak human rights organisations as well as other Australians across a broad spectrum, the situation remains the same with only a few cosmetic touches.

We have published the voices of the Elders and other Northern Territory Indigenous community leaders in their many communiqués, media releases and statements issued throughout the period. As time goes on, the tone of these statements becomes angrier, more despairing and anguished as their very reasonable requests are simply ignored by the authorities and the Intervention is kept in place.

We believe this collection of essays, fiction, poetry and memoir by leading Australian writers and statements by the Elders will give a new perspective, power and clarity to an issue that will continue to be highly controversial. And most importantly, we believe the role of the writer in this instance is to make Australian readers think about the plight of other largely voiceless Australians.

Many voices both Indigenous and non-Indigenous have been raised in eloquent protest against the Intervention ever since its first announcement by John Howard. Contrary to the carefully managed spin that there is deep disagreement within the Indigenous community, the fact is there is strong consensus about the Northern Territory Intervention among most experts, people on the ground and organisations.

Introduction

Most importantly, the majority of Elders and community leaders in the Northern Territory oppose it, some of whom have petitioned the United Nations. These include Rosalie Kunoth-Monks of Utopia, Djiniyini Gondarra of Galiwin'ku, Harry Nelson of Yuendumu, Djapirri Mununggirritj from Yirrkala, Yananymul Mununggurr from the Laynhapuy Homelands, Diane Stokes at Muckatty Station, Maurie Ryan and John Leemans at Kalkarindji, Reggie Wurridjal and Helen Williams at Maningrida, Joy White with the Larrakia mob in Darwin, Barbara and Walter Shaw in the Alice Springs Town Camps, Dhanggal Gurruwiwi from Wallaby Beach, Matthew Dhulumburrk Gaykambayu from Ramingining, Miriam Rose Ungunmerr-Baumann of Nauiyu, and Rachel Willika, Yalmay Yunupingu and George Gaymarani Pascoe of Milingimbi.

Local groups like Stop the Intervention Collective, Sydney, and Intervention Rollback Action Group, Alice Springs, which have worked so hard to publicise the facts, organisations representative of local Indigenous people like Yolŋuw Makarr Dhuni, eminent Indigenous and non-Indigenous figures like Tom Calma, Lowitja O'Donoghue, the late Malcolm Fraser, Alastair Nicholson, Chris Graham and Olga Havnen as well as international organisations like the UN, Amnesty and church groups have all stated their strong opposition.

One dissenting voice had a particularly powerful effect on me personally. Rachel Willika, a Jaowyn Elder from the remote community of Manyallaluk spoke at a protest meeting we at Women for Wik convened in 2007 in Sydney when news of the Intervention had broken. This meeting was chaired by Dr Anita Heiss and addressed by eminent Indigenous women we'd invited from the Territory. These women included Olga Havnen, the then national Indigenous leader from the newly formed Combined Aboriginal Organisations, Eileen Cummings, and former advisor to the Chief Minister of NT on Aboriginal and Women's Affairs, her daughter Raelene Rosase. An emotional and attentive audience packed the hall and spilled out into the foyer.

Rachel Willika had never been on a plane before, or to Sydney but she stood in front of us with quiet dignity and grace. Her speech was one of the most eloquent and powerful I've ever heard and moved many of the audience to tears. And, in my case anyway, to action. Her description of the fear in their community when the soldiers came has stayed with me permanently and so in part inspired this anthology.

In a statement to the *Guardian* at around the same time she said, 'That John Howard has no heart. This intervention is hurting Aboriginal families.'

It is no coincidence that eloquent speech has the power to spur people to political action.

And as always, writers, filmmakers, painters and other artists have been major players in this history of analysis and dissent.

There are some towering examples of this: *The Swan Book* by Alexis Wright and the movies *Charlie's Country* by David Gulpilil, *Our Generation*, a superb documentary film by Sinem Saban and Damien Curtis, and John Pilger's *Utopia*.

All of these have received serious recognition, mostly internationally. David Gulpilil received a standing ovation and the prestigious prize for best actor in the Un Certain Regard section at Cannes, also winning best lead actor for the Australian Academy Cinema Television Arts awards. *Charlie's Country* won best film and best director at the Film Critics Circle of Australia Awards. It's safe to say this film will receive more awards.

Our Generation was voted best campaign film in the London International Documentary Festival, and Pilger's *Utopia* was voted by the London Film Review as one of the five best films of the year. Alexis Wright's critically acclaimed book, which I believe will become an Australian if not international classic, was shortlisted for all the major prizes including the Miles Franklin, the NSW Premier's, the Stella and the Voss. A review in the *Sydney Morning Herald* described *The Swan Book* as possibly 'one of the most important Australian novels yet,' another in the *Sydney*

Introduction

Review of Books '... and perhaps the first truly planetary novel.'

Other more direct examples of eloquent voices raised are those of people like Rosalie Kunoth-Monks, Djiniyini Gondarra, Pat Dodson, Jeff McMullen, Tom Calma, Jon Altman, Judy Gurruwiwi, Barbara Shaw, Paddy Gibson, and many others. Their passionate speeches around Australia are powerful examples of inspiring oratory when all too often dumbed down, evasive, clichéd and impenetrable bureaucratic language is the norm for the authorities defending the Intervention.

These people are true Australian heroes. They spend many hours travelling around Australia speaking and campaigning about what the Intervention actually means to the people who are suffering through it.

When we decided to compile this anthology we were delighted with the calibre of writers who agreed to contribute and felt very confident about putting our proposal forward to publishers. Six months later not one publisher took the project on, though most said it was a great project with an excellent list.

But thanks to heart-warming support from the community – a dedicated group of women, who called themselves Women Inspired to Action, or WITA for short, raised funds for us through crowd-funding – with generous contributions from people all over Australia; a generous grant from the CAL Cultural Fund; keen interest and support from the late Michele Harris and the members of 'concerned Australians', an extraordinarily generous offer by Graeme Jones and Tracey Kirby of Kirby Jones to do our typesetting and design free, the committed work of Tara Wynne of Curtis Brown and people like Pamela Hewitt and Danny Vendramini who have donated their time and expertise; we have been able to continue with our plans to publish this book in 2015.

So this is our hope for the anthology – that our distinguished list of Australian writers and Elders will join in with these other artists, supporters and community leaders to provide an in-depth, eloquent and thoughtful dimension to this urgent debate, so long neglected by mainstream Australia. We believe that the truthfulness, clarity and passion of their language will provide an inspiring antidote to the spin and disinformation which has been the official language of the Intervention up until now.

Above all we intend this anthology of eloquent Australian voices to take the debate to a wider audience and through this unique compilation prove that the abuse of human rights by the Northern Territory Intervention has no place in this country.

The Intervention: An Anthology is an extraordinary document – deeply moving, impassioned, spiritual, angry and authoritative – it's essential reading for anyone who wants to understand what lies behind this passionate opposition.

ANITA HEISS

WE ARE MANY NATIONS BUT WE ARE ONE PEOPLE

I was in the Northern Territory at a writers' event in June 2007 when the Howard government with the support of Labor and the Democrats rolled out the NT Intervention. Three months later I chaired a public forum organised by Women for Wik at Australia Hall in Sydney on 14 September. It was there I heard first hand from Northern Territory Aboriginal women about what was happening in their affected communities. Olga Havnen, Eileen Cummings, Raelene Rosas and Rachel Willika shared stories to a packed hall of concerned Australians wanting to know how they could help get the power back into the hands of those who had lost control over their own lives. It was one of the most emotional gatherings outside of funerals I have ever attended.

I remembered those women as I wrote my first blog 'Rallying the Troops to Get Out of the NT'. It was 12 February 2008 and the evening before the National Apology to the Stolen Generations. But the much-awaited 'Sorry' would follow a day when thousands of Australians converged on the capital to demand the human rights of Aboriginal people in the Northern Territory be reinstated.

The rally saw people travel across the country specifically to declare their disgust at the racist legislation. I met young Nyungah woman Natasha Moore who had travelled from Perth just for the day. We met as the crowds gathered at the site of the Tent Embassy on the lawns of Old Parliament House. We stood there after Ngambri Elder Matilda House had welcomed politicians to the 42nd sitting of Parliament – a ground-breaking moment in Australian political history.

After we were given a welcome by the Tent Embassy mob at the ceremonial fire we marched, led by our brothers and sisters from the Northern Territory. I marched alongside friends I'd gone to university with twenty years earlier, supporters of Residents for Reconciliation in Western Sydney I'd met ten years before, family members I was meeting for the first time, local school students in full uniform, and many others (black and white) who were united under the banner 'STOP THE INTERVENTION – HUMAN RIGHTS NOW'.

There were many familiar faces there on the day, some locally from Sydney and others from across the country. The band Street Warriors and poets Kerry Reed-Gilbert and Elizabeth Hodgson were there. It didn't matter what nation you came from, we were one mob and we were united in fighting for the rights of our brothers and sisters in the Northern Territory. I noticed that even though I'd rallied in four different states in the previous fifteen years on issues such as land rights, black deaths in custody, budget cuts to Aboriginal affairs, the Stolen Generations and the Intervention, this was the first rally I had ever participated in that didn't have police lining the streets or watching our moves. There was not one cop to be seen, until we arrived at Parliament House and saw they formed a protective barrier around the building.

The wide range of media present spoke volumes about how the convergence on Canberra was being regarded generally. Apart from the expected Indigenous print, TV and radio media, there was mainstream media from every medium also. I was heartened by the media interviewing key members of the NT communities represented on site, because it meant that our issues, the issues of Australia, would get some mainstream coverage. It would further put the Rudd government on notice for what we expected from his term in office, aside from the Apology.

I spent much of my day with Aunty Eileen Cummings from the Northern Territory whom I'd met at the Sydney meeting of Women for Wik in 2007. Aunty was part of the Women for Wik monitoring project to keep a check on what is happening in the NT in lieu of any formal accountability process put in place by the government. When I listened and watched her interviewed by Gunditjmara filmmaker Richard Frankland she made it perfectly clear what needed to be done in the NT: the government needed to start talking to communities, the Community Development Employment Projects program needed to be restored so that people could work, and the quarantining of wages needed to end.

She said, 'Our people need to get back the power to control what's happening in our communities. We're now reliving what happened to us as children when the Native Police came in. Right now in the Territory, I'm reminded of growing up on a mission settlement.'

Most of us saw the Apology as an important symbolic and healing gesture for those who directly suffered under legislation that stole our parents, grandparents, uncles, aunts, cousins and friends. Many of us also hoped it would come with practical actions to ensure the future sovereignty of our people as well.

* * *

On 26 August 2011 I was part of the 45th Anniversary of the Wave Hill Walk-off. It was there that I felt the strength and dignity of those who walked off Wave Hill Station (then 'officially' owned by British Lord Vestey). The protest was a demand for rights to their traditional country, and to be treated equally with other Australians employed on the land.

Like most others, I went to Wave Hill to pay respect and to show gratitude to those who paved the way for the land rights movement nationally, and to acknowledge the great strength those involved demonstrated in the face of absolute racism and adversity. On Friday, 26 August to mark what is now known as Freedom Day, I marched along with local community members, friends and writerly peers, and those who had travelled over the country to be part of the celebration.

We were there also to pay homage to the memory of Gurindji/ Malngin leader Vincent Lingiari and to remember the significant and symbolic gesture of the then Prime Minister Gough Whitlam pouring red earth through the local leader's hands back in 1975. It was a moment that marked the return of the ancestral lands to the Gurindji mob and yet it was a moment declared null and void with the introduction of the 2007 NT Intervention, which shifted the power of Aboriginal lives and land away from individuals and communities, back to the Commonwealth Government.

The celebration therefore was heavily tainted with the reality of life for the local Gurindji mob today, and their new fight for old rights and their desperation to reclaim the freedoms they fought for in the 1960s.

With the event coordinated by Gurindji/Malngin/Mudpurra woman Brenda L. Croft (also an artist, curator and academic) and MC'd by Vincent Lingiari's grandson Maurie Japarta Ryan, we heard from staunch non-Indigenous unionists who played a key role in activating union members nationally to fundraise to support the Wave Hill mob. Aboriginal rights campaigner and one of the first to step up to assist the Gurindji cause, Brian Manning spoke with passion about his role supporting Vincent Lingiari, and stated in his address that 'The Walk-off succeeded in 1966 because of the unity of the people to stay solidly together in the face of all sorts of inducements. To decide on a course of action and remain united to achieve what you decided. That is the job ahead. You can do it!'

Another speaker, Jack Phillips of the Waterside Workers Federation who was involved in the Aboriginal rights campaign in 1966 – urged the politicians on the day – including the NT Chief Minister Paul Henderson – to go back to their parties and 'make them pull their socks up'.

A message delivered by the Central Land Council via Ngarla Kunoth-Monks demanded a formal government apology for the 'shame, hurt and trauma' the Intervention caused Indigenous Territorians, stating:

Throw the word 'Intervention' away. We demand an apology from our governments for the terrible recent policies that encourage assimilation and 'normalisation' – this amounts to cultural genocide.

Following formalities, we were treated with dancing by the local women before the crowds made their way down to Wattie Creek for a community barbecue. My head was spinning, my heart a mix of confusion – celebrating the past, concerned for the present and barely hopeful for the future – and so I headed back to the campsite to reflect on a most extraordinarily emotional morning.

* * *

On 29 June 2012, I was a guest speaker at Sydney Girls High School where they were celebrating NAIDOC Week. As the assembly occurred only hours after the Australian Parliament passed legislation to roll out another ten years of the NT Intervention (now known as Stronger Futures), I was preoccupied with what felt like someone standing on my heart. My head was pounding, trying to understand how the media had let this significant political moment pass Australians by. Following the Senate spending most of the previous day debating legislation aimed at re-introducing the offshore processing of asylum seekers and media covering it extensively, the Upper House continued sitting until early in the morning to pass the Stronger Futures legislation before a parliamentary recess. It was a non-debate, with many senators missing from the house.

As I sat on the stage I appreciated hearing the words of two Year 11 Legal Studies students Ruby Lew and Isabella Olsson, who delivered an address that demonstrated a better understanding of Aboriginal self-determination and native title than Australian politicians in the major parties. On the Intervention they said:

Self-determination has been the goal of Indigenous groups since even before Mabo, with the aim of it to have decisions regarding Aboriginal communities made by Aboriginal people rather than distant authorities. The Mabo decision and native title have been crucial elements in furthering self-determination and increasing the sense of pride and belonging in the Aboriginal community, but there are major barriers not only preventing progress for self-determination. For example, the Northern Territory Intervention was a drastic and inhumane measure against the chronic issues facing Aboriginal communities in northern Australia that stripped many Indigenous people of their basic human rights, and almost completely destroyed any concepts of self-determination worked for beforehand. It is one of many obstacles that are preventing Aborigines and the wider community from achieving self-determination.

Here were young Australian women who were already writing about the injustice that the NT Intervention and Stronger Futures serve upon their fellow Australians. I believe *all* writers have a responsibility to hold a mirror up to society, to reflect back to those who cannot see what is happening around them, and to make readers stop and think about it.

I am a Wiradjuri woman. I come from central NSW and have lived most of my life on the land of the Dharawal in Sydney. I am the beneficiary of the sacrifices of the old people I went to Wave Hill to honour. We in the state of NSW enjoy the land rights that were born out of the protests made by the Gurindji people, led by Vincent Lingiari.

With this in mind, I keep asking myself: how many of my extended family, my friends, my fellow Australians (black and white) know the true story of the Wave Hill Walk-off? More importantly, how many understand that these very same people, this very same community, have also been stripped of their self-determination, their sovereignty, their human rights, because of the racist NT Intervention?

Many older Australians who read my novel on the Stolen Generations will tell me 'they didn't know'. No Australian today can claim 'not to know' what is happening in the Northern Territory. This anthology is just another means of helping people engage, think and talk about the issues surrounding the policy, the practice and the repercussions for those impacted on – Australians who happen to be Indigenous.

In working on this anthology, I was not surprised at all by the willingness and urgency of the writers who agreed to participate and their need to speak out. They reflect a mere handful of those who generate conversations through their work daily on issues that matter to all of us as Australians.

ROSALIE KUNOTH-MONKS

REFLECTIONS ON THE INTERVENTION

Quotes Made between 2011 and 2014

Excerpts from Speech at Arena Forum, June 2012

I have lived seventy-five years of my life feeling that I'm an outsider in my own country. And that's not easy to do when you're clinging to your language, when you're clinging to your identity and when you're clinging to the essence of your being.

Tonight I thought I'd share with you some of the reflections since the Intervention. I don't want to talk to you as you being white people and me being an Aboriginal person. I want to talk to you and hopefully reach out with the pain in the last five years that the Aboriginal people have carried around.

We are all aware in Australia of the horrific journey that Aboriginal people have had to take right from the beginning. People say invasion but I say on our first encounter. It was kinder when we were shot than being under the care of Macklin.

Trauma, emotional and mental, a lot of us are going through – tremendous, tremendous trauma and that's not over exaggerating.

Because we live in terror of our languages, our ceremonies and our land being taken off us right at this time in our history.

My recollection of the Intervention in my home community Urapuntja, commonly known as Utopia, was the day that soldiers in uniform, the police and public servants arrived and we were ushered up to the basketball stadium and we were all told that we were now under the Intervention.

We don't have access to newspapers, a lot of us we don't have access to TV, a lot of us were going along our normal way, living at home, and just doing the normal everyday things but on that day that they landed it was incredible.

We really thought we were going to be rounded up and taken, because John Howard had made the statement and Mal Brough of course carried it out, that we were now under the Intervention.

So tonight I thought I'd share with you the greatest impact of the last five years of the Intervention has been on the mental and emotional health of the Aboriginal people in the Northern Territory.

People have developed a very deep sense of insecurity that undermines their feelings of certainty and safety because the age-old social structures are being eroded as we sit in this room.

People from the Homelands and the remote areas are being forced to recognise their own vulnerability and their dependency on the system that is being forced on them and consequently the lack of control over their futures.

People who've been made to starve on a daily basis to get their food, absolutely rely on that horrible Centrelink money, which is a pittance anyway.

Young people of course are our concern, as mothers, grandmothers, all of us, we worry about our children.

In the Homelands young people are staying close, in my Homeland that is, with their Elders but those who have drifted to the towns or who live there are in difficulty. We see that. Barbara Shaw talks about it quite a bit. She puts a nice picture on it because she can't really bring it out in the way, the raw way, that it's happening in Alice Springs in particular and also in Tennant Creek.

So these kids they drift away from our place but at the same time in the last five years those kids are not rocks. They feel. They feel the shift of what used to be their stable home, what used to be their stable family. They feel it.

We are traumatised. We are traumatised by the government policies that are in place right now.

I would imagine that a lot of the people when they became aware that they were going to be killed in the last [world] war – mainly I guess the Jewish people – when they became aware in their last moments that they were dying, that terror, I can now imagine what they went through because I'm going through it in the Northern Territory now.

So the kids – of course their response is going to be anger. Of course they're going to feel that they have lost belief in any fairness within the system and many of them are resorting to what is commonly known as antisocial behaviour in Alice Springs and in Tennant Creek and a lot unfortunately are turning against each other. And that I don't believe is accidental. I believe that is somehow engineered or so forth, by the policies that we do turn on each other and that we do fight with each other especially if you perceive someone to have maybe a little more than you have and in the poorest and the most deprived communities this does happen.

The bribery and corruption that is going on by the government also further separates people, separates them with a little bit of money because they've leased their land, and in leasing their land they've also brought on themselves this feeling of guilt, this feeling of having given up and they feel that … Even the Land Councils play a role in further fragmenting and separating Aboriginal people. Once we are separated and we suffer alone we are easy prey for Protector Macklin – I think Jeff McMullen used that term – to come along and to stomp all over us. It's an absolute nightmare.

* * *

It is the lack of awareness in communities around Australia that actually allows what is happening and what is done supposedly for the betterment of us Aboriginal people.

The other thing that I really believe is that we have not got long before we lose the essence and the continuance of our Aboriginal people ... We will have little ones growing up without their language. We will have them all being a carbon copy of the rest, so you will all be the same – there will not be the colour, there will not be the glorious songs, there will not be the dances that meant something. It will only be for entertainment and how shallow is that?

So tonight in sharing with you my pain I'm not doing it for your entertainment. I'm doing it with you tonight hoping that we can unite and in a free democratic country. I still have the belief that we can overcome things that are not fair, things that are wrong, things that are absolutely evil.

* * *

Aboriginal society today appears to fall into three categories and mostly government has difficulty recognising the differences.

Firstly, there are people living their traditional lives in communities. I am one of those people and so is the little girl sitting next to me ... Secondly, there are those who live in more developed centres living in nuclear families, deeply respectful of their roots and maintaining custom, customs looking back thousands of years. And thirdly, there are the highflyers and I think names have been mentioned here tonight especially up there in Queensland somewhere. Many of those have disregarded their heritage in their own lives but have been able to capitalise on their Aboriginality to their own advantage. This is human nature and we must learn to forgive.

They do a disservice all the same when they speak for us. We don't want them speaking for us. We will speak if not in this language, in our own language. We must speak truly for ourselves because the leaders – as Djiniyini Gondarra says over and over – of black Australia are the born leaders from their own group of people ... I have been endorsed by the Eora nation to be a speaker. The Intervention is based on materialistic approaches to negotiation which doesn't work – houses, big ones or I'd love to have a Lamborghini – that's not our priority, it is the quality of life that is our priority … The quality of our life is so important.

Otherwise it's not worth living.

Put a bullet between our eyes, as a lot of the old people are saying now, and the young people are joining us too.

Consultations and agreement with individual community leaders and the people should not be by bribery. 'We'll build you so many houses, we'll give you so much of taxpayers' money for this and that.' That's not what life's about.

You know what – a lot of the old folk say, tell them to take the nails and whatever else that it takes to build a house and take it back to their country. We can live without those if we're going to be punished for being who we are.

* * *

In closing, our greatest fear … is that we are losing, and fast, our fragile cultural background and identity and we feel in many ways we are being used and usurped by people who do not value our language or our ceremonies and indeed our land. The solution my dear friends who have taken time out to come here today is not through the government policies. The solution is to stand strong together.

You have two beautiful cultures here – one's English where we all speak and get on together, the other one is your Aboriginal culture within Australia.

We are your people and you are our people.

It is not on the basis of your colour that I would push you away, it is on the basis of a racist attitude and that is wrong and it devalues every one of us. It devalues me and it devalues you. Let's just say no to the Intervention and let's say no to our government of the day.

Unfortunately both of the governments feel that we all need to be normalised. We refuse that.

Discussion with Graeme Innes, Human Rights Commissioner 11 July 2011

We were told to gather at Utopia, the basketball area which is quite a big expanse of open area and all of a sudden we became aware, around us, were public servants, the police, and also – this is my recollection – and also the army. Some of these people were armed, if they weren't armed they had batons ... The shock – you could almost taste it – and our hearts – not only mine but quite a few of the people here with me – our hearts were sinking and we didn't quite know whether we were going to be shot or put into paddy wagons or whatever. And then the directives came like shots from these rifles anyway and we were told there was a new way that Aboriginal affairs is going to be handled. And that was our introduction to the Intervention. And I can tell you that it was horrific.

Just from this community I have had a tremendous amount of trauma, a tremendous amount of soul searching of Aboriginal people feeling that they have done something wrong but they couldn't put their finger on what it is that's wrong. They've come to the conclusion what is wrong is that we were born black into a different culture and that as quickly as possible we've got to become as one people – speaking the same language, forgetting about our lands, forgetting even about our customary practices because we were really brutally removed by the Intervention into this new world. And they're still recovering from being told by the government that they are paedophiles, that they are substance abusers, and the new thing that was hoisted upon them through the Intervention was this thing called pornography which they'd never heard of in their lives before. And to interpret that to a group of people, to get some idea of what pornography is, that shocked them further because that is not a practice that they had heard about among Aboriginal communities within the vicinity of Utopia. But these are new things that they have to learn because they were aimed at them like shots.

Because a lot of the younger people asked us what's the new word, what is that pornography, and I was the chairperson of our community here. And I had to explain that to a mixed group of people, women and men, for them to get a concept of what I was talking about and they asked me, 'Well which black people are doing it in the Northern Territory and where are those things?' and I said, 'Now, as far as I know, there were no black actors and actresses here doing pornography.' This is what men think had been forced on to us and there was no – as far as I knew from across the Territory – no Aboriginal people doing that kind of a job.

We haven't really seen a positive at Utopia. The only thing that we got from that, from the Intervention, is the police station. Whether we put that as a positive I'm not quite sure because we have always worked cohesively and wonderfully with the police from either Harts Range which is 150 kilometres from me or indeed from Alice Springs. We've not had any qualms or run-ins with police, we knew what the police were there for, law and order, and that assisted us in looking after our families and making sure we had law and order in our community along with the customary law and order. So it just enhanced what we already had on the land of Utopia and adjoining communities.

I believe – I've only come back actually from Tennant Creek and I believe what the people are saying – that to achieve true reconciliation with Aboriginal people of the Northern Territory the negotiations have to change, that there has to be some justice and justice put into place, whereby Aboriginal people will now tell the government what is needed on our Homelands to bring us closer to accessing some of the things that the rest of Australia takes for granted.

One of the things that we are terrified of is losing our identity through brutal treatment of us on our Homelands. We want to retain our language, we want to see schools remain, we want to demand that our identity and our culture continues to be secure, accessing all the other knowledge, not only within Australia but outside of Australia. So at the moment how we're feeling – and I think this is common across the Northern Territory – is that we call upon the Australian Government to have some principles of democracy on our land and that includes taking into consideration the living continuing culture of the first Australians of this country.

In response to a question about the trip she made with Graeme Innes and Djiniyini Gondarra to speak at the Convention on the Elimination of Racial Discrimination in Geneva

The impact from that journey was that for the first time since I've been aware, since I've had this black consciousness of myself, that is the first place where I was greeted as an equal, as a thinking person, and that people actually listened to me. It was a very moving wonderful experience. From that, I believe, I came back feeling stronger, feeling that I had a right to express myself and my people's – not ambition so much but our rights to continue living as Aboriginal people within our own country, having the right to our land, to our language, and having a right to say our children are educated. What I also became aware of was that on the human rights, we do not have to succumb and be passive to assimilation in the way that the Intervention actually was rolled out. We have a right to a quality of life. So that was my experience from coming back from there – and also continuing on – some of the wonderful people that I met there, continuing on a relationship with those people that do not look down on me but rather look at me as another human being and treat me as such.

I think the future negotiations for all Aboriginal people within Australia should be that the government actually has to have a diplomatic and respectful dialogue with us. It is again another opportunity to start and give the government a chance to negotiate with I think Dr Gondarra's faith in traditional lawmen and law women in the communities to be affected.

The fact that the *Racial Discrimination Act* was removed alone shows me that the way the government went about the last Intervention was that they felt they had complete absolute control over us. They must first of all remove that control and acknowledge there is a living vibrant culture in spite of everything that's been thrown at it that is still alive and well. And the fact is that black consciousness is becoming more and more aware of the hideous history that Australia and its government has against Aboriginal people.

And we don't want to sever the relationships between human beings – we're far more mature than that – within Australia. We just want to take our place right there in the midst of that, albeit with our cultural identity in place. And I think with the young ones – I have two beautiful grandchildren, one eighteen and one nine – this is the way they're thinking: they do not want to go back into the bushes and hide and feel second class, they want to take their place, speaking their language, being proud of who they are, and being accepted for what they are, accessing all knowledge in the dominant culture as well as their culture.

Stop the Intervention Speech, Sydney, December 2012

What this is about is our survival. We have been traumatised by the NT Intervention. The decision to continue with these policies under Stronger Futures for a further ten years must be reversed.

The government says they want to 'normalise' us. Well the sooner they free us from discrimination, the sooner our lives can go back to normal. We need to live on our own terms and with strength in our own customary practices. This must include a return to structures of governance in the outback that put our people in full control.

What does it say about our government when they receive a report on income management which shows clearly that it is discriminatory and yet they are willing to carry on? I feel such pain for our young people, like my granddaughter, who, like calves branded with an iron have been singled out as second-class citizens when they are trying to find their place in the world and build a bright future.

ABC *Q and A* Statement, June 2014

I have a culture. I am a cultured person [speaks in language]. I am not something that fell out of the sky for the pleasure of somebody putting another culture into this cultured being.

John [Pilger] chose [to depict] what is an ongoing denial of me. I am not an Aboriginal, or indeed Indigenous. I am an Arrente, Alyawarra First Nations person, a sovereign person from this country [speaks in language].

I didn't come from overseas. I came from here ... I am alive. I am here and now. And I speak my language. I practise my cultural essence of me.

Don't try and suppress me and don't call me a problem. I am not the problem. I have never left my country nor have I ceded any part of it.

Nobody has entered into a treaty or talked to me about who I am.

I am Arrente, Alyawarra female Elder from this country. Please remember that. I am not the problem.

Excerpts from interview with Jeff McMullen, August 2014 about her proposed candidacy for the Northern Territory senate

The Intervention to us was like Australia declaring war on us and in the process they demonised and dehumanised Aboriginal men, women and children. And that is the reason that I'm running for the First Nations. First Nation people are us, Aboriginal people.

It is our land. A lot of us have not moved off our land. Please note when I say our land. It's not just a few generations that we've been there. We've been on those lands for thousands of years. For thousands of years singing our songs that bind us to the earth, speaking our language, and performing our beautiful rituals, our ceremonies.

* * *

In the eyes of the legal system of both Westminster and definitely through my tribal law, I know I belong there.

* * *

I think it is well overdue that we challenge now the Australian Government to realise and admit – not go into denial – that the lands belong to us.

We are not people who will say nobody is allowed on this land. We are people who are inclusive – we grew up sharing whatever we had with our neighbours and guess what? We didn't look at the colour of those people.

If there was a lonely white woman isolated by the distance from any township on a station we looked after that woman, we also looked after the children. We embraced them as fellow human beings.

It is now time for the government of the day to say yes, the Aboriginal people are our brothers and sisters and they have a right, an absolute inherent right to share the wealth of this nation.

Celebrating the diversities of cultures that are in Australia and also celebrating the humanity that's in Australia and caring for those and sharing – that's a part of our makeup.

And this is what the First Nations Party is trying to bring into fruition I guess, or trying to achieve and right the wrongs that have been done.

I've asked the question in my mind: What is it about Aboriginal people that frightens our white brothers and sisters? Is it our white brothers and sisters or is it only the legislation that is drawn up by governments in isolation from us? We're not at the table talking about it, we're not saying we want to share in the thoughts of the people who are running the country, we're not a party to it.

We have just been cast right into the very depths of despair and control by the parties that are in government.

A lot of the mainstream vested interests such as mining companies, such as the people in government whether they're public servants or not they will probably say I'm naïve. No, sorry, this is the way we live right here and now in 2013. We do care and we do absolutely care for our land.

***

In saying that, we say we value our system and we are hungry to learn and access other knowledges that are outside of that culture, but first of all we have to feel that we are safe and secure, not only on our land but also with our language and as I said before, with our dances because that is who we are.

***

We really have been fed crumbs and made welfare dependent. That did not come about by us refusing to participate in the mainstream, it came about through almost a program that said this colour people, the First Nations people, that is the Aboriginal people must be kept right back, and right at the bottom of the socio-economic system.

And that's about where we're going now unless we take control right here and now.

***

It's part of being a human being as opposed to being a predator who is going to kill everything that is weaker than yourself. We are of the human race.

Elders in Conversation, Melbourne, 10 May 2010

We need to say enough is enough. Take away from me my language, take away from me my responsibilities for the land, take away from me my land and I am a nothing. I will become a carbon copy of a different culture. In the NT, and the top end of Queensland, and in Western Australia, you come as tourists to experience the culture that your government is trying to kill.

PAT ANDERSON

THE INTERVENTION: PERSONAL REFLECTIONS

June 2009

The 'emergency response', soon to become known as 'The Intervention', was announced supposedly in response to an Inquiry that I co-chaired with Rex Wild QC into the neglect and abuse of Aboriginal children in the Northern Territory – although I should say at the outset that the Intervention did not address any of the recommendations from our Inquiry.

I would like to share with you some of my own reflections on both the Inquiry and the Intervention. Along the way, I want to puncture some of the myths and assumptions that seem to float in the background of the public and policy debate, subtly but powerfully influencing the story that gets told about Aboriginal child neglect and abuse, the Intervention, and the relationship between black and white in this country.

Let me start by taking you back to 2006.

In May of that year, following a number of stories in the media about sexual abuse and violence in Aboriginal communities, the ABC TV *Lateline* program screened an interview with Alice Springs Crown Prosecutor, Nanette Rogers, in which she described in horrific detail some of the cases of abuse that had come before the courts.

While the details were both shocking and real, in a general sense much of what she had to say was not new. The issue of Indigenous family violence – and especially of the abuse and neglect of children – had been raised for many years at the highest levels by concerned Aboriginal people, communities and organisations. For example, the Royal Commission into Aboriginal Deaths in Custody, in its landmark report almost twenty years earlier stated:

> The history of disruption, intervention and institutionalisation to which Aboriginal and Torres Strait Islander families and children have been subject has left many of those families confronting severe difficulties in securing the adequate care and control of their children ... it is apparent that many Aboriginal families are in crisis.

In 1997 the Human Rights and Equal Opportunity Commission's 'Bringing Them Home' report went further, highlighting the alarming numbers of notifications and substantiations of child abuse and neglect in our communities. And in 2001, the National Aboriginal and Torres Strait Islander Health Council, formed to give advice at the highest level to Australian governments, made 'the protection of children from abuse and violence (including sexual abuse)' the second of nine priority areas for action by governments.

So, it is a myth that governments did not know about Aboriginal child neglect or abuse until the storm of media and public concern broke in 2006: our communities and organisations had been alerting government to the facts and calling for action for years.

But it seemed that our calls for action fell on deaf ears. But when the mainstream media take up an issue, that apparently is a different matter. The *Lateline* program started a media frenzy, especially when the following month, it aired another program alleging the existence of paedophile rings in a Central Australian community. Suddenly, it seemed that every newspaper and every television news report contained a shocking story about the abuse or neglect of Aboriginal kids. The issue became front-page news, and now governments were under the kind of pressure they understand, and to which they react.

Of course, the serious health and social issues faced by Aboriginal communities need to be brought out into the open, need to be debated, and where there is abuse and violence, this should be exposed and the perpetrators need to be brought to justice. The media can play an important role in this process. But the media's quest for drama and conflict can also be destructive.

Much of the reporting at this time and after, even if well-meaning, ended up reinforcing damaging mythologies about us, our lives and communities. Aboriginal families felt that they were all being accused of mistreating or neglecting their children.

Our men in particular found this a difficult and distressing time. All too often the media merely picked up the old stereotype of 'the violent black man', amplified it, and played it back to the public at full volume. I know good men, men who care for their communities, families and children, who felt shamed walking down the street, who felt that people were looking at them thinking 'there goes one of those paedophiles'. This tended to put some people and communities on the defensive and make the real issue – the welfare of children – more difficult, and not easier, to address.

Much of the public attention was focused on the Northern Territory, and the pressure on the Northern Territory Government to address the issue became intense. In August 2006, the then Chief Minister of the Northern Territory, Clare Martin, announced the formation of the 'Northern Territory Board of Inquiry into the Protection of Aboriginal Children from Sexual Abuse'.

I was asked to co-chair the Inquiry, along with former Federal Police commissioner Mick Palmer. Unfortunately, Mick had to withdraw soon after the announcement, and Rex Wild QC, a former NT Director of Public Prosecutions, was named in his place.

The terms of reference of the Inquiry broadly asked us:

i   to look at what contributed to the sexual abuse of Aboriginal children;

ii to identify barriers to the provision of effective responses to and protection against that abuse;
iii to look at how government and non-government agencies might contribute to a more effective protection and response network; and
iv to look at how the NT Government could help support communities to prevent and tackle child sexual abuse.

How were we going to go about getting the answers to these questions? The answer was by talking to Aboriginal people and organisations, and by talking to service providers and government agencies.

Over the course of a year, we travelled to more than forty Aboriginal communities around the Territory and held extensive community meetings to get Aboriginal people's views on how to ensure that their children grow up safe, healthy and ready to be part of their community and the nation. We took the time to establish a relationship with the communities we were to visit, particularly because, as I mentioned before, the media and public debate had left many feeling cautious and defensive to say the least. And overall, this approach worked. There were of course some troubled places where few people turned up to talk to us. And, even in those places with a good turnout, not everyone would speak to us: some people stayed away.

In other places – and I am thinking particularly of that Central Australian community that had been the subject of massive TV and media reporting – we were met politely but with some suspicion, as a lot of people there obviously still felt pretty pissed off by being targeted, as they saw it, by the media and the politicians.

But overall I was very heartened by the response. In some places the public meetings were attended by up to a hundred people – and this is in places that might only have a total population of a few hundred men, women and children. It is particularly positive and significant that where people did turn up, a high proportion of men participated.

What struck me most in these talks with the Aboriginal communities was their attitude. They had suffered much as a result of the historical processes in this country, and many of them had suffered violence and abuse themselves. Many were sad, distressed and shamed by what was happening in their communities and in their families. But they were owning the problem, they were not turning away and saying it was too hard. They wanted to work with the professionals, they wanted to work with the government and with the service delivery organisations, they wanted to be part of the solution. Throughout, there was a sense of great concern about children and young people, and the threats they face.

People were worried about kids not going to school, about girls having babies too young, about drugs and alcohol, the lack of jobs, and the presence of pornography. And while we did not uncover individual cases of child abuse, we found all the conditions present under which it happens: poverty, overcrowding, drugs and alcohol, pornography, and perhaps most disturbingly of all, a breakdown of structures of authority and meaning. We found, too, that many who came forward and spoke to us were child victims of abuse and neglect, who had never had their trauma acknowledged and dealt with.

Throughout our conversations with Aboriginal people, we were often received with openness and trust. There were daily reminders, up close and personal, about the complexity of people's lives and situations; we felt that we had been invited into an intimate space, that people trusted us, and believed that we would be the initiators of some action. Both Rex and I felt a huge burden of responsibility to faithfully record these concerns, ideas, and life experiences.

But alongside this open attitude, we found a huge lack of government services.

For example, many communities had no police presence. Child protection workers were few, far between and often burnt out, so overwhelmed with the most acute cases of abuse that long-term prevention work with families and communities was an impossibility. As for family therapists, child psychologists, social workers and all the other specialists you would hope to see as part of a system for effectively dealing with child abuse and neglect, they simply did not exist for remote communities – and it wasn't much better in the towns either.

Clearly, the warnings of the Royal Commission into Aboriginal Deaths in Custody (from, let me remind you, 1991) and the 'Bringing Them Home' report, and the National Aboriginal and Torres Strait Islander Health Council and all the other reports and studies – about family breakdown and abuse in Aboriginal communities – had been largely ignored. Perhaps this failure to act contributed to the attitude of some of the senior bureaucrats we consulted during the process of the Inquiry.

The sense of urgency about the protection of children that we found in Aboriginal communities was, I am sorry to say, in stark contrast to some of the government agencies to whom we spoke. I don't want to point my finger at any particular agency, nor do I want to over-generalise: there were some agencies which clearly had been putting thought and energy into how to deal with child abuse and neglect. The police, in particular, seemed to have put some effort into thinking through the problem.

But there were other government agencies that showed little sense of urgency, understanding or purpose when we went to talk to them about the plight facing Aboriginal children. There seemed to be a lack of an intellectual framework, and little idea of what they should be doing, how they could be doing better, and what they would need to do a better job. There were no practical, forward-thinking plans. These agencies seemed reactive and passive. They seemed to have become places where the problems were all just too big, and where the Northern Territory was not seen as a place where things could happen, a place that could come up with solutions.

I was and still am puzzled and shocked by this attitude. Where does it come from? Maybe the Inquiry that Rex Wild and I were conducting was seen as a threat, not an opportunity. Maybe some of those we spoke to were being 'good public servants' and they thought that being too open with us would lead to criticism of them, their department or the government. Maybe an ethos had developed in these agencies where we Aboriginal people were seen essentially as 'a problem': I got the sense that some of these agencies were blind to the positives of Aboriginal life and culture and didn't see the sheer potential of our people that was being lost.

I want to emphasise that this attitude was not universal – there were always public servants with energy and commitment. But this other attitude of passivity and reaction was common enough to shock me, especially after meeting with Aboriginal communities where people were determined to recognise and deal with the issue. After Rex and I had finished the consultations, we sat down to write the Inquiry report for the Northern Territory Government. We called it 'Little Children are Sacred' because this reflected what some of those communities told us, from Arrernte people in Central Australia to the Yolngu of Arnhem Land. Our main finding was consistent with what many Aboriginal people had been saying for a long time, namely that:

> there is a significant problem in Northern Territory
> communities in relation to sexual abuse of children. Indeed, it
> would be remarkable if there was not, given the similar and
> significant problems that exist elsewhere in Australia
> and abroad.

We put forward almost one hundred recommendations to address the issue. These recommendations covered a whole range of areas – child protection services, health services, policing, rehabilitation, prevention, family support, education, housing, alcohol, employment and more. But for me the very first recommendation was the most significant. It said:

> It is critical that both [the Northern Territory and Federal]
> governments commit to genuine consultation with Aboriginal

people in designing initiatives for Aboriginal communities [to address child sexual abuse and neglect].

This recommendation was strongly informed by the willingness and determination of many in the Aboriginal community to work with the authorities to address the problems they faced. Of course, we recognised that these recommendations would take a lot of money to implement, and we knew that the Northern Territory budget is tiny in comparison to the resources of the Commonwealth.

So, although we called for the Northern Territory Government to show leadership, we were explicit that this required national action and that the Federal Government needed to provide much of the resources for the solution. Our call was for Aboriginal child sexual abuse in the Northern Territory to be designated as an issue of urgent national significance by both the Australian and Northern Territory governments.

We delivered the 'Little Children are Sacred' report to the Northern Territory Government in April 2007.

Rex and I sincerely thought that given the level of public concern, and the fact that they had commissioned the Inquiry, the Northern Territory Government would want to act urgently to address the issues we found. We thought they would ask themselves: what can we do within our current resources? What more resources do we need? And we expected, and were ready to be part of, an urgent and formal approach to Canberra to get a Federal commitment to a joint effort to address the issues raised in our report.

But nothing seemed to be happening.

The inertia and lack of interest that we had noted during our consultations with some government agencies seemed to have struck again.

I ask myself, once again, as an outsider to those processes, why did the government find it so hard to act? Why did the NT Government commission a report which they must have known would identify areas of long-term neglect where money – and possibly large amounts of money – would need to be spent? Was our Inquiry merely a way to deal with the media and political pressure that had built up during 2006? Were we just part of the government's efforts to 'manage' the issue?

These are cynical thoughts perhaps, and to counter-balance them I remind myself that I know that there were also people in government who were pushing for real action on the basis of the report.

But before that internal struggle between action and inaction could be resolved, before the inertia could be overcome, the Federal Government beat them to the punch. On 21 June 2007, the then Prime Minister and his Federal Minister for Indigenous Affairs announced the 'emergency intervention' in the Northern Territory. This announcement was firmly predicated on the Northern Territory Government's lack of response to 'Little Children are Sacred'. But in fact, there was almost no relationship between what we recommended and what the Northern Territory Intervention encompassed.

Our key recommendation about working with Aboriginal communities was ignored.

Where we emphasised the need for resources and for flexible processes of engagement with Aboriginal families and communities, the Intervention emphasised external control and blanket provisions affecting all Aboriginal people. Not all elements of the Intervention were wide of the mark: there were moves to restrict alcohol availability, enforcement of school attendance for children, increasing police and banning pornography. However, no one needed an Inquiry to tell them that these measures were needed – there had been broad agreement for a long time about exactly these kind of actions, and numerous recommendations for action from studies and reports. But the 'headline' elements of the Intervention were deeply problematic.

They included compulsory health checks of Aboriginal children to check for evidence of abuse, blanket quarantining of welfare payments to all Aboriginal people leading to the suspension of the *Racial Discrimination Act*, plus the compulsory acquisition of

Aboriginal townships, and the scrapping of the permit system that allowed Aboriginal people some control over access to their land.

All this was accompanied by a 'get tough, quick fix' rhetoric that clearly implied where the problem lay: it was with us. It was Aboriginal people who were to blame.

Never mind the years of reports to government identifying the problems and suggesting solutions, never mind the consistent neglect and under-resourcing of services to Aboriginal communities, never mind the inaction and complacency. No, in the end, it was clear that we were to blame, we were now going to be given a good shake, told to sit down, and that they would sort it out since we were obviously incapable of doing it ourselves.

The paternalism inherent in the Intervention seemed to escape most media commentators, but it did not escape Aboriginal people. The Intervention presented a real dilemma for Aboriginal people, at the local community level as well as at the national level. For some, this was a long overdue recognition of the continuing disadvantage of Aboriginal communities and the need to act decisively to end it. On the other hand, there were those who opposed the Intervention for its attack on rights that had been hard won by Aboriginal and Torres Strait Islander Australians over many years. And there were many on the continuum in between these two positions: people who were trying to get more information about what was being proposed and how it would work, or those who opposed some of the elements of the Intervention, were unsure of some, and saw potential in others. However, driven by the media's appetite for conflict and drama, and by the government's own 'black and white' rhetoric, the debate quickly became polarised.

We were divided, whether we liked it or not, into 'those in support' of the Intervention versus 'those against', between those who adopted a 'rights based' approach or those who focused on the need to protect women and children – as if these were opposing principles.

In my view it is a real problem when public debate about such an important issue becomes polarised in this way – yet this was inevitable given the way the Intervention was presented to the Australian people. The question remains: What did the government want to achieve?

I don't think we'll ever fully understand the process by which the Federal Government decided on the Intervention: the key decisions were taken behind closed doors, and little effort went into uncovering exactly how they were made and who made them. There was lots of speculation about why the Intervention was announced. For some, the Intervention was a cynical political exercise to 'wedge' the Labor Party and gain narrow political advantage in an election year. Others have seen the Intervention as an ideologically driven attack on Aboriginal rights. The NT Government's inaction gave the Prime Minister the opportunity to advance his agenda in Aboriginal and Torres Strait Islander Affairs, central to which was the undermining of rights to land: the Intervention as the counter-revolution to Wik and Mabo.

This, I think was central to the Intervention, and explains why so many of its elements had nothing to do with children and why almost none of the recommendations of the 'Little Children are Sacred' report were included.

However, others saw the Intervention as a genuine attempt to address the suffering and neglect of Aboriginal children. Many of our people would have difficulty with this, and indeed looking at our then Prime Minister I find it hard to see in him much compassion for Aboriginal and Torres Strait Islander Australians.

I remember once seeing a small poster in an Aboriginal Medical Service which someone had made and put on the wall and which simply said CONCERN PLUS IGNORANCE EQUALS PATERNALISM.

This sums up neatly to me some of the atmosphere of the Intervention which so many of us found so frustrating and demeaning – the assumption that somehow, in all these years, no one had been doing anything for the health and welfare of Aboriginal children. This ignorance of the history and realities of Aboriginal life, and the disregard of the evidence of what works in such situations of disadvantage, seemed to me to be the key feature of the Intervention and those who led it.

But whatever the real motivations behind the Intervention, one thing I know for sure: it was not the welfare of Aboriginal children and communities alone that drove it. All sorts of these other agendas were at play: political positioning, ideology, electoral advantage, and good old-fashioned arse-covering.

And this seems to me to be a continuing theme in the history of the relationship between black and white in Australia: that action on Aboriginal disadvantage gets continually caught up in other, contradictory agendas.

This perhaps has been the biggest barrier to genuine progress. You would think that if the government was serious about addressing the disadvantage so many Aboriginal communities suffer, there would be a rational process to sit down and look at what the problems are, to look at what has already been tried and what we know works, to look at the kind of principles that we know should underpin action – and then, a commitment to action and of resources. Yet as far as we know, the whole Intervention was almost literally designed on the back of an envelope, over two or three days, in some offices in Canberra, by people who took little account of the evidence, and had no understanding of the historical realities of Aboriginal life.

People have said to me: 'But something had to be done!' Of course, I agree: something had to be done. But if you are seriously ill in hospital and 'something has to be done' you expect the 'something' that the hospital staff do to be both aimed at treating the illness, and to be based on good evidence. Doing something that is neither well intentioned nor well evidenced is unlikely to be helpful. The Intervention was neither well intentioned nor well evidenced.

I have argued strongly that urgent action was needed, but that it needed to be based both on the evidence of what we know works and on our rights. The issues of evidence and rights deserve more attention, but here I do want to say that the artificial distinction that the government set up between 'rights-based' and 'practical' approaches was false. An approach to addressing Aboriginal disadvantage that is based on respect for our established rights is necessary because in the long term it is the only one that, practically speaking, will work.

You cannot address endemic social problems without the collaboration of the people affected. You certainly cannot pretend that the state can intervene in a sensitive and difficult area such as the relationship between families and children without the community fundamentally accepting this approach and endorsing it.

My experience tells me that our people are more than ready to support an intervention to create better, safer futures for their children. But if this is at the expense of their rights, rights that historically have been hard won – people, even those with the most goodwill, won't cooperate.

I know there are some communities where Aboriginal people – and especially Aboriginal women – support some of the aspects of the Intervention that others of us see as violating our rights. There are a number of places, for example, where Aboriginal women have spoken out in support of the compulsory quarantining of welfare payments, which although it necessitated the suspension of the *Racial Discrimination Act*, they say has led to improvements in their communities. If those communities want to collectively make the decision to restrict welfare payments in their community or for particular families, we need to respect those wishes and learn from their experience.

Such a model is being trialled in Cape York – the Family Responsibility Commission there is enforcing standards of behaviour and helping people resume responsibility for the wellbeing of their community and of the individuals and families who live there, especially children. They do this in a way that aims to encourage and support local authority and justice – not undermine it with blanket, externally imposed solutions.

And I ask myself too – what is being put in place to assist those communities and families to resume full control of their welfare payments? Or is the welfare quarantining permanent? Is this how all Aboriginal families are going to have to live, into the future?

With the Intervention in the Territory, there are many places where the welfare quarantining measures in particular have caused much resentment, and led to people 'disconnecting' from services and processes to address disadvantage. They have stirred up memories, memories not that deeply buried, of times when the state believed it had a role in the personal lives of all Aboriginal people, and exercised control over them in a way that it never attempted to do for non-Aboriginal citizens.

This is part of my family history – a history shared by many, many Aboriginal families – when it was taken for granted that Aboriginal and non-Aboriginal families should be treated differently, and that the state and its institutions had a right to be present, as it were, around the kitchen table.

Acknowledging this history, and working with the complexity and diversity of Aboriginal life across the Territory and across Australia, accepting that what will work in one place may not work elsewhere, or at least not without adapting it to the local community, its priorities and capacities – this is one of the key policy challenges that Australian governments must take up.

In November of 2007, a new Federal Government was elected. We had a commitment to Closing the Gap. An Apology was delivered. The Intervention was reviewed – but remained in place.

This article was prepared with the assistance of Edward Tilton.

RACHEL WILLIKA

A STATEMENT

2 October 2007

I live at Eva Valley in the Northern Territory. It is one of the communities affected by the Federal Government's Intervention. I am a single mother. I look after my family, and I support my family. I have six children, some grown up, but we still live together in the community.

I was living at Barunga when I first heard about the Intervention. I was told by mobile phone. It was on the news. When we found out, everyone was worried. The girls wanted to go to hide in the bush. When we saw the army on TV, I felt frightened. Some people, not just children, but adults, too, thought they might come with guns.

I have been thinking about those words 'Little children are sacred'. Who are the little children? Are they talking about all the children? Black children and white children? That's what it says to me. We should be protecting all the children. Aren't white children sacred, too?

I work at the local school, tutoring. I love the children, and teaching them to write and how to sound the alphabet and how to read books. After school, I prepare for church. Our church is a little shed on a cement slab. No power, no water. We use an extension cord from a nearby house so we can have lights and play music. We pay for our electricity with power cards. We try to make sure that there is enough money on those cards so we have electricity all the time, but when it runs out we go outside and make a fire.

A Statement

When I was a young woman I used to drink. I'm a Christian person now. Christianity helps people to fight bad things, like alcohol. My belief in God gives me courage.

Eva Valley is a dry community. Before the Intervention the drinking people would sit at a community place, along the road to Barunga. All the drinking people sat there together, and it was a safe place. Now, they are drinking along the highway. The roads are dangerous and I'm worried there might be an accident.

We don't know what the government is planning to do. At Eva Valley, we have got no email, no internet, no newspapers. Most people don't have a TV or a radio, so we can't keep track of what's going on. You need a big outside antenna to get TV reception. Only four or five houses have this. We don't have mobile coverage and we have to use a pay phone – but to use the pay phone we have to drive 100 kilometres into Katherine to buy a phone card. We haven't got a bus. Our bus is too old now, so we have no transport to go into town to get food. We all put in whatever money we've got to pay for a taxi. That costs $190, one way.

The permit system made me feel safe. People could only enter the community with the permission of the traditional owners, so we knew who was coming in. Anybody can come in now. We don't like to have strangers come in. They might bring in drugs and alcohol, and we don't want that.

This government Intervention is making life harder for Aboriginal people. I am worried we might lose our land, our rights. I feel like the government is attacking our culture, and that it wants to change everything. The government should be helping to make families strong, but what is happening now is hurting us.

These are really serious matters, and we need to deal with them seriously. We are talking about the future of Aboriginal children. Everything needs to come out in the open. We need to be honest if we are to make better lives for our children. I want to work with Aboriginal organisations, because I feel comfortable with them. The Federal Government has lost our trust.

I am writing this because I want to stand up and protect Aboriginal children in the Northern Territory. We don't want to go back to the days when we got paid in rations, and every community had a white superintendent. We want to move ahead. We want to live and work on our own land. We're not going to let them come and run the show. We're going to stand up. We have rights.

DJINIYINI GONDARRA

QUOTES FROM SPEECHES ON THE INTERVENTION

On return from the International Convention
on the Elimination of All Forms of Racial Discrimination
– 77th Session, August 2010

I want to begin by expressing my thanks to the Quaker United Nations Office whose personnel accompanied Rosalie and myself in Geneva.

I also want to thank members of the NGO team, the Australian Racial Discrimination Commissioner Graeme Innes and his staff, Les Malezer from Foundation for Aboriginal and Islander Research Action, and the representatives from the National Association of Community Legal Services, Amnesty International and the National Native Title Council, for hearing our story and helping us to put this in our report to the committee. I want to thank the Committee on the Elimination of Racial Discrimination (CERD) itself, with the rapporteur Jose Cali Tzay, for truly hearing our personal experience of what is happening in the Northern Territory (NT) for the First People of Australia, and then sharing that concern back to the Australian Government delegation when they appeared before the committee.

Finally I wish to thank 'concerned Australians' who negotiated our appearance before CERD and enabled our travel to Geneva from our communities in the NT.

It was encouraging for us to meet people interested in our struggle for justice and peace. We were able to meet many individuals personally. They are people who will stand in solidarity against this system that has made us victims.

The trip to the UN headquarters in Geneva was very worthwhile for us because it allowed the world to hear what is truly happening to the First Peoples of Australia in isolated communities in the NT, places that have not been represented well by media and government reporting. We have repeatedly tried to bring attention to our cause through the government, and other organisations. This has not been a possible doorway.

We have not received any response from the government – this was a good time to go to the UN. The UN was able to hear us express that the Northern Territory Emergency Response (NTER) and Intervention are not special measures. It shows that what the Australian Government is trying to do is target the First Peoples of this country. By going to the UN, we are asking the Australian Government to take our concerns seriously. I can now see that the UN is the vehicle for the voice of Aboriginal people to be heard. That is before the highest council in the world. This is the same way other countries resolve issues of race and discrimination.

The Australian Government has supported the UN Declaration on the Rights of Indigenous People and must remove the NTER measures from the legislation, and start to look at more positive ways of working with all Australians. We must be treated equally. This is justice for everyone.

We all agree that children should be looked after, that there should not be domestic violence, that there should not be violence from alcohol. These are issues that affect all Australians. We should not have been targeted as the only people who are affected by these issues. We should be finding the solutions together.

Many Australians are concerned with how the First Australians are being treated by the Australian Government.

They can see that this is unjust. Ordinary Australians can see this injustice in a democratic country and know that it shouldn't be happening. When you share with a body such as the UN – straight away they see that Australia is racist and that the government does not govern with the spirit of peace and order.

The survival for Aboriginal people relies on changes to the Constitution and the establishment of a treaty. The treaty needs to be borne out of the people who have a very strong connection with land, culture, spirituality and law rather than being established by government, or a committee formed by government. It should be established by the people who maintain tradition because the necessary tools are already in place.

Now that we are back in Australia, we want to establish an ongoing forum where there is a relationship between traditional peoples of central Australia, Arnhem Land and groups like the Human Rights Commission and other interested parties to continue the conversation that has been started.

Visiting the UN has helped me to see that we are not alone in the struggle for human rights. There is a platform for all Indigenous people of the world where we can go and share our concerns. Both Rosalie and myself felt great relief at being able to share our pain, on behalf of our people in Central and Northern Australia, in this forum.

Excerpts from the Australian Senate's Stronger Futures Hearing held in Maningrida, 22 February 2012

Creating legislation like this is changing the Northern Territory Emergency Response (NTER) into Stronger Futures, but the formula of the legislation is the same as in the NTER. Therefore, our concern is that that needs to be considered properly ... You know it breaches the international charter of human rights. I think we need to be sensitive enough and try to help people. If we want to see Aboriginal people better in education, better in jobs and better in any other area, we need to work together to build better legislation, because this particular legislation is not on.

Dhurili Clan Nation

People are frustrated. People are sick and tired of being controlled. When people are sick and tired of control they just give up hope: When our lives are being threatened and taken away, we just sit and do nothing. I have already emphasised that people are dying, not just dying spiritually and emotionally but dying physically. They cannot live for the day because their lives are controlled by somebody else. They have given up hope: what is the use?

Food Security

The Stronger Futures Bills address fraud security by once again creating more powers for the Minister for Indigenous Affairs and her department. We object to this on the basis that it is again a backward step from self-determination. Nor does it address underlying problems to people eating well, like cost and other things, and it is the same with education. In Arnhem Land, in places like Milingimbi, Galiwin'ku and Gapuwiyak, the Arnhem Land Progress Aboriginal Corporation have run the stores for the last forty years. They have been controlled by the people. We know how to run the stores ourselves and there are 300 local people working there. The Arnhem Land Progress Aboriginal Corporation is a non-profit non-government store which is run by us. We do not depend on government. What profit we make we use to employ our people. If we are talking about self-determination that is how we go about doing it. We do not need government money. We generate what we get, and we always give the money back to the people for different purposes and different reasons.

Customary Law

When the Northern Territory Emergency Response legislation was established, do you know what the government has done? You took away our traditional customary law, which is very key and important because it emphasises the rule of law, not the rule of man. In customary law, you have three basic elements: peace, order and good government. There is consistency in the law and people are sent into the law.

You just did away with something that was very important. The reason why that was done away with was so that the government could go ahead and do what they liked, so they can play around with our lives and our people. I think you need to consider that very seriously.

The Stronger Futures Bills will also continue the powers for police to take people away from our town without telling anyone and to interrogate our citizens without representation. Once again, I consider this racist as it does not apply to any other Australian citizens. It is also a major disrespect to the jurisdiction of the Yolngu nation while at the same time limiting my people's individual rights.

P.M. NEWTON

567,000 KM DRIVEN

567,000 km driven.

They like those kind of stats in Defence. Kilometres driven. Kilometres flown. Nautical miles steamed. Litres of fuel burned. Measurables. Logistics. It's all about the stats, the numbers. Log them at the start. Drive, fly and steam where you're told. Do what you're told when you get there. Log the numbers at the end. Add it up and there you have it. That's the operation. Done and dusted.

Dusted. 567,000 kilometres driven. One of those numbers to make you slap one another on the back and trot out lines about the wide brown land. Over half a million klicks and we never even left the Territory, mate. Didn't even touch the sides.

But measurables, they can't tell you everything. They can't tell you about the dust. Red, ochre, brown, tan, yellow, pink, pale, dazzling, choking, coating. Baby powder fine, then sandy, like it's a bloody great big beach without a drop of water, a blade of grass, a tree. And when the wind kicks up that's when you feel it, all the different sizes of the grains, pitting, abrading, gouging, reminding you just how deep it can carve stone. Those northern types with their hundreds of words for snow, they'd be struck dumb out here. Struck dumb by dust.

There's always that second of disorientation, jolting awake in the cabin of the truck. Bone-deep weary and then looking out and seeing red. Trapped in the coarse sandy cloud thrown up by the truck in front. Blank for a moment. Too many thoughts collide, sort themselves out into the most important question. What number in the convoy?

There were some IEDs designed to take the first one. First set of wheels that roll over. Nothing personal. But there were some took the second or third or the last but one. Depended if they were automatic, or if someone was watching, up in the hills. Made it worse, that second option. Thought of someone sitting, patient, just waiting, watching, sparing and smiting as they choose.

Meantime, the sapper just drops through the gears and wrenches the big wheels out of the red cloud, turns into the desert and laughs. Overtaking one, two, three, four trucks. Roars round them, straight up into the lead. It's our turn for clean air, to make first tracks on the long red ribbon of dirt running gun barrel straight into the Tanamai. No fear of the road. Of the edge of the road. Of anything lying hidden there.

The sapper laughs again, sniffing the passenger's fear, spotting the white knuckles hanging on to the door frame, the legs ready to spring.

'Chill,' the sapper yells, 'you're not in fucking Uruzgan now.' 185,876 litres of fuel used.

An army, air force and navy on the move. Not marching on their stomachs but consuming none the less. All those kilometres driven, flown and steamed, figured in litres of fuel expended. Throw them at the problem. Because problem solvers – that's what they are – from the Solomons to Timor Leste to Baghdad and Kabul, what can't they do?

Seventy-three communities.

People, equipment and stores to haul in there by land and sea and sky. Logistics – just another problem to be solved. It's politics decides on what's the problem; and politicians who decide the how of solving it. Us? We just solve what's left over after the deciders have done deciding. We drive 567,000 km, fly 168,000 more, steam 46,000 nautical miles, prepare 16,500 meals, and build what we're told, where we're told to, and live like we're ready to leave.

We always send the NORFORCE mob in first, before the balanda turn up with their convoy of trucks. Calm them down a bit, speak the language, trade on ties of kin and skin to smooth the way, convince them that an army rolling into town isn't really an invasion.

First place we lob, there's TV cameras thick as flies, filming trucks, sappers unloading trucks, people standing about watching trucks, dogs cocking a leg on a truck tyre, wide-eyed kids clinging to the legs of parents giving narrow looks and turning away.

There's a call for a football and one is produced. A leather interloper entirely the wrong shape for this end of the country. Still, it gets tossed about. Khaki and kids play mixed codes. Parents watch from the fringes and the cameras have something to pad out the evening bulletins.

The minister has his sleeves rolled up. Some brass and underlings flank him, to frown, smile and nod on command. It's not much of a presser. Everyone is hot and dusty and thirsty and tired and calculating how many hours' drive to the closest cold beer and swimming pool, to spend a night under air-con watching tourists comparing their shots of rocks and gorges and crocodiles. It's a small convoy of four-wheel drives that heads out of town and the dust cloud it raises falls quickly back to earth.

In the night, that first night, people in town whisper, like they're in church. We find ourselves doing it too, setting up tents for the experts we've carted across country. We crank up a barbecue as part of the extending-a-hand approach but there's sand in the sausages, they crunch against our teeth and no one from the community comes anywhere near. A pile of snags lie hardening in the fat and start fights among the dogs when we toss them out.

We bivouac that night. I lie beneath the Milky Way, so bright I see it even with my eyes shut. And as I lie there, I hear it, the susurration of stars moving slowly across the sky, wrapping around me as the planet moves, I feel it curving away beneath me, spinning, dizzying. I open my eyes and see shapes darkening the star field, blotting out the light, streaming away from town out into the desert. Feet moving through sand, make the same timeless sound as my stars.

After that the cameras and the reporters and the politicians fade away and it's just the trucks and us and the NORFORCE boys blowing generations of credit as the convoys roll from township to community to outstation. We mark each place on our maps and on the land itself.

Five hundred projects, 116 villages.

The sapper's diagnosis watching blue-draped shapes lining up with their children at the clinic is simple.

'Problem with this lot is they could all do with a bit of porn, eh? And a beer and a few glasses of wine. Mellow 'em all out a bit, you know? Make 'em less bloody aggro.'

The Dutch Army's team of women medics are organising the queues, triaging by interpreter and guesswork. The blonde doctors and nurses in uniform are a conundrum to perplex the men gathering across the square.

We pose beside the clinic. The Dutch take a snap, then we return the favour.

In Uruzgan, we khaki civil engineers build clinics for women and kids and schools for girls. We improve roads, put the power on, hells bells we even build an airfield. And then we leave it and go home.

Some of the men, they tap their wrists and smile at us as we drive past in our Bushmasters, a gunner on top, the rest of us crammed inside. Our interpreter tells us later what they mean, 'You have watches. We have time.'

Funny old world, eh, that same sapper says, driving in the final nail. He leans against the signpost he's just put up, shirt black with sweat and alive with flies. On the edge of the community, cemented well in, the sign warns all who enter that they are under Intervention Rules. No grog. No porn. The sapper packs up his tools, grumbles, gagging for beer, counting the klicks back to the closest bar.

We inherit a task. We build. We are builders. The plans come standard. Bridges, clinics, schools, wells, roads, airports – army engineers don't do pretty. We do fast, we do difficult – difficult terrain, difficult access, difficult weather, difficult people who shoot at you, try to blow you up. The plans come standard but there's artistry in adapting to the conditions, there's satisfaction in watching that line of blue camouflaged women moving towards the front door. Or seeing a row of little girls line up outside the one-room school we built in a weekend.

We're well gone, we're out of country and safely home by the time the ones who lurked in the corner of our eyes, on the edges of our nightmares return in the night and burn it to the ground.

There's a woman arguing with the health team outside the dilapidated community centre. She knows what her kid needs. A dentist. Fill the tooth or take the damned thing out. Kid can't eat, can't sleep. But we didn't bring a dentist and the doctor's not here to make that kind of medical check. The woman turns away in disgust, her kid cups his jaw and follows her. His feet are red with dust.

We've put the finishing touches on our last building. A police station. The eighteenth one.

And now we're out. The logistics are being tallied. $17.7 million on Operation Outreach. We can account for every cent in kilometres and litres of fuel and meals provided and communications and transportation and in the things we built.

You did your job. That's all you can do. My therapist tells me this. My therapist came as part of my own Intervention package.

A weekend of pills and booze and bloody wrists in the bathroom ended with Mum and Dad and my brothers and sisters and a psych team and stitches and weekly appointments on the comfy couch. Veterans Affairs are slow to get going, but once they get into gear they can be ruthlessly efficient.

We talk, I talk, she listens. I ask questions, some she can answer. There's one she can't and it's the one I keep asking.

How come, over there I built schools but over here I built police stations?

CHRISTINE OLSEN

CROSSING THE GAP

Rupert Maxwell-Stuart, Arunda Mat-utjarra and Mu-tujulu Elder, on being asked how much the sacred tjurungas were worth – the ones given into the care of Ted Strehlow by the old Arunda men. He thinks a bit then gives a quizzical, bemused look to his interrogator. 'Oh,' says he, 'about tuppence ha'penny.' Laughs. Shoots another look at him. 'The only riches we have are in our heads.'

I spent some time in Jigalong researching the script for the film *Rabbit-Proof Fence*. It was based on Doris Pilkington Garimara's book about her mother, Molly, and her two aunties, Gracie and Daisy, walking back to Jigalong following the rabbit-proof fence. That was in 1931 when they were young girls. I would go out to Jigalong with Doris and we would stay with Molly in her camp. Jigalong is in the Pilbara. It's in Western Australia, not the Northern Territory. (Now the Western Australian Government is trying to close down Aboriginal communities in that state so they're in the same position as people in the NT after the Intervention.)

I spent a lot of time in the Battye Library in Perth. That is where all the Western Australian Aboriginal records are kept. Day after day I would immerse myself in the world of the Chief Protector, Mr Neville – a highly bureaucratic world of files and memos and telegrams and officialdom. The problem with Mr Neville was that he was a supreme bureaucrat – he prided himself on it – and if you were Aboriginal and you fell under his gaze you could never extract yourself. Molly herself, even though she escaped him twice, lost both her children to him.

Central to Mr Neville's power was the *Aborigines Act 1905* (WA). This Act gave Mr Neville power over every Aboriginal person in the state. He became their legal guardian. He could decide where they worked and lived and who they married. It was Mr Neville's policy to 'breed the black blood out' and he would go around the country giving lectures on this very topic. He had a lantern slide projector and photographs of 'half castes', 'quarter castes' and 'octoroons' to illustrate his ideas.

When John Howard announced the Intervention in 2007 I was immediately struck by two things. It was being done under the guise of child protection and it was as if Australia had suddenly gone back 100 years to the 1905 Aborigines Act where Aboriginal people had no power. The parallels were striking.

It was like a scorched earth policy. The army was rolled in to every town and Aboriginal community. Communities lost the right to decide who could come on to their land. Every Aboriginal initiative was got rid of. Aboriginal programs run by women to educate about violence against women – gone. Aboriginal employment in looking after their land – gone. And, once again, Aboriginal people had their money taken off them to be administered by the government.

I don't watch much television but I caught Paul Keating's Redfern speech and I also saw Tony Jones's interview with the disguised public servant who, as it turned out, blatantly lied about having worked in Aboriginal communities. Two – what's the word? – lightning rod pieces of television. The Redfern speech I remember vividly. I was walking out of the room when Keating began to speak. I turned and stood in the doorway scarcely believing what I was hearing, then edged my way back in, standing to listen to the whole speech. And how dispiriting to see, in the Tony Jones interview, the government engaged in using the national broadcaster to slander a whole group of its citizens as part of a massive land grab.

Of course, that kind of double dealing would be nothing new in the history of black and white relations in Australia. It's the twenty-first century version of poisoning the well, only this time it's the minds of white Australians that are being poisoned.

'Outrage is useless,' my friend, anthropologist John von Sturmer advises me.

I see a documentary on television, on the ABC. It's about some Aboriginal women artists from Utopia who have taken their paintings to New York where they have been feted in shows around the town. They're back home now. In the desert.

'You know,' says one of them. 'I feel really sorry for those people in New York. They have nothing. And we …' she gestures around the wide open desert country. 'We have everything.'

I'm driving north-east of Marble Bar along Skulls Creek Road. We're looking for a native title meeting which we never find. I'm in the back of the ute with Nora and her two daughters and Ricky, Doris's son. We're all squashed in. I'm sitting between the two girls, cushioned by them, my legs stuck straight out. Nora is cradling my foot in her lap. We're driving through some of the most spectacular country I have ever seen.

Every now and then an arm will be lifted, a hand pointing out something in the landscape – a tree, a bush turkey. Nothing is ever said. Except by me. Nora chides me. 'Ooh it's lovely.' She's mimicking me. 'Just like a white woman. Ooh it's lovely.'

I ask my friend Kamahi Djordon King for his thoughts on the Intervention. 'In the end people were saying no to mining companies and I think that's what the Intervention was all about – just mining.' Kamahi is a painter and an actor, born in Katherine, a member of the Gurindji tribe. He goes on.

'So now adding us into the Constitution and with this Intervention still going on in the Territory it's a very, very confusing time to be an Aboriginal in Australia.'

I don't know about this Constitutional rights, adding us or recognising us as the first owners. But what happens with sovereignty? Like with the Apology there won't be and never will be any compensation. It's not good enough.

If it's Aboriginal land, any single piece sold, all the real estate agents should be signing up every place sold, no matter where it is, gets a five per cent commission. It goes into the Aboriginal land fund for that particular area. If it's sold in Eora area then it goes to Eora nations.

If this was to happen it would be huge. It would be restitution. And the thing is, if we start having something like that, within thirty years of that being in place, we would be happy. We would be telling our kids everything's okay. You're an Aboriginal. This is your land. We actually get paid for this. We're self-sufficient. We're moving ahead and we're building a better future.

Jigalong. I'm down one end of the verandah. Molly's down the other. I'm sleeping in my swag and two little tiny frogs have joined me. It's the wet season. There's water everywhere. I get up and make us a cup of tea. Molly has a ratty looking cockatoo in a cage. We sit and drink our tea and look out. Grey clouds, grey water, it's all closed in.

So the question is how do we approach the sacred? And why are we so stuck? Maybe they're the same question?

John von Sturmer 'The whole society can't recognise the beauty of that world.'

YINGIYA MARK GUYULA
A STATEMENT

June 2011

My name is Yingiya Guyula from Liya-dhalinymirr clan of the Djambarrpuyŋu People. I am a Yolngu Studies lecturer at Charles Darwin University in Darwin.

The Intervention has only created problems in East Arnhem Land communities as well as remote Homeland centres. The Intervention has made our people more frustrated and confused, the white man's way of thinking is forced on us, and forcing us to abandon our culture.

Government ministers have flown into Arnhem Land communities just for a few hours on the ground to gather a little bit of information, then they fly back into the cities thinking they know how to fix the problems in the communities, thinking they know what's best for us.

Governments only looked at the fringe camps and towns and wet areas where people drink alcohol in places such as Nhulunbuy, Katherine, Tennant Creek, Jabiru, Alice Springs and Darwin.

White people see Aboriginal people in these places and think that these people don't care about life, don't care about living. But who are they to judge them? They class all Aborigines the same, but they are wrong.

These white people and those bureaucrats do not go out to the East Arnhem Land communities, where my people live, where there has never been alcohol, and there is no child abuse. There are Aboriginal people living in remote communities of Arnhem Land, in Homeland centres, away from towns, away from the binge-drinking areas, poker machines and gambling venues.

These are people who are able to manage their funds and work, or who want work, education, discipline, and practise ceremonies.

Quarantining of Centrelink payments should be optional and not compulsory. Quarantining might be okay for people living in town camps and cities, where alcohol and gambling is a problem, but it doesn't work for my people living in remote Arnhem Land Homelands where there is no gambling, no alcohol and no child abuse.

We are asking simply for understanding that in life, there needs to be an understanding between the two cultures. There needs to be respect between cultures.

Mapuru Homeland has a co-op store which won a national award for selling healthy food. Centrelink won't approve it to accept quarantined money. This means an aircraft charter flight from the mainland Homeland at Mapuru to the closest shop on Elcho Island costs $560 return. This means it's costing $560 for a return flight just to buy $150 worth of food. Where's the sense in that?

Arnhem Land is like the European Union, made up of many different nations, each clan-nation with their own language, each with its own national estate. Bringing everybody in from the

A Statement

Homeland centres into the major settlements is not the right thing to do because people do not feel secure or happy living in another man's land. Children are forced to go to school, but really they do not feel safe and secure on other people's land.

There are about forty children who willingly run to school every day at Mapuru Homeland because it's their home and they feel secure. Yet the NT Government wants to close down the Homeland schools and bring everyone in to the major communities.

They think it's not worth spending money on Homeland schools who have forty or more children freely, and with their own willingly attending school, but they are providing internet services, facilities and technology to white schools with attendances as low as five. The Education Department provides computers and internet and distance learning for hundreds of cattle stations and small schools across the Northern Territory, but Homeland schools are neglected.

Furthermore, I would like say that these Homelands are our homes. There is no violence in the remote Homeland communities, no child abuse happens, no alcohol, no pornography, because out there in the bush is where the cultural ceremonial grounds are, and it is from the Homelands that strong discipline comes through spirits of our fathers talking through the land.

Both the Commonwealth and the Northern Territory governments haven't given equal opportunity to us the First Australians to be able to exercise our rights.

Through the Intervention white man police stations have been put in the major communities for dealing mostly with cultural conflict issues (problems that can only be solved through traditional cultural justice), but instead the white policemen force white man law onto us, disrespecting our blackfella law. They think they've done the right thing. But often they're only making it much worse by locking up senior leaders, the very ones who are wise and keeping our Indigenous law strong.

This time we are taking the case further where it can be heard loud and clear by people whose ears, brains, feelings have a heart for Indigenous Australians. It is now being taken further where there is an ear that will listen.

We are taking it further, to the United Nations and we will talk about the Intervention, about how income management in the Northern Territory has had a devastating and debilitating impact on remote communities in Arnhem Land.

Finally, we need you to support us. We need you to tell governments that we want the same opportunities as white people, to live and enjoy our own cultural life, but they must stop trying to make us like white man, we have our own cultural identity. Let us be who we are, and together we will have hope for the future.

Thank you.

LARISSA BEHRENDT

THE DIALOGUE OF INTERVENTION

It was the 'national emergency' that had sat neglected for over thirty years. In the wake of decades of reports, each with in-depth analysis of the issues and complex blueprints on how to address the immediate and the underlying issues, the Federal Government announced that it was finally going to prioritise the endemic violence in some Aboriginal communities and relied on the recently commissioned report by Pat Anderson and Rex Wild, 'Little Children are Sacred'.

For a federal government that has been much quicker to blame the Northern Territory Government for their neglect of law and order issues or to blame Aboriginal culture, the change in priorities was a profound turnaround. So profound that initial reactions from many Aboriginal people were cautious support of the intention to finally do something, combined with healthy cynicism about the timing and the proposed means of dealing with the issue.

When originally announced, the Federal Government Intervention, unveiled by Aboriginal Affairs Minister Mal Brough on 21 June 2007, included:

- widespread alcohol restrictions
- quarantining welfare payments and linking them to school attendance
- compulsory health checks to identify health problems and signs of abuse
- forced acquisition of townships through compulsory leases with just compensation

- increased policing
- introduction of market-based rents and normal tenancy arrangements
- scrapping the permit system
- banning of pornography and auditing publicly funded computers
- appointing managers to all prescribed communities.

All of this was to be overseen by a taskforce headed by the Western Australian magistrate Sue Gordon. Gordon was also the Chair of the handpicked Howard National Indigenous Council. The Council had previously produced a paper critical of communal land holding and developed a set of principles around land tenure that included support for the compulsory acquisition of Aboriginal land.

As the details of the Intervention plan emerged, one of the first things that became apparent was that the strategy had no reference to the Anderson Wild report it purported to rely on, following none of its recommendations. The Anderson Wild report specifically noted that a crucial part of the response to child sexual abuse was interventions to work in conjunction with the community, especially on measures such as establishing dry areas and dealing with substance abuse. Experience and research pointed to the crucial need to involve communities intricately to ensure the success of these approaches.

Heavy-handed, top-down interventions such as enforced prohibition have never proven effective in the black or the white community. Apart from the protocols and niceties, the research clearly shows that the most effective way to develop policies and implement programs in Indigenous communities is to have those communities integrally involved in them. It's not just a matter of good manners; it is effective practice and policy. The top-down, paternalistic imposition of half-baked policy ideas is a recipe for failure.

Beyond the practicalities of purely interventionist approaches were some larger questions about the strategies employed in the

Intervention. Why were issues related to Indigenous control of their land being tied to the issue of child sexual abuse? Fundamental criticism and concerns were also raised about the changes to the permit system and the intention to compulsorily acquire land. Even the Northern Territory Police Association stated that the repeal of the permit system would actually make it harder to monitor the movements of people into Aboriginal communities, therefore making it harder to stop drugs, alcohol and paedophiles from entering vulnerable Aboriginal communities. The change seems to be much more focused on opening up Aboriginal land to non-Aboriginal interests, a philosophical approach that accords with the Howard government policy towards Aboriginal communal land holdings generally.

The other crucial issue raised in the Anderson Wild report and overlooked completely by the Federal Government response was the failure of any of the measures to deal with underlying issues, specifically the under-funding of basic Indigenous health services and housing needs. In the lead-up to the last election, Access Economics estimated that basic Indigenous health needs were under-funded by $450 million. Aboriginal housing needs in the Northern Territory have been under-funded by approximately $2 billion. Yet nothing in the Intervention package seeks to address these underlying issues of disadvantage. This is a profound flaw because the whole approach is predicated on dealing with the symptoms rather than the causes of dysfunction in Aboriginal communities. Research and reports into the high instance of violence and abuse in some Aboriginal communities consistently point to the fact that cyclical poverty, including poor health and poor environmental health, contributes to the breakdown of the social fabric in communities. When that happens, communities become dysfunctional.

Another issue raised by the Anderson Wild report but overlooked by the raft of changes proposed in the Intervention was the fact that a large number of perpetrators of abuse of Aboriginal children were non-Aboriginal. Nothing in the Intervention attempted to deal with these non-Aboriginal perpetrators and instead seemed to work on the assumption that the problem was primarily within Aboriginal communities.

In many ways, the Intervention in the Northern Territory is a textbook example of why government policies continue to fail Aboriginal people. The policy approach:

- is ideologically led rather than making reference to research or understandings about what actually works on the ground
- directly contradicts what the research shows us works and what experts recommend as appropriate action
- masks other policy agendas unrelated to dealing with systemic problems of violence and abuse under the rhetoric of doing what is in the best interests of Aboriginal people, or children, and seeks to undermine community control over their own resources
- is paternalistic and top-down rather than a collaborative approach that seeks to include Aboriginal people in the outcomes.

While community leaders and representatives, particularly the Coalition of Aboriginal Organisations, worked tirelessly to develop an alternative policy response and lobbying parliamentarians to amend the harshest aspects of the legislation, it passed without amendment and with only one day allocated to a Senate hearing to enable public submissions. With little time to analyse the 500-plus pages of legislation, Indigenous people from the Northern Territory – and their supporters around the country – raised more concerns when it became apparent that the legislation specifically sought to take away the protection of the *Racial Discrimination Act* and to subvert the rule of law by characterising the actions in the Northern Territory as 'special measures' for the purposes of the Act. Only the Greens and Democrats, with some ALP parliamentarians from the Northern Territory, gave adequate scrutiny to the Bill. The ALP had quickly given its in-principle assent to the Intervention when it was announced and so was limited in how much it could subsequently raise objections. As an opposition party, it did not question any of the aspects of the plan that were patently flawed to anyone who knew anything about Indigenous affairs. The ALP's quick agreement with Howard without consideration of the details highlighted their ignorance of the Aboriginal Affairs portfolio and foretold how little things were to change under the Rudd government.

Some observers rightly commented that the legislation contained plenty of aspects that should have provoked the ALP, especially the proposed changes to the permit system, the changes to the *Aboriginal Land Rights (Northern Territory) Act 1976* and the attempt to subvert and override the *Racial Discrimination Act*. But Kevin Rudd and his government didn't blink, and were not drawn into making an Indigenous issue a wedge issue. While some admired his political astuteness in outsmarting Howard's pre-election tricks, the Aboriginal people in the Northern Territory paid a high price for this politicking.

At the first Federal Parliament on 13 February 2008 after Howard lost the election and Kevin Rudd became Prime Minister, he delivered the National Apology to the Stolen Generations and undertook to set goals to 'Close the Gap' with a report to be presented to the Parliament at the beginning of each year.

* * *

It is now eight years since the Intervention; seven since the National Apology. The speech was seen as the start of a new era – a counter to the 'pendulum's swung too far' attitude that Prime Minister John Howard had towards Indigenous issues. Debates about the national narrative and the role of Indigenous people in it were caught between the acrimonious extremes of 'black armband' and 'white blindfold', and the result was one of deep division. A circuit breaker was needed.

In his speech, Rudd not only addressed the wrongs of the past but made an undertaking for the future:

> For the future we take heart; resolving that this new page in the history of our great continent can now be written. We today take this first step by acknowledging the past and laying claim to a future that embraces all Australians. A future where this Parliament resolves that the injustices of the past must never, never happen again.

The key promise in moving forward undertaken by the Rudd government was to 'close the gap' – an important aspiration and one that is critical if Aboriginal and Torres Strait Islander people are to enjoy the same opportunities as all other Australians.

But he maintained the approach to Indigenous affairs laid out in the intervention and, in fact, expanded the welfare quarantining to other primarily Indigenous communities across Australia.

At the start of the first Parliamentary sitting of 2015, the Productivity Commission released its annual report on the progress on 'closing the gap' – 'Overcoming Indigenous Disadvantage – Key Indicators 2014' – and it contained, by its own account, some mixed results:

- Economic outcomes have improved over the longer term, with higher incomes, lower reliance on income support, increased home ownership, and higher rates of full-time and professional employment. However, improvements have slowed in recent years.
- Several health outcomes have improved, including increased life expectancy and lower child mortality. However, rates of disability and chronic disease remain high, mental health outcomes have not improved, and hospitalisation rates for self-harm have increased by 48 per cent.
- Post-secondary education outcomes have improved, but there has been virtually no change in literacy and numeracy results at school, which are particularly poor in remote areas

- Justice outcomes continue to decline, with adult imprisonment rates worsening (a 57 per cent increase in incarceration rates) and no change in high rates of juvenile detention and family and community violence.

But hidden in the report were figures that indicate that Rudd's promise of not repeating the mistakes of the past had become very hollow. The report shows that there has been a 436 per cent increase in care and protection orders on Aboriginal and Torres Strait Islander children between 2004 and 2013. Most children on these orders live away from their parents.

The Secretariat of National Aboriginal and Islander Child Care has pointed out that Indigenous children aged 0–17 make up 4.6 per cent of the population but 35 per cent of children in out-of-home care. This is an increase of 65 per cent from the time of the Apology. That is not a result that would indicate that we've learnt from our past experience.

In the 2014 Federal Budget, $534 million was cut from the Indigenous portfolio, cuts that the then Treasurer Joe Hockey claimed would eliminate waste. There is no doubt that some of the money spent on Indigenous issues is based on funding approaches that don't work but it is also the case that many key areas – health, education, housing, employment, community infrastructure – are all under-funded. Cuts to domestic violence centres, Aboriginal legal services and community-based organisations mean that there is less support for families in crisis, for people who are vulnerable because of poverty, health issues, homelessness and the like. The $534 million cut from the Indigenous portfolio as 'waste' could easily be redirected into essential services that would make a big difference to the least advantaged within the Indigenous community.

When Opposition leader Bill Shorten delivered his speech on Closing the Gap on 11 February 2015, he mentioned the over $500 million cuts that are affecting frontline services in Indigenous communities. In response, several Coalition MPs walked out, leading to criticisms that Bill Shorten had broken the bipartisanship on Indigenous issues that had existed since the Intervention was passed in 2007. If so, this could be very good news.

There have been moments when bipartisanship on Indigenous issues would have been helpful. Perhaps around the time of the Mabo decision and the implementation of native title legislation, or positive action to the recommendations of the Royal Commission into Aboriginal Deaths in Custody, or a positive response to the recommendations in the 'Bringing Them Home' report. Those are moments when bipartisanship would have helped progress issues of national significance and Indigenous wellbeing.

But the current bipartisanship that some lament as broken began not at the moment of the National Apology in 2008 but in 2007, when the Howard government announced it was implementing the Northern Territory Emergency Response (NTER), or the 'Intervention'.

Inevitably, a 'National Emergency Response' that was designed over a forty-eight-hour period in Canberra, with no consultation with people working at the coalface in the Northern Territory, and rolled out by people who were flown in was always going to be fraught. And in this circumstance, bipartisanship hasn't been helpful because it stopped the usual scrutiny that government legislation, policies and expenditure are subject to. A strong, healthy Opposition can seek to hold the government of the day to account and will ask the questions that need to be asked.

And those questions needed to be asked about the policy approaches taken with the Intervention. It was a high-risk, highly experimental approach to Indigenous issues in the most vulnerable communities in Australia. It took approaches that went against what the research and the experts on the ground said worked. If ever a policy needed diligent scrutiny about its implementation and effectiveness it was this one. This was especially so since the 'Intervention' legislation as it passed – with ALP support – suspended rights of review and appeal under the *Racial Discrimination Act* and the Northern Territory anti-discrimination legislation as well as suspending the right of appeal to the Social Security Appeals Tribunal. Those most vulnerable had no recourse if they felt the impact on them was discriminatory or unfair. Someone should have been asking those questions to government for them. Not only are these processes of scrutiny important to ensure that individuals are not disadvantaged, they are an important way in which unintended harsh and unjust consequences are identified so they can be ameliorated.

While Indigenous policy that was spawned by the Intervention is subject to Senate Estimates and other parliamentary processes, with both sides vested in its success, there has been much more defending than questioning of failures. It has fallen to the Greens, particularly Senator Rachel Siewert, to ask the key questions.

While the cynical view in 2007 was that Howard and his government were playing electoral politics, a similarly cynical approach was taken by the ALP. In meetings around Canberra as Indigenous groups gathered to express their concerns about the approaches in the Intervention and their possible negative impacts – and offering alternatives to deal with the issues of family and domestic violence and substance abuse – a subtle message was sent to those concerned that Rudd was simply agreeing to the measures so they wouldn't become an election issue. It was implied that after he was elected, the policy could be revisited. It is easy to see why Noel Pearson so often reminds us that we can't always assume the left are our strongest and best allies.

The sad facts in the Productivity Commission's report 'Overcoming Indigenous Disadvantage – Key Indicators 2014' is not simply the result of the Abbott government's policy failure. Nor is it simply the fault of the Howard government, which started going down the current policy pathway. It is also the fault of the Rudd and Gillard governments, which implemented the same policies and extended them – especially increasing the income management aspects.

If bipartisanship is broken, Bill Shorten may have started to do something significant in improving Indigenous affairs. Shorten's speech might contain a significant and positive shift. In providing an example of a community-owned approach that worked in reducing crime, he noted that it worked because it was 'championed by local people, local knowledge and local expertise'. Shorten went on to note:

> We are blessed, in Australia, with inspirational Indigenous leaders: educators, advocates and role models in every field … and we need to be better, as a Parliament and as a nation, at channelling their knowledge and their ideas.
>
> A re-engagement with people who are experts in the key areas of Indigenous advantage seems a commonsense approach but it will be a change from one that engages only those people who will say what the government wants to hear. A practical step forward would be to harness the expertise and knowledge of organisations such as the Australian Indigenous Doctors' Association' the Secretariat of National Aboriginal and Islander Child Care, National Aboriginal Community Controlled Health Organisation, and National Aboriginal and Torres Strait Islander Legal Services (NATSILS) as key advisors on the development of Indigenous policy for government in their areas.
>
> The biggest flaw in the policy taken by the Intervention was the exclusion and ostracism of experts in Aboriginal communities who had been doing the effective work on dealing with entrenched social problems. Their marginalisation from policy development is a key factor that explains why it continues to fail to achieve results. Effective responses – and a real alternative to Intervention – will only come when Aboriginal people with the capacity to be agents of change in their own communities are empowered to just get on with it.

NATALIE HARKIN
INTERVENTION: A POEM

*Criticise the Intervention and associated costs
then prepare to be profiled as someone who
is 'either not a parent or doesn't have a soul'*
Mal Brough, *The Age*, 8 August 2007

deja-vu back-to-the-future a haunting familiar emergency response 2007 pre-election manoeuvre opportunity-invites a fraudulent-truth alleged endemic 'pedophile-rings' soldiers invade to stabilise-health overnight laws special-measure-absurds suspend legal-protection Racial Discrimination Act seize control of lives assimilation-coercion open-up lands exploration-bound a gross-manipulation human-rights-violation echoes of Tampa 2001 another wedge-politic pre-election-fantasy military-led emergency response opportunity-sailed on a float of deception 'children-overboard' Royal-Navy deployed so clever the symbols emotive-strong children-at-risk and the Military-State bunker-down Australia through discourse Protection strike hate and intolerance let fear stop your heart in hardened-conviction ignore Treaty rights help mythology unfurl this election-win! but ... there is always resistance global-campaigns calls for sanctions and boycotts international-shame lobby United Nations to cross our shores demand a rapid peace-keeping deployment-force then bolster our troops storm Capital Hill stabilise this Government command our Emergency-Response.

what price can be placed on souls
whose Stronger Futures
are not secured?

DJINIYINI GONDARRA

RESPONSE TO THE PRIME MINISTER

Julia Gillard's Announcement of a Second Intervention in the Northern Territory, 26 June 2011

The government and the people of Australia are only able to achieve true reconciliation with Aboriginal people of the Northern Territory if the environment for negotiation is changed and justice, that was so brutally removed by the Intervention, is restored. Only through respectful dialogue and working together can we call Australia a nation based on the principles of democracy.

Future negotiations will rely upon:

i   The Aboriginal people in the seventy-three prescribed communities of the Northern Territory do not welcome any further consultation with the government until it acknowledges the failures of the current Intervention.

ii   The Aboriginal people of the Northern Territory will only endorse a new initiative by the government to improve the lives of Aboriginal people if the government first establishes a diplomatic and respectful dialogue, negotiation and relationship with the traditional lawmen and lawwomen in the communities to be affected. These are the people who are seen as the true leaders by their communities, who are charged with maintaining ceremony, language, law and order. They must be properly consulted before any new initiative can take place in their communities.

iii The name 'Intervention' and 'Emergency Response' must be removed from any future initiative, which should instead focus on the goals of education and empowerment of Aboriginal people in the Northern Territory. It must dispel the prejudice and racial discrimination of Aboriginal people that is embedded in the Intervention, and which has created deep emotional pain and shame among Aboriginal people.

iv Any initiative aimed at education and training must support the right of Aboriginal people to maintain their Indigenous languages, cultural practices and the capacity to live and work on country.

v To effectively support appropriate and beneficial development in Aboriginal communities, the government must replace Government Business Managers with mentors who support and facilitate education, capacity-building and locally controlled development in Aboriginal communities.

This is the will of the Aboriginal people of the Northern Territory.

DEBRA ADELAIDE

WELCOME TO COUNTRY

Later that night, I was sitting out the back smoking a rare cigarette and drinking a not so rare glass of wine. White, some sort of sav blanc. Not my usual preference but something left over from ages ago, the last time I'd had people over. It was dry enough, and cold enough. The day had been exceptionally hot but the breeze was nudging the humidity away. In another half hour or so it could even be cool.

I lit a second cigarette and turned the radio up. Set on the sort of radio station that people like me find themselves listening to, in the end, it had been humming in the kitchen behind me, in the dark. Now I listened while I smoked and sipped my wine and thought. Eventually the muffled chatter clarified from background noise to actual words, and song. I could hear distinctly the wind from the desert town of a far-off country. A place where it would be hotter right now than here.

Earlier that afternoon I had taken a small load to the charity store. This is what people did at this time of the year. In my case, cleaning out the other bedroom was a long overdue task, and still a difficult one. I had taken most of the day to sort through the remains of clothing, outgrown or discarded, and all the cards and folders, the trinkets, toys and games, the faulty or obsolete electronic gadgets, and finally the books that surface in every generation: school atlases, paperback dictionaries bursting with stray leaves, and those novels all kids seem to acquire, even those who aren't big readers. *American Psycho. To Kill a Mockingbird. Trainspotting.* All the Harry Potter books, though only the first three of these had been read.

There were old shoes, mostly stained sneakers and outgrown boots. The boots were good quality, and my size. Still, I packed them as well. I knew I would never wear them. I put them in cartons along with the old board games, including a backgammon set that I never remembered being used, and playing cards that I remembered were. There was also a guitar, several cartoon character doona covers, and an empty CD stack.

What I had thought would take an hour or two took me most of the day. I have always considered myself a tidy sort of person, not obsessive, but tidy enough, but confronted with the entire room and its half-emptied wardrobe, I felt a mild sense of panic, as if I had no idea where to begin, or what to follow through with. I had a feeling that the task would never end.

Some of the cartons with lids which I had accumulated over the past months for this very purpose, I filled with the belongings I had decided to keep, packing them neatly and marking the outsides with black Texta before stacking them back into the wardrobe. I had already vacuumed the bottom of the wardrobe, and sprayed for insects. When that part of the task was done I had made a coffee and before I had even finished drinking it went back to retrieve them, to take away too, because what was the point? I knew there was no point. But when I reopened the wardrobe door and saw the cartons I had only just marked SCHOOL STUFF and SPORT AWARDS ETC, I closed it again.

Loading up the car, I realised there was not that much. It all fitted comfortably in the boot. Despite my best intentions I had really only cleaned and rearranged most of it. And with all my dithering about, by the time I pulled up at the charity store the place was closed. In the parking bay beside the skip bin belonging to the store someone had already left the skeleton of a bike, a baby's cot and mattress and a pile of bulging green garbage bags. And a CD stack, just like the one I was bringing. The empty CD stack: symbol of the charity throw-out, wherever you went, the world over I should imagine.

I unloaded an old suitcase that I'd filled with soft toys, some of them damaged, but it was unthinkable that these go in the garbage bin. As I placed it down I noticed a rabbit's ear sticking out of the side. Rosie. Rosie the rabbit. She had received a great deal of love once. Rosie the rabbit, she has a funny habit. I could still hear the childish refrain. What funny habit? I could not remember, or perhaps I never knew. I opened the suitcase and tucked Rosie's ear back. She had also lost an eye, and I did remember how that happened. The dog at the time, a lumbering beast with a devoted nature and an excess of enthusiasm that was never tempered by age, made off with Rosie and chewed away an eye before we could rescue her. I remembered the wails, which went on all night, the sobbing to sleep. The even fiercer love that ensued. I almost took Rosie back to the car before I realised the futility. As if keeping Rosie meant anything when its owner was gone forever.

I unloaded the cartons and on top of the stack placed the guitar in its cheap vinyl cover. The guitar was missing two strings. It had been cheap too, but it was serviceable, or had been. A three-quarter size, it had been replaced by bigger and better ones, which themselves had long gone from the house. It had always had a decent tone, at least I had thought that. But then maybe I was just a sucker, back then, for the special sound of a child first learning a musical instrument. Standing there beside the charity store, I could almost hear the chords of 'House of the Rising Sun' floating in the early evening air.

There was no one about. The store was at the end of a lonely strip of shops that were always shut by five pm. I took it down again and unzipped the cover. There was an inside pouch containing a spare set of strings. I took a pair of pliers out of the car's tool kit and sat on the kerb of the parking bay while I replaced the missing strings. I tuned the guitar, as well as I remembered how, replaced it in the cover and placed it on the top of the stack of cartons. On the way home I stopped at the servo and bought cigarettes.

Halfway through the second cigarette, and I was contemplating a third. The movement of my arm from table to mouth was not enough to set off the light sensors so the dark was now complete and in the still night the radio seemed even louder.

I hadn't even looked in that skip, I realised now. I'd assumed it was already full. But now I wondered if I hadn't wanted to look in case of rats or something. I'd read about people sleeping in skips. Homeless kids and refugees. Town drunks. It seemed unlikely in this quiet part of the suburbs, but still, I wondered.

The background noise on the radio faded and the sound of someone speaking in soft accents filled the night. I realised the topic under discussion was the rebellion. Some people were even calling it war. Then I heard the call of a song, in another tongue, one both familiar and unknown. More words, then a request. The presenter commenting on the conflict. More singing, soft and plangent. A single musical instrument, something reedy sounding, a wind instrument, but a primitive sort of one. It was playing a simple but unbearably beautiful tune over the desert wind, which could be heard murmuring in the background. Someone talking again, this time about desert conditions. About the wind itself. The hardship. The rebels. Instruments – but were they talking about weapons or musical ones? The beautiful reedy sound kicked in again, this time with a voice, pure, full-throated, urgent, almost angry. A woman's voice, I thought. It seemed to cut across the country and through the soundwaves and the thick humidity where I sat in the dark, my cigarette held in suspension, burning to the filter.

The words may have been in another language but I knew what they meant. One long note stretched out for what seemed like minutes, the singer's voice deep and resonant yet rising and falling like the desert wind itself. Then the presenter's voice kicked in again only to cut out, mid-sentence. I went to the radio in the kitchen to fiddle with the dial but I knew what had happened. It was becoming more common. Sometimes it was the wind itself, but more often the programs that got through were detected and shut down. After a few seconds an announcer came on air to state the time and then introduce a chat show about do-it-yourself home repairs, as if the previous program had never happened.

I grabbed the wine from the fridge and went outside but even as I was pouring my third glass I knew what I had to do. People like me, we don't act often enough. Perhaps if I were not the kind of man I am I would not have been sitting there alone, contemplating an ashtray, an empty glass, and the prospect of drinking more or just leaving the bottle and going to bed to stare at the ceiling in the dark. I did not know which would be worse. I tossed the wine away into the garden instead, and went inside and shut the back door. Getting into the car, I drove like crazy, but as I approached the charity store my headlights scanned the pile of discarded belongings and I sighed in relief. The guitar was exactly where I'd left it.

I made the last flight out. It was always a late flight to that country, as if the airline decided that only the bold or the foolish held that sort of commitment; would care enough to be leaving so late, so close to the airport curfew. As if they'd provide a flight to support the official stance – that the country was not inaccessible – but only as a token gesture. Because who would willingly go there, given all that had happened in the last decade? And given all that had happened, I wasn't even sure if I'd need my passport or not, but I took it just in case. Anyway, after I was finished there I might want to fly elsewhere, to a place even farther away.

At the check-in counter the assistant barely looked at my papers, uncaring who might be flying out there or why. She waved me and the guitar straight through to the boarding gate.

'You can take that on board,' she said. 'You'll have a whole row to yourself.'

It was probably deliberate that you had to fly through the night, the dark and the humming of the engine meant to lull you to sleep, so you didn't have to think about what would face you at the end. But I remained awake the entire time. The plane was barely a third full. I could have taken out the guitar and strummed a few chords if I wanted, if I could remember any.

We landed just before dawn and by the time I exited the terminal, light was seeping through the indigo sky. I had forgotten about the desert chill. I stopped and took a jacket out of my backpack, knowing that in another hour or so I'd be taking it off again.

You couldn't fly all the way to that country of course. We had flown west for hours, but the place where I was heading was now east. To get to it we'd had to fly all the way over it, to the closest town to the border. Now I would have to wait for a supply truck, one authorised to take travellers, as there were no longer any coaches, and private cars had long been banned. When one came along, seeming barely to pause to let me in, I realised we would be driving for hours with the rising sun in my eyes. Leaving in haste, at night, I had not thought to bring sunglasses. I threw my backpack and the guitar in the rear seat and climbed on board.

The truck driver did not speak, though he was not unfriendly. He clearly preferred his own company and the sound of whatever he was listening to through earpieces that attached to a player on the dashboard. I closed my eyes and tried to rest as we sped through the morning. We drove for hours in the unbroken silence, the road unexpectedly straight and hard and fast, though when I thought about it, I supposed it needed to be. Now that the conflict had accelerated, troops would have to be able to get quickly from place to place.

'Checkpoint ahead,' the driver finally said, dislodging me from a near sleep.

By now the light was bright. I squinted and saw ahead the long glittering line that stretched as straight as the road we were on, seeming to cross it. But the road stopped at the checkpoint. The driver waved me out with him, spoke briefly to the security officer at the gate, and returned, tucking his ID card back into his wallet. I wondered if he needed a passport to get through. I wondered about the load he was carrying, what goods were now being allowed through, and why. I barely had time to get my things out of the back before he accelerated and drove through. The gates closed behind him and I stood on the road with the sun falling down like a blessing I did not need.

This was the infamous fence. Three sides of a square at the bottom of the autonomous state now just called Country, stretching to the ocean way up north. Forming a country within the country. The cyclone wire fence so straight and neat: if it were a perforated map you could just tear this bit off and toss it away. There had been dingo fences and rabbit-proof fences before – now we had the ultimate fence. A see-through Berlin wall, containing all the people who refused to submit or conform, swept up out of every corner of the country and installed here, forever. Told they could live wherever they wanted in Country, do what they liked: hunt, sleep, fight, sing, make love and music wherever they liked, but they could never come back.

And at the start they literally did not get a thing more: not a ration of bacon, not a sack of flour, not a packet of Band-Aids or a single headache pill. You wanted your lands, you got them back, the government decided. You want your sovereignty, so take it. You wanted country, you now got country, they said. Welcome to Country, said signs posted at all the entry checkpoints along the fence, a message for every new load of people rounded up and brought in.

Except here, at the most accessible side, there was a war, with supplies drip fed or smuggled through by sympathetic people outside Country. The entire coast, of course, was the weakness despite fences on every landing point and razor wire on all the beaches. Charities or just charitable people regularly threw supplies over the fence all the way around. No one could ever stop that. And they had never been able to stop the music coming out over the airwaves, despite cutting off the electricity years ago, right at the start.

That community I'd heard singing on the program, that person asking for help, were located around this side of Country. It was probable that if I waited long enough or walked along enough of the fence near one of the checkpoints I would encounter someone on the other side. It happened all the time. People stationed to receive or pass on news and telegraph it back via smoke signals, runners, even just by coo-eeing across the desert lands.

I didn't have a hat, I didn't have anything much, but I had a bottle of water and there was a clump of mulgas, enough shade if I sat patiently. The security officers at the checkpoint, just a donga with an air-conditioning unit almost as big, stared indifferently through me. I wondered, if I was desperate for water or anything, would they help?

But luckily I didn't have to find out. In the early afternoon some figures appeared through the shimmering heat. I walked right up to the fence.

'You heard,' a woman said. 'You came all this way.' She had a couple of kids with her, teenagers.

I nodded and tossed the guitar as high as I could. For a moment I thought it was going to catch on the razor wire, but it only brushed the top of the fence, then wobbled, then fell down straight into her outstretched arms.

I knew not to wait for or expect thanks, so I turned to leave, then stopped, fished the packet of cigarettes out of my backpack and tossed them over too. One of the kids stretched out a hand and caught it like a pro. I hoisted my backpack again.

'Hey!'

I turned around.

'My boys will love this.' She was holding the guitar horizontally, in two hands, as if it were an offering.

'Good,' I said. 'My boy did. My son loved it too.'

NICOLE WATSON

FROM THE NORTHERN TERRITORY EMERGENCY RESPONSE TO STRONGER FUTURES

Where is the Evidence that Aboriginal Women are Leading Self-Determining Lives?

It is now eight years since the Northern Territory Emergency Response (NTER), otherwise known as the Intervention, was imposed on thousands of Aboriginal people living in townships throughout the Northern Territory. The NTER was the Commonwealth's response to allegations that Aboriginal children in remote communities were being subjected to sexual abuse. The measures that fell under the umbrella of the NTER included child health checks, prohibitions on alcohol and pornography, the auditing of computers, the compulsory acquisition of Aboriginal lands and the quarantining of social security payments.

There was no prior consultation with those who would be forced to live under the measures. Sue Gordon, the former Head of the Northern Territory Intervention Taskforce, justified the absence of consultation by reference to the nature of the crisis:

> I have pointed out very clearly that this was an emergency, and if you have an emergency like a tsunami or a cyclone, you don't have time to consult people in the initial phases.[1]

Eight years later, Aboriginal communities are no longer compared to natural disasters, but the Commonwealth's power over Aboriginal lives remains undiminished. In June 2012, the Commonwealth Parliament passed a suite of legislation, called 'Stronger Futures in the Northern Territory', effectively extending some of the NTER measures for another ten years. Bipartisan support within the major parties effectively denied the Australian people any meaningful debate over the provisions of the Stronger Futures legislation. Its passing attracted minimal media coverage, and with the exception of a small number of bodies, criticism within the Australian human rights community was relatively muted.

To some extent this lack of engagement can be explained by the former Labor Government's position that the measures were widely supported by Aboriginal women. A small number of high-profile Aboriginal women have also publicly expressed their approval of the measures. This article takes the position that although the opinions of such individuals should be respected, they are not a stand-alone justification for the imposition of racially discriminatory measures. A mature public debate would be informed by an analysis of the ways in which the NTER measures can impact on Aboriginal women, engagement with evidence-based research and consideration of Aboriginal women's historical experiences of state interventions.

I will argue that earlier state interventions that were in the name of protecting Aboriginal women invariably resulted in a binary, which simultaneously rendered their rights invisible while subjecting them to excessive regulation. This binary finds resonance in key NTER measures.

There is little evidence to suggest that Aboriginal women are any safer as a result of those measures. Yet they have been deprived of a myriad of rights, so that the state's longstanding imperative to control Aboriginal women is fulfilled. This article will be divided into three parts. Part one will discuss the history of the binary of invisibility and control. Part two will provide a background to the NTER, and part three will argue that the binary of invisibility and control finds resonance in the NTER measures of income management and the seizure of Aboriginal lands.

For over two centuries, racism and patriarchy have shaped the lives of Aboriginal women. As stated by Behrendt:

> The bodies of black women are contested terrain, the spoils of colonial conquest. Aboriginal women, who enjoyed power and respect within their traditional communities, fell to the lowest rung on the socio-economic ladder in colonial society because of the double taint of a subordinated race and a subordinated gender. Through this transferred misogyny many black men have been quick to learn that exploitation of black women was acceptable and quick to forget the status Aboriginal women held in their own communities.[2]

Racism and patriarchy have served to make Aboriginal women's rights invisible. At the same time, their bodies have been subject to excessive regulation. This binary saw the theft of Aboriginal women's land and rampant sexual violence on the frontier. Members of the colonial police forces not only overlooked the abuse of Aboriginal women, but were often complicit. Although they were denied the protection of the rule of law, Aboriginal women were subject to a form of wardship under protectionist legislation, which existed in most parts of Australia during the earlier part of the twentieth century.

The protectionist system made Aboriginal people vulnerable to indefinite incarceration on remote reserves. Aboriginal family life suffered through invasive measures, such as inspections of the family home, and the removal of Aboriginal children into dormitories. Many Aboriginal women exercised considerable bravery in their attempts to keep their families together, in spite of the protectionist regimes. While Aboriginal women's lives were subject to excessive regulation, their rights and in particular, labour rights, were invisible. The most common employment for Aboriginal women during the protectionist era was domestic service in white households. Many were denied the ability to manage the paltry wages they were paid, as such wages were usually given to the protector on the ward's behalf.

One of the most humiliating aspects of this system was the need to ask the protector for permission to spend one's own wages. During its inquiry into the treatment of former Aboriginal wards, the Senate Standing Committee on Legal and Constitutional Affairs received evidence from one former ward that she preferred to run away, rather than face the continuing degradation of having to ask for permission to spend her own money:

> I ran away ... in 1967, just two days after my father's funeral. I borrowed $12 from my married sister rather than go to the police station and be interrogated about what I wanted my money for. Growing up, that is all you saw – our people, my parents, my sisters and other family members being questioned: 'What do you want your money for? You don't have any money.' It was humiliating and degrading. So I left, a 16½-year-old, and started a new life in Townsville. That $12 was the best investment I have ever made. I educated myself.[3]

Like their ancestors, Aboriginal women of today continue to grapple with invisibility, while at the same time, being prone to excessive regulation.'

In the early 1990s, researchers such as Bolger powerfully elucidated the invisibility of female victims of Aboriginal family violence. Although invisible as victims, Aboriginal women are subject to excessive regulation by the criminal justice system. The first survey of the needs of Aboriginal women in custody was undertaken by the New South Wales Aboriginal Justice Advisory Council, in 2003. The result was the ground-breaking report, Speak Out Speak Strong. At the time of the study, Aboriginal women constituted 31 per cent of the female prison population in New South Wales, representing the fastest growing prison population in the country.

In common with their ancestors, the participants had lengthy experience of the law's regulation, but had been denied protection, with devastating results. Speak Out Speak Strong made disturbing revelations about the links between childhood sexual abuse, addiction and incarceration. Seventy per cent of the participants had been sexually assaulted as children, and almost all of those women reported having a drug problem. Few of the women had ever had access to a professional counsellor.

In light of this history, it beggars belief that anyone would rationally argue that perpetuating the binary of invisibility and control is an answer to the multiple levels of disadvantage endured by Aboriginal women. Yet this is precisely what the NTER has delivered.

The Northern Territory Emergency Response

In the two decades that preceded the NTER, numerous reports had attested to the suffering of Aboriginal victims of sexual abuse. Perhaps, what was different in 2007 was its public airing. In the lead-up to Prime Minister Howard's announcement of the NTER on 21 June, the ABC television program, *Lateline*, publicised shocking allegations of paedophile rings operating in the Northern Territory. Those allegations were followed by the public release of a report by the Northern Territory Board of Inquiry into the Protection of Aboriginal Children from Sexual Abuse, Ampe Akelyernemane Meke Mekarle, 'Little Children are Sacred'.[4]

The report painted a horrific picture of communities that were in the throes of addiction and dysfunction. The report was unequivocal in its demand that governments abandon imposed solutions, in favour of working in partnership with communities. The need for a new approach was all the more pressing given the, 'sufficient evidence to show that well-resourced programs that are owned and run by the community are more successful than generic, short term, and sometimes inflexible programs imposed on communities.'

While the Commonwealth accepted that there was a crisis, it

rejected the report's consultative approach. Howard and his Minister for Indigenous Affairs, Mal Brough, both described remote Aboriginal communities as disaster areas where the rule of law had either broken down entirely or was on the verge of collapse. But rather than implement the Inquiry's recommendations, the Commonwealth imposed a five-year long Intervention, to 'stabilise' Aboriginal people.

In August 2007, the Commonwealth Parliament passed the voluminous legislative package that would authorise this dramatic stabilisation of Aboriginal people. In spite of the protection of women and children being its stated goal, the legislation was not specifically concerned with the rights of either group. Rather, wellbeing was to be improved by a series of measures that would serve to discipline, such as the income management regime. Under the regime, varying amounts of income support payments are quarantined for expenditure on priority needs. The quarantined funds are held in individual accounts that are commonly accessed by way of a debit card. Quarantined funds cannot be spent on alcohol, pornographic materials or gambling.

Various means of surveillance were imposed under the rubric of the NTER, such as the auditing of publicly funded computers. The brief of the Australian Crime Commission, a body ordinarily associated with the investigation of large-scale and organised crime, was also expanded to include 'Indigenous violence or child abuse'. In order to coordinate implementation of the NTER measures, Government Business Managers (GBM) were sent into communities. The GBMs exercised broad powers over bodies integral to community life, on behalf of the minister.

Aboriginal populations were to have even greater contact with the criminal justice system, as a result of blanket prohibitions on alcohol, and changes to the administration of the Northern Territory's criminal justice system. In determining bail and sentencing applications, courts can no longer take into account customary law or cultural practices that would have the effect of mitigating the seriousness of the behaviour in question.

The Commonwealth's grasp over community life extended to land, which is both the most substantial asset owned by many communities and the lynchpin of culture and identity. The Commonwealth's acquisition of interests in Aboriginal lands was governed by Part four of the *Northern Territory National Emergency Response Act 2007* (Cth). Leases over certain Aboriginal lands were granted to the Commonwealth for five years.

Although the protection of children from sexual abuse was the ostensible motivation for the NTER, the Commonwealth failed to invest in strategies to address the underlying causes of abuse. Programs to develop parenting skills and community education to break the cycle of intergenerational abuse were also overlooked. Likewise, the Commonwealth failed to invest in mechanisms to measure child wellbeing in the Northern Territory.

Recent Developments
Spurred by the looming expiry of some of the NTER measures, the Commonwealth engaged in widespread community consultations in the latter half of 2011. The process began with the launch of a discussion paper – Stronger Futures in the Northern Territory: Discussion Paper – on 22 June 2011.[5] The discussion paper listed eight areas for future action, with an emphasis on school attendance, employment and alcohol abuse. The tone of the paper suggested that the NTER had improved the lives of Aboriginal people in the Northern Territory.

Just six days after the launch of the discussion paper, the first consultation meeting was held in Tennant Creek. Between what remained of June and August, consultation meetings were convened in over a hundred Aboriginal communities in the Northern Territory. All meetings were facilitated by staff of the Department of Families, Housing, Community Services and Indigenous Affairs, who controlled the agenda and recorded the conversations that took place. The Commonwealth is yet to make those records publicly available. However, a representative sample of transcripts suggests that specific proposals being considered by the government were not revealed.

On 23 November 2011, the government tabled three Bills under the umbrella of 'Stronger Futures in the Northern Territory'. The package effectively continues many of the NTER measures discussed above. Together with the Explanatory Memoranda, the three Bills ran to over 300 pages. Even for lawyers, unravelling the legislation is an onerous task because it requires reference to earlier legislation. It beggars belief that the general consultations conducted between June and August could have provided the foundations for such an intricate result. Nonetheless, the legislation was passed by the Senate in the early hours of Friday 29 June 2012, after a debate that only began on Thursday evening.

The Public Debate over the Northern Territory Emergency Response

Debate over the NTER measures has to some extent been overshadowed by the diversity of opinion among a small number of high-profile Aboriginal women. This has been represented in the media as a manifestation of a division between Aboriginal people in the remote north and those in cities on the eastern sea board. In reality however, Aboriginal women's opinions are not defined by geography. Supporters and opponents of the NTER alike can be found throughout Australia.

This diversity of opinion should be expected. An individual's opinion is shaped by an unknowable number of conscious and subconscious factors, such as family history, education, religion and professional associations. Such factors will inevitably come to the fore in any discussion about an issue as complex as child abuse. What I find startling is the often unarticulated but strongly held view that Aboriginal women should not disagree with each other. Debate among Aboriginal women scholars in particular, is a logical outcome of not only our vocation, but also the diversity of our backgrounds and expertise.

Arguably, the most prominent Aboriginal woman scholar who has written in support of the NTER is Professor Marcia Langton. Langton has written two essays on the NTER, both of which were published in the *Griffith Review*. The title of the first, 'Trapped in the Aboriginal Reality Show', is a reference to the voyeuristic imagery of violence within Aboriginal communities, that has become a macabre form of entertainment played out in Australian public life.

Many critics of the NTER would agree with Langton when she argues that the crises in remote communities are rooted in twenty-five years of neglect by successive Northern Territory governments. Likewise, the violence against women and children that Langton so powerfully describes is not denied by most critics of the NTER measures. Langton argues that by the time that the NTER was announced, the crises had reached the point when prior consultation would have been an 'indulgent fantasy'. Once again, few critics would claim that decisive and urgent action was not required, but most have deferred to the consultative approach in 'Little Children are Sacred'.

Langton appears to defend the NTER on the basis that it is precisely what many have sought for decades – 'protective interventions to prevent the abuse, rape and assault of Aboriginal women and children, and decisive action against the perpetrators'.[6] But in neither 'Trapped in the Aboriginal Reality Show', nor her subsequent essay, 'The End of Big Men Politics', does Langton explain how the measures described above actually protect women and children.

Langton argues that Aboriginal opinion is divided into 'two camps':

> There are, as some journalists are delighted to report, two camps on these matters, one concerned with symbolic outcomes and the other with the practical. In reality, the two camps are divided by historical issues: those who have lived through the many tragedies and their aftermath in remote Australia committed to preventing the destruction of their

societies in a haze of alcohol and drug abuse; and those with cosmopolitan urban experience who have allowed libertarian leanings, and deep political disappointment, to confuse their logic.[7]

This argument overlooks the Aboriginal women who are at the forefront of the grassroots movement against the NTER, such as Rosalie Kunoth-Monks, the community leader from Utopia in Central Australia. In a report by 'concerned Australians', Kunoth-Monks strongly objected to the top-down approach of the NTER:

> The biggest thing that we have an argument with the government is, we're not white people. We have our own language. We have our own ceremonies. We have our own land. What we want from the government is real help and real funding rather than putting law on top of our law.[8]

Other Aboriginal women from the Northern Territory have voiced similar concerns about the loss of autonomy and cultural authority. Among them is Barbara Shaw of the Mount Nancy Town Camp near Alice Springs. Shaw has been a passionate advocate against the NTER, who has spoken in domestic and international forums and was an applicant in litigation in 2009 that attempted to prevent the Commonwealth's takeover of the Alice Springs Town Camps.

As would be expected in relation to any important public policy, there are also Aboriginal women in the Northern Territory who have spoken in favour of the measures. Among them is the parliamentarian, Bess Nungarrayi Price, whose community of Yuendumu is subject to the NTER. In a speech to the former think-tank, the Bennelong Society, Price said that she embraced the NTER because, 'it meant at last somebody was acknowledging that there was a crisis and that it needed to be addressed'. Price's personal story is compelling and when she discusses the human costs of addiction, it is impossible not to be moved. But like Langton, Price does not base her support of the NTER on evidence of improved outcomes for women and children.

The debate thus far has been at times personal and has failed to address some core questions. The most important of which is an analysis of how the various components of the NTER actually impact on Aboriginal women. This analysis can be contextualised by Aboriginal women's historical experience of state interventions that, at least ostensibly, have been in aid of their protection.

Key NTER measures and the binary of invisibility and control

Income Management

The income management regime was initially applied on the basis of physical presence on certain Aboriginal lands, irrespective of personal circumstance. The former minister, Mal Brough, insisted that a blanket approach was necessary in order to protect vulnerable women and children. In his second reading of the Social Security and Other Legislation (Welfare Payment Reform) Bill 2007, Brough said:

> The welfare reforms outlined in this Bill will help to stem the flow of cash going towards substance abuse and gambling and ensure that funds meant to be for children's welfare are used for that purpose.
>
> … This broad-based approach is needed to address a breakdown in social norms that characterises many of our remote Northern Territory communities.
>
> In particular, this approach is essential to minimise the practice known as 'humbugging' in the Northern Territory, where people are intimidated into handing over their money to others for inappropriate needs, often for alcohol, drugs and gambling.
>
> If certain groups, such as the young and old, are excluded from this measure, it could leave them potentially even more vulnerable.[9]

Brough's sentiments were contradicted by a subsequent report on women's experiences of income management, prepared by the Equality Rights Alliance. The study found that 70 per cent of respondents considered that the BasicsCard had not improved their personal safety, and some even believed that the new scarcity in cash had led to an increase in crime. Rather than offering protection from 'humbugging' by their relatives, 91 per cent of the women surveyed believed that income management had made no difference to their family relationships. The study was confined to Alice Springs and Darwin. Consequently, the study may not necessarily reflect the views of Aboriginal women in remote communities.

The indignity described by former wards during the protectionist era finds resonance in the shame felt by some women in relation to the debit card, or 'BasicsCard'. Seventy-four per cent of the women involved in the Equality Rights Alliance study said that they felt that others 'aren't as nice to me when they see that I use BasicsCard'. One woman argued that:

> It was just enforced over everybody and I don't see why it should happen to people who are doing the right thing. I would have been embarrassed to go to Woolworths with BasicsCard. I have no history of mismanagement or social problems.[10]

Their difficulties were compounded by a lack of trust in Centrelink staff. Particularly concerning was the suggestion that some women had been deterred from seeking a crisis payment in order to escape an abusive relationship, for fear of triggering a referral to income management.

Like earlier interventions, the income management regime appears to have curtailed women's freedoms. The report by the Equality Rights Alliance suggested that compulsory income management has restricted women's choices as consumers. Whereas some women preferred to buy their children's clothing from second-hand stores or small chains, they were now compelled to shop at larger department stores with facilities for the BasicsCard. Others encountered difficulties in buying prescription medicines, as not all chemists accepted the BasicsCard.

The Compulsory Acquisition of Aboriginal Lands
One of the most controversial aspects of the NTER was the compulsory acquisition of Aboriginal lands. In his second reading of the Northern Territory National Emergency Response Bill, Minister Brough justified the Commonwealth's acquisition of Aboriginal lands on the basis that it would, 'give the government the unconditional access to land and assets required to facilitate the early repair of buildings and infrastructure'. For many communities however, the timely or even untimely repair of buildings and infrastructure is yet to occur.

Few commentators have considered how the compulsory acquisition of Aboriginal lands has impacted upon women's law, identity and health. But it is crucial that Aboriginal women are able to fulfil their custodial obligations. Rosalie Kunoth-Monks has spoken of the importance of land to health:

> Health is about being emotionally sound, mentally sound, and knowing who you are, as well as being physically fit. You know who you are when you are on your land, doing what generations of Aboriginal people have done, taking care of that land, singing the songs that the mythology brought forward, right up to today.[11]

Her statement found resonance in a health impact assessment of the NTER measures carried out by the Australian Indigenous Doctors' Association in 2010:

> Ownership and control of land and housing have a positive influence on psychological and physical health. Aboriginal identity is tied to land, cultural practices, systems of authority

and social control, intellectual traditions, concepts of spirituality, systems of resource ownership and exchange. Loss of control over land, a lack of engagement with non-Aboriginal Australia and resulting powerlessness has had ongoing, serious negative impacts on health.[12]

The compulsory acquisition of Aboriginal lands is yet another example of the binary of invisibility and control. In common with income management, the rights of Aboriginal women have once again become invisible. The state's control over Aboriginal women is consolidated just as their ability to assert ownership over their lands is curtailed.

Conclusion

The tragic allegations contained in 'Little Children are Sacred' demanded an urgent and considered response by Australian governments. Although the NTER was a timely response, its measures were at odds with the tenor of 'Little Children are Sacred', which placed an emphasis on empowering Aboriginal communities to own the solutions. All the more galling was the absence of prior consultation. Many of the key NTER measures were subsequently repackaged under the benign guise of 'Stronger Futures' and effectively extended for a further decade.

In spite of the profound consequences for Aboriginal people, the public debate over the measures has been minimal. This article takes the position that a mature public debate would engage with the perspectives of a diversity of Aboriginal women, take account of research on the impacts of key NTER measures, and allow for consideration of Aboriginal women's historical experience of state interventions.

JOHN LEEMANS

MEDIA RELEASE FROM THE GURINDJI

28 July 2011

Gurindji tell consultations meeting: stop the Intervention immediately.

Gurindji people from the communities of Kalkarindji and Daguragu spoke with a united voice during a government consultation meeting yesterday, demanding an immediate end to the NT Intervention.

Gurindji said the loss of control over community land, new Community Development Employment Projects arrangements forcing people to work for the BasicsCard and the takeover of community council assets by the Victoria Daly Shire are making life harder every day.

They are upset that Minister Jenny Macklin did not attend the consultation meeting personally and are demanding she face the community on Freedom Day, the 45th anniversary of the Wave Hill Walk-off on 26 August.

Community spokesperson John Leemans told the consultation meeting:

> The NT Intervention must end immediately. It is a violation of our human rights, our integrity and liberty.

Media Release from the Gurindji

The world is condemning it through the UN. The churches are condemning it. The majority of the voice of the Australian people know this is wrong. The government can no longer ignore the reality of failure and abuse.

We want control of our land back. We want to be able to practise our culture and speak our language. We want jobs created so we can work in our community.

There is a big movement of people into Darwin and Katherine, because there are no jobs in the community any more. This is exactly what we don't want – people must be able to live and work on their Homelands.

We have a brain to think for ourselves on how to run our own communities. It's called self-determination. But since the Intervention everything has been taken away from us.

Following the meeting John Leemans said:

We know Minister Jenny Macklin stayed away from Gurindji country because we are strong and organised against her Intervention. We are going to keep this battle going. I am organising a protest on Freedom Day, forty-five years since our old people walked off Wave Hill station.

I am challenging Jenny Macklin and the Prime Minister Julia Gillard to come and face us here on Freedom Day. She must see all the damage that's been done to this community.

No King, Queen, Prime Minister, dictator or whatever should be above laws of fundamental human rights.

Gurindji worker Peter Inverway said:

I told the consultation people I've been trying to get a job for more than two years now, but they just keep forcing me to work for the BasicsCard. It's like in the old days, before our walk-off, when the station workers were just paid in rations.

So many young people are walking around with no jobs. The Shire bosses over Aboriginal people and has sacked many of our workers who have good qualifications and have worked for years. Non-Indigenous contractors coming in from Katherine get all the work and make big money, while Aboriginal people are thrown aside like rubbish.

We haven't seen anything of the $672 million Indigenous housing program. Many of our houses are from the '60s. They are falling apart and there's no one to fix them. You can fax off to NT Housing in Darwin but nothing happens. The overcrowding is terrible. We need the housing under community control. Local workers need to be employed to build new houses.

We're sick of the racism.

We're upset the government only sent public servants here for this consultation. We need to see the minister herself to tell her – stop the Intervention.

MELISSA LUCASHENKO

WHAT I HAVE HEARD ABOUT THE INTERVENTION

*Trigger Warning: Rape. Paedophilia.
Racist Violence*

As I write this, media headlines are full of recent public tragedy – the murder of two innocent people in Martin Place, Sydney. A deranged gunman attempting to use the symbols of radical Islam took hostages yesterday. After seventeen hours, three people, the gunman included, were dead.

These past twenty-four hours have been an exercise in very tight information management by Australian police, security agencies and the media. As the Sydney siege unfolded, few of us (and virtually nobody in the general public) really knew any of what was happening in the Lindt Café. People's lives were at risk – that's all we knew. Misinformation ebbed and flowed throughout the seventeen hours. We watched TV and listened to radio and social media, but were hardly better informed than if we hadn't.

As I write this, the Abbott Federal Government continues to intervene in the lives of Aboriginal people in the Northern Territory. Little information is available. An exercise in very tight information management is underway. People's lives are at risk. Misinformation ebbs and flows. I have been to the NT only once in the past decade, and then for less than a week. I am far from well-informed about the situation for blackfellas on the ground up north. But here is just a little of what I have read and heard – from my home in the south

– about Northern Territory Aboriginal life and about the Intervention, from many thousands of kilometres away in Brisbane.

I heard that, when the intervention began, under the Howard government in June 1997, it was preceded, six months earlier, by attempts to bribe remote Aboriginal communities to lease their ancestral land to the feds. These bribes took the form of offers of additional housing and other services in desperate communities starved of these normal Australian services. These offers were, at least initially, refused.

I heard that an Aboriginal novelist, now deceased, wrote in the 1990s about working alongside senior Conservative political figures in the south. She wrote that those Conservatives believed that 'bringing back missions' was a sound policy idea for Aboriginal Australia.

I heard Uncle Tiga Bayles on 98.9 community radio describe the people responsible for the Intervention as 'Genocide Johnnies and Genocide Jennies'.

I heard that when the Intervention was first announced, Prime Minister John Howard said, 'The decisions we have taken are non-negotiable.'

I heard the Reverend Dr Djiniyini Gondarra talk about the history of his Yolngu people in the NT as 'being taken away by the Church, taken away by the Welfare, and herded into the white man's yards, like cattle'.

I heard that when the army was first sent into remote Aboriginal communities, some of the black people fled because they feared that the army soldiers had come to shoot them, or take their children – again.

I heard the Reverend Dr Djiniyini Gondarra explain cuttingly in the documentary *Our Generation* that it 'was never our dream to come to the white man's yard. It wasn't our dream to come and work for the white man as a slave.'

I heard Pat Anderson, Aboriginal head of the Little Children are Sacred Inquiry, say in the documentary *Our Generation* that 'where there is unemployment, poverty, alcoholism, drug-taking, overcrowding, you can guarantee that those children, at some point are going to – are severely at risk – and at some point are going to be sexually abused, or abused in some way.'

I heard that when the writer Bill Bryson came to Australia in 2000 he ended his travel book with an impassioned plea for Australian governments to 'Do More. Try harder.' Bryson was astounded and shocked that so little was being done to eradicate the poverty and misery of many remote Aboriginal lives.

I heard that the last officially recorded massacre of Aboriginal people occurred in the NT in 1928.

I heard that other Aboriginal people tell of massacres which followed in later years, within living memory, but that these massacres were not recorded in white history.

I heard friends say that Aboriginal people are routinely harassed and threatened by police in the NT to this very day.

I heard that a common white sentiment concerning Aborigines in the NT during the last century was 'shoot, shovel and shut up'.

I heard from a journalist that in the late 1990s senior members of the ALP in Darwin routinely referred to the esteemed Aboriginal leader Galarrwuy Yunupingu as a 'coon', and mocked the accented English of this man who can speak a dozen Aboriginal languages.

I heard an Aboriginal friend from the remote north say, in relation to certain whites of his hometown, 'they'd shoot me as soon as look at me'.

I heard two Aboriginal mothers in Brisbane tell me that they would not live in Northern Australia by choice due to the dangers of paedophilia.

I heard a friend in Arnhem Land tell me in 2001 that her five-year-old son had been offered marijuana at the local creek.

I heard an Aboriginal ex-serviceman who lived in Jabiru for several years describe that remote Aboriginal town on days when royalty payments arrived as 'reminding me of war zones, when I was in Somalia and Rwanda'.

I heard first-hand reports of a white man from Perth expressing a wish, in early 2014, to travel to the Northern Territory to 'shoot an Aboriginal'.

I heard an Aboriginal alcohol and drug worker from Alice Springs tell me that initially after the Intervention 'the kids were fatter and better fed'.

I heard that the suicide rate of Aboriginal people in the NT increased five-fold after the Intervention.

I heard it hotly disputed that paedophile rings operate in the NT. I heard first hand that one such ring, run in a major Northern Territory town by white so-called Christians, raped my Aboriginal friend repeatedly from the age of two.

I heard that the same Aboriginal friend was raped in her own home by multiple men including two NT police, in 2010.

I heard that my friend escaped the NT and now lives a far safer life down south.

I heard that charges were never laid against Donald Bruce Henderson, a white paedophile who for years was a house parent at the Retta Dixon home in Darwin, a home for Aboriginal children removed from their families under the assimilation policies of white governments.

I heard a white man say that he prefers to beat Aboriginal women because 'the bruises don't show'.

I heard that Patricia Turner, the Head of the National Indigenous Television Network, described child sexual abuse as 'the Trojan horse (the government is using) to resume total control of our lands'.

I heard that Sydney-based social anthropologist Dr Gillian Cowlishaw went to Katherine to do research, where she met an older Aboriginal woman. I heard that after some weeks she realised that her new friend – who was not literate in English – was uneasy. I heard she later realised the Aboriginal woman believed a four-wheel drive from the University of Western Sydney had a 'W' on its side because Dr Cowlishaw worked for the NT Welfare. Her Aboriginal acquaintance was fearful she might have come to take her grandchildren away.

And I heard what the esteemed Aboriginal writer Alexis Wright, who has spent the bulk of her life living and working in Alice Springs, told me, when I asked her about the Intervention. I heard her when she said vehemently:

> Yes. Yes, of course the government should do something about the living conditions and the violence. But not this ...

LIONEL FOGARTY

Philosophies Exterminated

As laws contemplate isolation, seasons cries
Has contained company flames personality.
We connection general disinterest within,
The intellectual process.
Squeal; labelled manipulated judgments
Are made by boulders by lawyers.
The destroyer now galloped empowered,
Ongoing developments.
Northern Territory seems not the dreaming potential,
As the current over used neglected are outdated trickle inescapable.
Elemental suffering are not limitative.
Perpetually was perfect for the governmental,
Orienting condition.
Lifelong innocents are balance to vote for attachments.
Unconditionally appear if friends are adversary interaction.
As laws wall entire existence, we find tolerance policy lacking.
Betrayal interpret was the surged stunned silent when laws looks,
To touch the community of the Territory.
Imitation repeated intrusion by takes a life for exasperation laws.
In contemplate bloody recalling the stories did not work.
Punishment composited arose matter of facts,
The transgression veins were perversely evil symbols,
When literally the Blackfellas intactness because township.
Valid crowns of sovietisation gave more association for us to
Resistance, even to rewrite.
Place near campsite were deliberately moved and caused
    indifference.
Devastate habitats made barrier over encroaches so outbreaks can

escalate.
Expensive plots was now the forces,
Reducing load of crop diseases went on to share remotes.
The moral eyes was to negotiate,
The prominent was to hear memorable
Yet simplistic approaches caused monstrous crime of slaughter.
Importance subject from dimension came to confront predators,
To written laws over laws.
Arguably financial languish on Aborigines negates for the
Whole world endangered to greed.
Extreme candidates were expert on how native Australians are to parent,
An investigation of what viruses the virus hazards.
As laws made by natives no; but play it out?
Has the write it down no; but play it out?
To philosophies our own exterminating.

DJINIYINI GONDARRA

is the spokesperson for the independently established Yolŋuw Makarr Dhuni (Yolngu Nations Assembly) which represents the people of 8 nations in the Western, Central and East Arnhem Land areas of the Northern Territory: Miwatj, Laynha, Raminy, Marthakal, Garriny, Gumurr Rawarraŋ, Gatjirrik and Midiyirrk.

Statement 2011

The Yolŋguw Makarr Dhuni first met in Galiwin'ku in 2011 and made the following statement:

> There is no more turning back.
> We declare that we have not been conquered.
> We declare that to this day we are a sovereign people.
> We declare that we are subject to our Maḏayin system of law constituted by the Unseen Creator of the Universe and revealed to the Givers of Law:- Djaŋ'kawu and Barama, and we continue to steward this system through our lawful authorities and government.
> Our Maḏayin system of law establishes Mägayamirr- peace, order, and good government; is dhapirrk consistent in its statutes; and is assented to by all Yolŋu citizens through the Waṉa Lupthun assent ceremony.
> Our Maḏayin system of law is guarded by the Yothu Yindi separation of powers.
> Our Maḏayin system of law is a rule of law not a rule of man.
> Our Maḏayin system of law is the equal of any other system of law.

JEFF McMULLEN

ROLLING THUNDER: VOICES AGAINST OPPRESSION

Ever since the frontier wars a dread rises up from the dust and bones of the past whenever the great white protectors in far off places start talking about imposing law and order. When the Australian Government ordered boots on the ground, with army troops and federal police taking control of seventy-three Northern Territory remote communities in June 2007, the Intervention was so clearly discriminatory that the hurt inflicted was instant and deep. Nothing like this had happened since Aboriginal people had been rounded up onto the old government missions in the first waves of dispossession. An overwhelming majority of First Peoples opposed the Northern Territory Emergency Response (NTER) from the start because they recognised the Howard government's actions as an assault on their Homelands, their culture and their traditional way of life. From Galiwin'ku on Elcho Island, Milingimbi in the Crocodile Islands, Maningrida and Yirrkala in north-eastern Arnhem Land, out west at Kalkarindji and Daguragu, across Central Australia in Yuendumu, Utopia and Ntaria, at Mutitjulu in the shadow of Uluru, as well as in the town camps of Alice Springs, Tennant Creek and Darwin, I heard a rolling thunder saying NO to the land grab.

With a taskforce of over 600 troops and federal police travelling from interstate with powers to enter Aboriginal homes, the Intervention sent waves of fear into these isolated and strongly traditional communities. My oldest friend in the heartland, the Utopia Elder, Rosalie Kunoth-Monks, told me how some mothers were afraid for their young ones, an echo of eras past when government cars and trucks arrived on dusty roads, removing children to far away institutions creating the Stolen Generations. 'This is a huge violation of our human rights,' said Kunoth-Monks. 'They want to use this scare over our children to break us as human beings, to starve us off our Homelands, to herd us into the towns and of course if they ever get their way we will still be second-class citizens. The government refuses to support our own attempts to be sustainable. It's our land that they want to control. But they don't understand that it is the land that holds us.'

In response to the Howard government's brazen Big Lie that there were paedophile rings sexually abusing children in all of the targeted communities, a claim later vigorously denied by the Australian Crime Commission,[1] the Arrernte/Gurdanji woman, Pat Turner, nailed the truth at the outset. Growling at the television cameras she declared, 'We believe this government is using child sexual abuse as the Trojan horse to resume total control of our land. What the Prime Minister and his minister, Mal Brough, are proposing is in the view of the Combined Aboriginal Organisations of Alice Springs totally unworkable. Mal Brough is drawing too heavily on his military background to swoop into our communities and do a quick fix.'[2]

The ex-army captain, Mal Brough, Minister for Indigenous Affairs in the Howard Coalition government, outlined to Federal Parliament a military-style campaign replete with jargon about a five-year emergency phase proceeding to normalisation. The Prime Minister, always hostile to land rights and self-determination, believed that he had found the perfect man for the job. Just a few months earlier Brough had appeared on *Difference of Opinion*, the ABC television series I anchored. After a tense, hour-long debate about the massive changes coming, Patrick Dodson leant across the panel desk and said to Brough in a quiet but measured tone, 'Minister, it is not fundamentally about policy. It is about how you value Aboriginal people as human beings.' Brough seemed disturbed and as we walked from the television studio he confided that he was frustrated by the lack of progress around the country, insisting that he was determined to stop the collapse of Aboriginal life, because, he added fervently, he had Aboriginal family. Although publicly he had never sounded certain about this Indigenous heritage, Brough's sister, Caroline, identified as an Aboriginal person on the basis that their maternal grandmother, Violet, strongly believed that her missing father had been an Aboriginal man.[3] Highly emotional and cocksure of his own political strength, the Queenslander Brough led the charge in an extraordinary attack on local self-determination in the Northern Territory and yet he was always on shaky ground because of his limited relationship with these communities and his superficial understanding of the complexities.

Whatever Brough thought he could accomplish, the Intervention was built on all too familiar white politics with the ever-present aims of assimilation and control. The new oppression could only be enforced with the help of black advocates in positions of influence who truly believed in a radical development agenda. As we will see, it is doubtful that the government's extraordinary propaganda campaign could have succeeded to the same damaging degree without these loud and persuasive voices. In the eyes of so many white Australians this relatively small number of prominent Indigenous supporters of the Intervention who were afforded so much attention in the national news media, added authority to the deeply offensive and shameful stereotyping of Aboriginal men and families, linking all of the remote communities and, indirectly, all Aboriginal men with organised paedophilia.

Elders opposing the Intervention from the beginning, including Dr Djiniyini Gondarra on Elcho Island, Rosalie Kunoth-Monks at Utopia, George Gaymaroni Pascoe at Milingimbi, Harry Nelson at Yuendumu and Reggie Wurridjal at Maningrida, warned the new invaders that the government legally must consult and work with the community leaders and organisations. Aboriginal Medical Services and the Australian Indigenous Doctors' Association, underscored this sensible advice, pointing out that they already knew the factors having negative impact on children and what was required was adequate government support for programs to reduce the hunger, malnutrition and neglect in overcrowded houses and under-serviced communities. Instead, in a massive overreach by Captain Brough's command central, local Aboriginal organisations with the most knowledge of the issues were sidelined. While the government had no legitimate evidence, moral authority or lawful reason to crush this very limited form of self-management, as well as violate human rights en masse, it launched the Intervention by manufacturing and then manipulating a perception of national crisis.

The 'Little Children are Sacred'[4] report of June 2007, one of some thirty recent assessments of the plight of Indigenous children around the country, set out a tragic pattern of abuse, neglect and poverty in the Northern Territory. What the Howard government did not tell Australians in seizing on this report as the pretext for the takeover of the NT communities, was that substantiated neglect and abuse occurred in considerably greater numbers in Queensland and also at a higher rate in Victoria, the Australian Capital Territory, South Australia and New South Wales.[5] The government similarly had no interest in offering the necessary context to explain how generations of poverty and forced child removal had contributed enormously to the neglect and abuse of children.

If the rate of substantiated abuse was seven to eight times higher among all Indigenous children as many claimed, then surely Australians needed to be told why it was getting so much worse during Howard's years in power. We must remember that then Health Minister, Tony Abbott, steadfastly refused to approve an estimated $460 million per annum required to address the critical shortfall in spending on Indigenous primary health care. For many decades the government had ignored the need for a great society program to build adequate housing for everyone who called this country home. When over 70 per cent of one's health is determined by socioeconomic status it should have been perfectly clear to the government why Indigenous children were suffering the most and where the real emergency lay in remote Australia. The Northern Territory Department of Health has estimated that up to half of the Indigenous gap in life expectancy is due to crippling, generational poverty.[6] Instead of empowering communities to take the lead in their development, governments responded to the pain of the First Peoples by locking them away in a fast growing industrial-prison system. Today about a quarter of the nation's prison population is Indigenous and in the Northern Territory about 84 per cent of prisoners are Indigenous.

Take a look at Rolf de Heer's confronting film, *Charlie's Country*, as David Gulpilil leads us through an explanation of what the new invasion of law and order looks like in the remote communities of the Northern Territory. Through the eyes of strongly cultural people it appears to be a choice of being driven off their country into the fringe-dwelling camps in the long grass outside the larger towns, long periods of incarceration for trivial offences or being abandoned to shrivel and die in poverty.

Throughout its eleven years in power the Howard government stubbornly refused to admit that it was starving remote communities of support and aggravating some of the very social problems it purported to address through the Intervention. I have correspondence from Abbott's office in which he defensively rejected my warnings about the gathering plague of preventable chronic illness that is the greatest threat to the health of all Australian children, especially the poorest.[7] I provided international evidence showing that the well-being of mother and child should be the starting point and that infants in deep disadvantage needed additional support. Abbott replied that the Coalition government had committed millions of dollars to the health of Aboriginal children and what was required was behavioural change in the remote communities. As always, the government cast Aboriginal people as 'the problem', as if these serious social challenges existed only in the remote communities.

No one in the Howard government ever discussed with reporters, breathless about the manufactured crisis in the Northern

Territory, the disturbing truth that about one in four Australian girls and about one in seven boys nationwide were subjected to some form of sexual abuse. In the years to come, the Royal Commission into Institutional Responses to Child Sexual Abuse[8] would investigate about 4000 individual stories from around the country, providing a glimpse of the persistent inability of society to protect children in general, not only Indigenous children. Of course, no one ordered NT-style Interventions into the church and state institutions, or into the barbed-wire detention camps where the children of asylum seekers had been locked up for years.

By ignoring almost all of the recommendations by Indigenous health expert, Pat Anderson and former magistrate, Rex Wild, in their 'Little Children are Sacred' report, especially the call for careful community consultation, the Howard government doomed the Intervention to failure. Not only was the assault on Aboriginal communal life an absurdly clumsy 'top-down' strategy with very little grassroots involvement, Brough's strident style, barking orders at people, was totally counter-productive. The government's over-the-top propaganda was unnecessarily aggressive, alienating and deeply humiliating for Aboriginal families. Despite the evidence that about one in three Australian women in general are victims of domestic violence at some time in their lives and almost one a week is murdered by a partner or former partner, the Intervention never addressed the broader issues in our society but singled out Aboriginal men who were made to feel that they were all failures, nothing more than child molesters, wife-beaters and hopeless drunkards. 'Do they think we are all bad?' the old people would ask me, over and over again as I travelled the remote communities. This 'shame job' guaranteed that few if any communities would support the Intervention. Bringing in Government Business Managers, mocked by the locals as Ginger Bread Men, repeated the oldest patterns of Australian government assimilation as most of the blow-ins were white, handsomely paid and provided with vehicles and air-conditioned accommodation. Some resigned in embarrassment and others quickly realised they too had been duped by the government. Enlisting khaki soldiers to handle the logistics pointlessly strained the long-established good relations between Aboriginal people and NORFORCE, which of course had many Indigenous troops drawn from this region.

Looking back, it is hard to see how anyone could have conceived a more insensitive government offensive as large blue signs posted at the entrance to the communities warned of penalties for possession of alcohol or pornography, branding Aboriginal people as different, shaming them as less deserving of the fundamental human rights that other Australian citizens took for granted.

For the third time in history, Aboriginal people lost the protection of the *Racial Discrimination Act* (RDA). The Intervention's provisions were so blatantly discriminatory that the then all white zone of Federal Parliament simply by-passed this important law aimed at preventing racism. It demonstrates the hollowness of the Australian Constitution, its historic stain of racism and exclusion of any genuine protection of human rights, especially for the unrecognised First Peoples. As former High Court Justice Michael Kirby would later put it, 'Constitutionally speaking, we are still basically White Australia, however much we boast that we have changed.'[9] Because there was no consultation with the communities and no prior, informed consent, the Intervention breached Australia's international legal obligation to respect the rights of the First Peoples. A constitutional lawyer, Professor Larissa Behrendt, argued prominently in the early weeks of the Intervention that its discriminatory, damaging provisions could never be legally justified as 'special measures' for the clear benefit of Aboriginal people. Gauging the deep humiliation felt by Aboriginal people as their communities were stigmatised, Dr Tom Calma, the ATSI Social Justice Commissioner and Race Discrimination Commissioner, aimed his strongest criticism at the abandonment of these fundamental human rights. To get basic services including support for their children, he said, Aboriginal families should not have to trade off their citizens' rights.

Ending permit control over access to the Aboriginal lands; compulsorily controlling townships under five-year leases; impounding community resources; disempowering local organisations and replacing their authority with new bureaucrats; ending the economic mainstay of the Community Development Employment Projects (CDEP); introducing blanket bans on alcohol and pornography; barring judges from considering customary law and cultural practice when setting bail or issuing sentences and notoriously, imposing compulsory management of half of Aboriginal income, all of these deep intrusions into personal and community responsibility amounted to social-engineering on a scale not seen since the era of the Aboriginal Acts and Chief Protectors. This was never a partnership with Aboriginal people but the most damaging policy inflicted on them since the Stolen Generations.

Bristling with the same righteousness and hypocrisy as the Chief Protectors of the past, Prime Minister Howard declared to the national media, 'It is interventionist, I accept that, but what matters more, the Constitutional niceties or the care and protection of young children?'[10] What kind of a democracy would allow a leader to make such a misleading statement and let it go unchallenged? Why didn't the Federal Parliament break into an uproar over the government's decision to remove from these Aboriginal citizens the protection of the RDA? Instead, Kevin Rudd's ALP Opposition rode along with the Intervention, rather than being wedged on their way to near certain victory in the November 2007 election. For over a decade the Howard government had waged war on Aboriginal land rights and self-determination, abolishing the democratically structured Aboriginal and Torres Strait Islander Commission (ATSIC) and undermining Native Title with the ten-point plan of extinguishment. In time, Rudd and then Gillard as Labor prime ministers would display the same willingness as Howard to abandon any form of self-determination in the Northern Territory and to dramatically weaken the Aboriginal Land Rights Act (NT) of 1976. The real agenda underlying the Intervention was control of these lands and abandonment of the smaller remote communities. 'What about my people, are we not human beings too?' asked Dr Djiniyini Gondarra at Galiwin'ku. The Yolngu Elder had rejected the Howard government's earlier attempts to force ninety-nine-year leases on his community in exchange for housing. He could see that the Intervention was a wolf in sheep's clothing. 'I don't believe they ever really cared about our children or they would have done so many things to help,' he said. I paid great heed to these warnings by Dr Gondarra and Rosalie Kunoth-Monks that the Intervention had little to do with the welfare of their children who were barely mentioned in the 500 pages of the NTER legislation.

After campaigning for many decades for improvements to the health and education of Indigenous children here and overseas, since 2000 I had been working closely with more than twenty of the remote communities now subjected to the Intervention. I consulted the Aboriginal Medical Services, legal aid services and the Menzies School of Health and found no enthusiasm for the Federal takeover. I also listened carefully to the handful of Territory-based supporters of the Intervention including Dr Sue Gordon, the former magistrate who became chair of the NT Taskforce. Her 'backs-to-the wall' rationale was that life had become so brutal for women and children that the remote communities had to be brought under a state of emergency, an argument echoed by Professor Marcia Langton at the University of Melbourne. Yet so many more Aboriginal people I consulted in the Northern Territory agreed with the widely respected Olga Havnen, raised in Tennant Creek and later appointed NT Coordinator General, who warned that marginalising the Aboriginal organisations and local leadership structure would be a 'top-down social disaster'. Milingimbi leader, George Gaymaroni Pascoe, said Australians should not be misled by John Howard's talk of 'practical reconciliation' and 'mutual obligation' because the real agenda was to break the influence of Traditional Owners and Aboriginal Lands Councils. The old and canny Harry Nelson from Yuendumu said there was a lot of smoke coming from

Canberra but after it cleared people would see the Intervention was a land grab. Patrick and Mick Dodson, national leaders with decades of experience, both were certain that the Intervention was a sinister plan to end traditional life, introduce private land ownership and open up the NT to rapid exploitation.

In opposing the Intervention the principle many of us invoked was straightforward. We had to speak out to ensure that Australians understood the truth … that this was state-sanctioned discrimination based on a Government Big Lie. To see what was happening to tens of thousands of Aboriginal people and do nothing would be to collude with the oppression. Yet surely here in this country we had the greatest inspiration to rise above that centuries-old crime of silence?

During the Nazi Holocaust, back in December 1938, the Aboriginal Elder, William Cooper, led a small group to the German Consulate in Melbourne to demand that they stop the slaughter of Jews. This was soon after Kristallnacht, the Night of the Broken Glass, when Hitler's brown shirts began their rampage, smashing shop windows, looting Synagogues and dragging Jewish people off to the concentration camps. According to the Holocaust Research Center in Jerusalem there was no other protest in the world quite like William Cooper's. Here was a man not seen as a citizen in his own land and still he raised his voice for other human beings because he believed in the common good. It is my conviction that this great Australian with his quiet dignity and enormous courage challenges us forever to demonstrate our sense of fairness and our shared humanity.

On Monday 25 June, as the Intervention troops began to roll, I called for national action against this discrimination in an address entitled, Children of the Sunrise, the first of scores of speeches I would give on this subject around the country. If you believe strongly in human rights, you must personally act to oppose injustice.

I can tell you that my wife and I would not allow our children to be inspected en masse for possible sexual abuse or neglect. Wouldn't you see a personal physical inspection as reasonable only if there were reasonable evidence that something may have happened to one of your children? But we wouldn't agree with our entire schools or local community being called in for medical inspections.[11]

While the Intervention brought out the most cynical self-interest, especially in those federal politicians who knew the facts but did not want to take a stand against draconian measures dressed up as child protection, it also prompted extraordinary courage from Aboriginal people on the frontlines of the struggle. Irene Fisher, CEO of the Sunrise Health Service Aboriginal Corporation in Katherine, risked her career, displaying a personal and professional dedication by putting her people's wellbeing first. We both flew to the Gunditjmara lands in Victoria to be part of a powerful forum opposing the Intervention. Joined on stage by musicians, Archie Roach and Shane Howard, Irene and then one Aboriginal speaker after another, thundered against the Intervention's exploitation of the child abuse claims and the resulting collective smearing of an entire people.

Thanks to the outcry from Aboriginal health professionals, like Irene Fisher and Dr Mark Wenitong, then President of the Australian Indigenous Doctors' Association (AIDA), the government abruptly stopped talking of mandatory sexual abuse inspections of young Aboriginal children. Instead, Brough's propagandists quickly reworked the message, describing the Intervention as 'an audit of the children's health'. It was a reminder of that cynical observation by the American political strategist, Karl Rove, that governments can create a 'new reality' before the public ever catches up with the spin-doctors.

The day after my Children of the Sunrise speech the text was circulated among ABC network management and lawyers. Someone had expressed concern about perceived conflict of interest. I was never approached directly by the Culture War warriors on the ABC board, including Keith Windschuttle, Ron Brunton and Janet Albrechtsen. After all, my television series had examined diverse views on Indigenous policy, including those of the late neo-conservative, Helen Hughes, who in many ways shaped the intellectual assumptions underpinning the government's assault on remote communities. My critics were hot and bothered that I was presenting to a national audience a thirty-three-part series and yet now publicly advocating that Australians should strongly challenge the government's false claims about the NT Intervention. Throughout the series I made sure that Australians heard from a spectrum of Aboriginal voices ranging from Dr Tom Calma, Professor Lowitja O'Donoghue and Olga Havnen who criticised the government's attack on Indigenous rights, to those like Warren Mundine, Dr Sue Gordon and Mal Brough who yearned for 'tough love', that sickly sweet euphemism for radical intervention. Revealingly, when I invited the Intervention's most influential Aboriginal supporter, Noel Pearson, to join in the analysis of these dramatic policy changes, he angrily bellowed down the telephone line, 'I've climbed the fucking mountain and you are trying to tear it all down.'

'Well come on down from the mountaintop and sit with other Aboriginal people to talk,' I invited, but the man who saw himself as a prophet of change was not ready to debate other equally strong Aboriginal intellects.

I made no apology then to ABC management or Noel Pearson for speaking up against the Intervention and I make none now. Given my knowledge of what was happening, I strongly believed that I had a responsibility to tell Australians the truth, especially when media in general, including some programs on the ABC, peddled government claims without investigation or context. For example, a senior bureaucrat from Mal Brough's office appeared in silhouette on *Nightline* in 2006 clearly giving viewers the impression that he was a youth worker, there to tearfully substantiate the minister's sweeping claims about paedophilia.[12] Journalist Chris Graham called on the ABC to investigate this ethical failure and lack of transparency but the network, foolishly, was reluctant to bite the government hand that fed the national broadcaster.

News Limited newspapers carry a particular responsibility, acknowledged by Tony Koch, then one of the *Australian*'s leading journalists, for promoting the pro-Intervention views and the rise to public prominence of Noel Pearson. His sermons on the mount about Aboriginal responsibility were adored by Rupert Murdoch's editors and other social conservatives but widely shunned by Aboriginal people around the country. The founder of the Cape York Institute, a skilful polemicist, political powerbroker and big businessman, Pearson is a Napoleonic figure whose attraction to politics was never matched by sound judgment about what this would mean for his people. After once deriding conservatives as racist scum, in 2007 Pearson wrote a lengthy letter to John Howard making a bold case that the Prime Minister could still win the election that year by convincing Australians that he had a renewed national agenda. Constitutional recognition of Indigenous people was one goal, but so was welfare management and a responsibility-based agenda, along the lines of Pearson's heavily funded trials in a handful of Cape York communities.

While Pearson's performance from the bully pulpit frequently dazzles white Australians, he antagonises and has been bitterly condemned by many strong Aboriginal leaders over his explicit, if qualified, support of the Intervention approach. Patrick Dodson told a Yolngu audience that Pearson was part of an ideological group including Marcia Langton and Warren Mundine that 'don't recognise you, they don't recognise your culture'.[13] Dr Djiniyini Gondarra told Australians not to listen to 'leaders who want to divide and conquer us. You appointed these people as Aboriginal spokesmen, not us. He is not our man, he is your man.'[14] Just weeks before the November 2007 election Pearson and Langton orchestrated a stunning political gambit as the Northeast Arnhem Land leader, Galarrwuy Yunupingu, reversed his original strong condemnation of the Intervention. After his dramatic announcement at Melbourne Law School, I asked Yunupingu why he was now supporting the Interventionist government that had been one of the most damaging to the rights and progress of Aboriginal people. He replied that

Pearson had convinced him that Howard was going to win the election. A respected Aboriginal scholar, now deceased, was standing with us and said, 'Jeff, you don't think Howard is going to win the election?' I told them that I was certain the Howard government would fall. Tragically, Galarrwuy Yunupingu had been persuaded that giving control of community lands to the Federal Government under a ninety-nine-year lease would bring on Noel Pearson's neo-liberal revolution, the 'radical centre' that he claimed would drive rapid development, transforming traditional people in remote communities into acquisitive individuals willing to give up communal tenure in favour of private home ownership and a job somewhere in the so-called free market.

While Noel Pearson and his allies always thought they were using the government, the truth is the Aboriginal neo-conservatives have been exploited over and over again by the corporate bosses and politicians. The government's divide-and-conquer strategy in the Northern Territory was painfully evident when we screened an early rough-cut of the anti-Intervention film, *Our Generation*. In Darwin's open-air theatre, the ailing voice of Yothu Yindu, the late Dr Yunupingu (brother of Galarrwuy) and his wife, Yalmay, strongly encouraged us to stay on the road to let Australians around the country hear the poignant voices in this authentic account of the Intervention's disastrous impact. At the Gama Festival, Galarrwuy Yunupingu and Marcia Langton noticeably did not attend the film's screening on the last night of that gathering but other senior members of the Yunupingu family stayed there until almost two am, crying and speaking out in language with unforgettable power to explain the pain caused by the Intervention. The Intervention created one of the deepest splits in the Indigenous leadership in my lifetime. Yet within two years, Galarrwuy Yunupingu had become so bitterly disappointed with the Intervention that he announced that he had been misled, that it went over the heads of the most senior leaders, had brought no change on the ground and was driving everyone crazy.

Because of the Intervention's shock and awe, and particularly because of the show of support from Pearson, Langton, Mundine and belatedly, Galarrwuy Yunupingu, the Australian media did not investigate how the Howard government had long been preparing to take control of the remote communities. Minister Brough's December 2005 Blueprint for Action in Indigenous Affairs, as well as his frequently stated desire to introduce private land ownership in place of communal control, signalled the broad outlines of the assault on land rights that was coming. In 2006 the Howard government amended the Aboriginal Land Rights Act (NT) to allow the government to lease townships on Aboriginal land for ninety-nine years, a land grab that would effectively end Indigenous control forever. Former Prime Minister Malcolm Fraser and his former Minister for Aboriginal Affairs, Ian Viner, have both stated unequivocally that these Commonwealth measures seek to smash traditional ownership of the lands. If you divide and then marginalise lands councils and sideline traditional owners you clear the way for a mere handful of powerful corporations to become the administrators of neo-liberal development. Most Aboriginal leaders understood this and resisted the flash of the cash, the temptation to sign a ninety-nine-year lease in return for slight improvements in their essential services. At this point, the hard-line Cultural War warriors saw the Intervention as the best means to ram through profound change to land rights.

It is curious but telling that the Intervention's ideological architects have been remarkably hesitant to stand before Aboriginal people and accept full responsibility for the social disaster. In Dispossession: Neo-Liberalism and the Struggle for Aboriginal Land and Rights in the twenty-first Century,[15] I set out many important links between prominent critics of contemporary Indigenous culture and the market fundamentalism asserting that these communally owned lands must be 'modernised' and opened up for private land ownership and rapid development. The neo-liberal view of remote communities is based on a particularly narrow view of modernisation, ignoring the insights of Djiniyini Gondarra and Richard

Trudgen[16] who explain how the 'modern' invasion of the traditional way of life also brought devastating epidemics, the ravages of alcohol and drug abuse, racism and social friction on the edge of large mining communities. The undermining of Aboriginal authority has always been followed by profound disorientation among traditional people. The neo-liberal argument that the remote communities are not viable also ignores the many decades of scholarship by Professor Jon Altman and others at the ANU's Centre for Aboriginal Economic Policy Research, showing that it is possible to develop effective local economies without the obliteration of culture that accompanies neo-liberal style intervention.

To understand the Northern Territory Intervention, why and how it happened, we need to grasp that it is neo-liberalism that is shaping the agenda for control of Aboriginal lands and assimilation of Indigenous people in the twenty-first century. Neo-liberalism connects the goals of 'modernising' Aboriginal culture and allowing mining companies and other corporations to exploit at minimum cost the resources buried in the 2.5 million square kilometres or 33 per cent of terrestrial Australia still under some form of control by Indigenous people.[17] While most of Australia's 400 or so current mines are not on lands occupied by Indigenous people, it is the vast El Dorado of the unexploited country that is irresistible to the neo-liberal developers.

David Harvey, the British social scientist, describes this ravenous strain of development as 'accumulation by dispossession'.[18] He identifies the essential features of neo-liberalism as privatisation and commodification of public/community goods; financialisation to treat good or bad events as opportunities for economic speculation; management and manipulation of crises to establish the neo-liberal agenda and a state redistribution of wealth, not to the poor but to the rich and powerful. Applying this neo-liberal pattern to Australia, what we are seeing is not 'trickle down economics' but exploitation of mineral wealth that is said to belong to the nation but, in fact, mainly benefits the capital managers.

Harvey is adamant that the global pattern clearly demonstrates that 'redistributive effects and increasing social inequality have in fact been such a persistent feature of neo-liberalisation as to be regarded as structural to the whole project'.[19]

In the ranks of the neo-liberals, Noel Pearson singled out Helen Hughes, Senior Fellow at the right-wing Centre for Independent Studies, as the most relentless of field marshals. This Czech-born immigrant who had come to Australia at the age of five intensely disliked socialism and derided the very existence of remote communities as an 'experiment that was to give Aborigines and Torres Strait Islanders a socialist utopia, leading to the establishment of a separate nation'.[20] Hughes ignored the obvious fact that although these communities were sensibly organised on traditional cultural divisions, they were never empowered to develop genuine autonomy, the kind that I have witnessed bring rapid improvement to the wellbeing of many First Nations societies in the United States and on the Saami lands in Norway, Finland and Sweden. Three decades of research by Stephen Cornell and Jo Kalt of the Harvard Project on American Indian Economic Development underscores that genuine sovereign control is the key to progress in wellbeing, education, housing and employment.[21]

Like most of the Intervention cheer-squad in Australia, Hughes overlooked the global evidence and instead identified as the first and urgent priority the introduction of individual property rights on communal Aboriginal lands. She vigorously argued for ninety-nine-year leases of remote communities to the Federal Government to facilitate a switch to private home ownership.[22] Not only was Hughes constructing David Harvey's first pillar of neo-liberalism, she was creating for the Howard government the intellectual antecedents and the strategy of shock and awe, the idea of failing communities with children in grave danger, to 'justify' the Intervention.[23]

After the Intervention taskforce arrived in Maningrida, a traditional owner, Reggie Wurridjal, challenged Senator Nigel Scullion (now Minister for Indigenous Affairs) on why the Elders had not been consulted in advance about the takeover of their homes, organisations and so many whole communities. 'I acknowledge that these people like Reg have every right to be a bit upset with me because there was no consultation. And the only thing I can say is that there was no consultation with anyone else either.'[24] Wurridjal and other Elders at Maningrida mounted a bold legal challenge to the injustice of the Intervention pointing out that using Aboriginal mining royalties to supposedly compensate communities for the imposition of emergency leases was not just compensation. The High Court slammed the door in the face of Aboriginal people and Justice Michael Kirby lamented that if other Australians had seen non-consensual leases imposed on their property interests they would have been afforded a transparent public trial denied to the remote communities.[25]

The government's unlawful failure to consult the remote communities also was condemned by United Nations human rights authorities including the Special Rapporteur, Professor James Anaya, who concluded that this overt discrimination was incompatible with Australia's obligations to the rights of Aboriginal people.[26] Rosalie Kunoth-Monks and Dr Djiniyini Gondarra travelled to Geneva to appear before the Committee for the Elimination of Racial Discrimination to carry the accounts of many remote communities trampled by the Intervention. A remarkable network of supporters known as concerned Australians led by Michele Harris and featuring the advocacy of former Prime Minister Malcolm Fraser, former Chief Justice of the Family Court Alastair Nicholson, former Victorian Supreme Court Judge Frank Vincent and former Liberal minister Ian Viner, focused national and international attention on the Intervention's abuse of Indigenous rights.

In Aboriginal communities, at universities, in town halls and cinemas around the country, Sinem Saban and Damien Curtis, screened the passionate voices in their film, *Our Generation*, and slowly more Australians began to awaken to the truth. Sinem had been a schoolteacher in Galiwin'ku when the Intervention rolled in. She picked up her camera to gather an authentic rendering of the fierce Yolngu resistance to the attempted takeover of their way of life. Our small band travelled cities and towns around this country with Elders such as Rosalie Kunoth-Monks and Djiniyini Gondarra directly addressing thousands of citizens. We had the backing of some of the finest musicians including Archie Roach, Shane Howard, John Butler, Danielle Caruana, Shellie Morris and Xavier Rudd who stood shoulder to shoulder with the Elders on our 'rolling thunder' campaign. Shortly before he died, our great friend, that gentle troubadour, Dr Jimmy Little, penned an eloquent plea, urging the government to 'listen to the wisdom of the Elders' who understood what was happening and would have the responsibility, inevitably, of cleaning up the social mess after the Intervention. How overwhelmingly sad to see such wonderful people giving so much to the struggle but dying with a clear portent of the dispossession that was coming. Djiniyini Gondarra's beloved sister who had spoken so eloquently in *Our Generation* about the lack of adequate housing, health care and nutrition for remote community children, gave her last breath to this campaign and died tragically, way too early, from totally preventable chronic illness. She was my sister too.

A child born in that first year of the Intervention will spend the first fifteen years of life under Federal control, because of the ALP Government's ten-year extension of most of the provisions of the NTER (2007). Despite over 400 submissions to the Senate's Inquiry on the ironically named Stronger Futures legislation of 2012, only a handful of these politicians even graced the Senate chamber for the vote continuing the assault on the Aboriginal Homelands. Even before the return to power of the Coalition in September 2013, neo-liberalism had swamped Canberra's political establishment, both legislature and bureaucracy. How shameful that the one burning national issue that produced firm bipartisanship between the major political parties was the imposition of Federal control over Indigenous lives.

Tony Abbott came into government admitting that the Intervention was heavily flawed by its 'top-down' approach yet his promise to be the 'Prime Minister for Aboriginal Affairs' has been characterised by unprecedented centralisation of control in Canberra and drastic cuts to most crucial services to Indigenous people. His gaffe about the arrival of the First Fleet being the defining moment in the history of the continent and the whiff of terra nullius in his comment that it was 'just bush' before the British came, are extraordinarily insensitive to the First Peoples who have lost faith in the gubba system. Despite his rhetoric about Constitutional recognition, the policy Abbott has outlined disempowers them around the country by shifting most Federal Government funding into a carefully controlled cabal of corporations, misleadingly named Empowered Communities. The government's acid attack on land rights continues, with further changes positioning these corporations and others for administration of vast tracts of mineral-rich land. The Northern Territory Government has been sticking to the Intervention blueprint, allowing the Homelands to die on the vine. The Western Australia Government follows suit, announcing that more than 150 of its remote communities will be closed and South Australia wants to end more than fifty small communities in the Anangu Pitjantjatjara Yankunytjatjara lands. Having dismantled CDEP under the Intervention, now Minister for Indigenous Affairs, Nigel Scullion, proposes work-for-the-dole with remote community residents required to work 25 hours a week for 52 weeks a year to receive the Newstart allowance. The new rules are clearly discriminatory because they will not apply to people in the cities but only to the 30,000 unemployed under the government's Remote Jobs and Communities Programme.

'I want an absolute halt to the punitive assault on the First Australians,' declared Rosalie Kunoth-Monks at Utopia. 'The trauma of the Intervention has cost lives. They are killing me and my people. Depression is now very high in so many communities and suicide is in numbers we have never seen before. I fear that the call for five-days-a-week slavery on welfare wages will lead to the elimination of communities that still hold culture central to our very being. We must rise above this dictatorship that wants to move us into the ghettoes of poverty in the townships, where there is no housing for us, no understanding even of who we really are. I am a black woman fighting for survival. Once again I state that we are not "the problem" … Stop the government violation of our human rights!'[27]

Travelling thousands of kilometres in a four-wheel drive with my sister, Rosalie Kunoth-Monks, visiting many of the remote communities now in danger, it is clear to us that as Intervention-style social engineering gathers momentum, traditional culture and attachment to country are facing a grave threat. In the last federal election, we rallied support for the fledgling First Nations Party, believing that a united majority of black and white Australians could defend land rights in the Northern Territory. On this battleground, at least, the First Peoples have the numbers if the rest of us follow William Cooper's urging to speak up for our shared humanity. As the lands of the First Peoples and especially the smaller remote communities are endangered around the nation, only a national awakening and a unified, powerful resistance can halt this gouging of country. Listen as the land sings to us all. We must all be custodians.

DJINIYINI GONDARRA, ROSALIE KUNOTH-MONKS, MAURIE JAPATA RYAN, HARRY NELSON, DJAPIRRI MUNUNGGIRRITJ, BARBARA SHAW, YANANYMUL MUNUNGGURR

PRESS CONFERENCE

Statement by Northern Territory Elders
and Community Representatives

Melbourne, 4 November 2011

No more! Enough is enough!

United First People's Law men and women who are born leaders representing people of Prescribed Areas in the Northern Territory make this statement. Once again, they have gathered to openly discuss the future of our generation who have been subjugated by the lies and innuendo of the Federal Government, set out in the Stronger Futures document (October 2011).

The Stronger Futures report has created a lot of anger and frustration due to the lack of process and the ignorant way in which the views of the people have been reported. We therefore reject this report.

We will not support an extension of the Intervention legislation. We did not ask for it. In fact we call for a genuine apology from the Federal Government for the hurt, embarrassment, shame and stigma, and for the illegal removal of the *Racial Discrimination Act*.

It is our intention to officially call upon Government for reparation. The recent consultations report shows that Government has failed to take seriously our concerns and feelings. This report is simply a reflection of predetermined policy decisions.

This is shown clearly by the absence of any commitment to bilingual learning programs as well as the proposal to introduce welfare cuts and fines to parents of non-attending school children. Once again, a punitive policy that is neither in the best interests of the child or the family.

Blanket measures have been central to the Northern Territory Intervention and have been the source of much distress. Where there are problems, they must be addressed on a case-by-case basis and preferably with assistance through the appropriate community channels.

Since August 2007 till 2011, more than 45,000 First Nations peoples living in the prescribed areas were traumatised when a bill was passed through both Houses of Parliament (The House of Representatives and the Senate).

This legislation suspended the *Racial Discrimination Act 1975* to put in place the Northern Territory Emergency Response.

The Australian Greens were the only party to oppose the legislation. These actions have placed Australia in breach of its international treaty obligations to the First Nations Peoples. Respectful discussion and negotiation with community Elders did not take place before the introduction of the Intervention.

Discussions on a diplomatic basis are essential. There are Elders in every Aboriginal nation invested by the authority of the majority. These are the people with whom Minister Macklin should be negotiating, rather than with the chosen few, as has been her habit.

There has NEVER been acquiescence in the taking of our lands by stealth. Aboriginal people are sovereign people of this nation. The process that will lead to legal recognition of customary law should be immediately commenced.

We believe that there should be an honest and comprehensive

treaty negotiation with the Australian Government and facilitated by the United Nations.

We have a right under international law to self-determination and after almost five years of the oppression of the Intervention, we demand that Government hand back to us control over communities and provide adequate Government, long-term funding to ensure the future of Homelands.

Community councils have suffered from years of underfunding. The same is happening today with the shires that have been imposed on us. There is a lack of funding for our core services. There is no capacity for Aboriginal communities to engage in long-term services planning without the certainty of long-term funding.

We have had enough! We need our independence to live our lives and plan our futures without the constant oppression and threats which have become central to the relationship between Government and Aboriginal communities in the Northern Territory.

We will not support policies that have not been negotiated with all Elders of prescribed communities and we will not support an extension of the Intervention, or an Intervention under other names.

Since the Apology and since reconciliation, the level of incarceration of Aboriginal men has increased three-fold; our families are being punished for failure to attend a foreign school design; our capacity to govern our own lives has been totally disempowered; Aboriginal youth suicide rates in the Northern Territory are higher than anywhere else in Australia; and our people have been demonised, labelled and branded. This is not what an apology is and it is not reconciliation. These outcomes are the very opposite to their intent.

Australia is in breach of its international treaty obligations to the First Nations People through its membership to the United Nations in the elimination of racial discrimination.

We as leaders of the Northern Territory acknowledge other people's views. We acknowledge that some may agree and some may disagree with parts or all of the 'Intervention'; whatever the name the Government chooses to call it. The only right we now have left is to remain silent.

We as Aboriginal people call on the international community to hold Australia to account for its continuing crimes against humanity for its treatments of its First Nations People. Again, we say of our visits by the minister's department – this is not consultation. Proper consultation is about listening and inviting and including the views of Aboriginal and Torres Strait Islander people.

Consultation is about outcomes that are progressive and agreeable to all parties. The future is based on our children having a quality education, but to date this continues to be a systemic failure. A quality education for our people needs to include:

- Bilingualism in schools to be returned and strengthened to ensure our children learn their traditional languages, dialects and cultural knowledges.
- Attendances need to be rewarded, rather than children and families being punished for non-attendance.
- Aboriginal teachers in classrooms and school educational leadership roles are essential to building quality, localised schooling programs. This means also equal pay and entitlements, rewards and opportunities consistent with their important roles.
- Curriculum needs to change and reflect traditional knowledges not just for Aboriginal and Torres Strait Islander children, but importantly for the broader Australian population who know very little about their own First Peoples.
- Aboriginal teachers need to be treated fairly and equally to their non-Aboriginal counterparts in delivering quality education to our children. This includes the opportunity to tell oral stories of kinship, creation stories, and about important cultural knowledge and skills. Failure to accept these views and work seriously towards their inclusion will simply mean more of the same.

BRUCE PASCOE

BREAD

Someone swept her hand through the grassheads at Cuddie Springs and looked down at what she had gathered and walked back to her camp wondering. She looked around, selected two stones and ground the seeds into a powder. She probably tasted it with her tongue and later that day, or one not too distant, she mixed it with a little water and cooked it by the fire.

She made bread. Thirty thousand years ago. Apart from her sisters, the next to try that alchemy were the Eygyptians 17,000 years ago. So, this woman came up with an idea, far more important to humanity than the moon landing, nearly 13,000 years after that Australian Aboriginal woman. If Newton hadn't latched onto the idea of gravity there were six or seven others working on the same idea in the same year, so it would have become known to the world soon after, but that woman came up with an idea that no one else contemplated for 13,000 years. That's genius isn't it?

Am I guessing that it was a woman? Of course, but Aboriginal culture tells us that the grindstone was the province of women way back in ancestral time so to credit a woman with the science is logical.

I tell conference gatherings about this invention and mostly the room shows a brief, quizzical disturbance before settling back into further contemplation of the gap to be closed between black and white Australians.

Close friends of mine eating my fish at my table look bemused by this little glimpse back in time and then come up with a rational explanation of why it is not a scientific breakthrough. Could you really call it bread? Was her ground oven really deserving of the word?

These are my friends and the fruit and ice-cream is yet to come so I am happy for the conversation to change because my hurt is so deep I can barely speak. Here is one of the greatest moments in human civilisation and people of great learning and unfailing support for Aboriginal people find ways of rationalising it into insignificance, into dependency.

This is what Australia is like. Not cruel, not nasty, just so wedded to a story of human history that Aboriginal Australia is forever outside it.

Nothing started here! Nothing was invented here! It all happened somewhere else while Aboriginal people existed in pristine hunter–gatherer ignorance.

While Australians insist on viewing their early history in this light we are destined to call in the army instead of the doctor, the policeman before the teacher. We will intervene to close the gap in life expectancy when the gap to be closed is in our knowledge of our own country. We will intervene like a bull in a crockery shop and never think to ask Aboriginal people for their opinion.

Women in the Kimberley knew how to resist the degeneration in their community wrought by alcohol. They begged governments and their agencies to allow them to reduce the hours of alcohol sales, and the volume and strength sold.

Authorities threw up their hands in horror. It was impossible, criminal to intervene between retailers and their customers; it went against the grain of free society, our free market. After fighting the authorities for a decade and seeing the further dissolution of their people the women went ahead, broke the law, and set up their own alcohol sales policy. The doctor in their community having kept comprehensive records of town health watched over the next decade as life expectancy rose, infant health skyrocketed, diabetes plunged, school attendance skyrocketed and family violence fell away. These results have been published by the Australian Medical Association but Australia would still rather subject people to welfare penalty than to do something they know works; inviting Aboriginal people to invent the solution.

Our insistence that Australian Aborigines lived a traditional life as hapless, wilful children with no real history, condemns us to mishandle the national response to Aboriginal disadvantage. No conversation of any depth between white and black is possible while Australia persists in believing a self-serving history.

I write this essay on the morning people died in the Martin Place siege in Sydney. Yes, it's tragic, yes, I'm appalled, no I don't think that's when Australia lost its innocence for that happened as soon as Europeans stepped on Australian soil and determined that they would ignore Aboriginal prior ownership and achievement in order to allow a space where a justification for colonisation could be expressed in Christian terms.

A few days before the siege I had a very depressing conversation with two women I admire. We argued about whether academic Australia had given true credit to Aboriginal Australia and whether the church had been a boon for the First Australians. It was depressing because I end up having that conversation in one form or another every day of my life. Australia cannot believe what its science is aching to tell it. It does not believe what the explorers saw: Aboriginal houses, towns, ovens, food preservation, food storage, clothes and … bread. It does not believe what Aboriginal Australia says about its history and economy. People wonder why conversations with Aboriginal Australia break down into incomprehension. We simply cannot believe what the other is saying.

It is painful to contemplate the nation in this light because I love Australia, obviously, and I love Australians, they are a great people, but we will never reconcile our black and white selves while we do not share a history, or rather, cannot see that our history comprises everything that happened here since homo sapiens began to make tools, and with those tools, bread.

Don't allow yourself to be repelled by the plaint of a tortured and innocent soul because that is not the case. I received the same education as most Australians of my age and with my mighty intelligence and refined morality I believed what I was taught: Aborigines gave way to a superior race and meekly went into the missions to eat refined flour and drink alcohol.

I didn't shout 'Eureka' when I learnt that Aboriginal people cooked 'damper' and never questioned why it wasn't called bread. Some historians have said to me that it is not called bread because it does not contain yeast. So how come Lebanese bread is called bread and Jewish equivalents have the word bread on their packaging? It is called damper rather than bread to distance it from the achievement of Europeans.

Why were we hammered in school with the Aboriginal diet of witchetty grubs and kangaroos? Why is the Aboriginal vegetable diet referred to as roots and leaves instead of names that hinted at their equivalence to English salads and potatoes? Why were we asked to colour in shields, spears and boomerangs and never flour mills and harvesting knives?

I went along with all this, I wrinkled my nose at the thought of witchetty grubs, I pitied a people without houses and clothes, until I was confronted by my own family's past. Even then it took me another decade to believe. Gradually, ever so gradually, I was inducted into the true history of the country and after slow and sceptical cogitation of those facts re-read my history books and realised the absences within them.

I then became strident in my new and superior knowledge, much to the embarrassment of my Elders, until finally I was acquainted with those other great determinants of Aboriginal success; modesty and tolerance.

I might have had the advantage of family connection but even without that I should have reached the same conclusion but for my slavish devotion to the story of European exceptionalism and the inferiority of all other races.

The gap between us is not the superior morality or attitude of one group over the other, it is a difference in our knowledge of the country's history. Some are born into households where that knowledge has been hard won but the rest of us have to search for it, even if that requires us to go outside the curriculum we thought was the bedrock of civilisation.

It is within our intellectual and moral power to acquire better knowledge, not in slavish worship of the noble savage, but through inquisitive review of the early European records. This is not a matter of good blackfella and bad whitefellow but an enlightened examination of our country's history.

It would be ridiculous if the whole nation began to tug the forelock at anything a blackfella said because we are as human as the next and some are as craven as Clive Palmer and Lang Hancock.

What would be wonderful, however, is that when overseas and asked about our nation we refrained from mentioning Gallipoli, Vegemite and Bondi and puffed out our chest and said, 'I come from the country that invented bread. And art, and building.'

Building! When Sturt, Mitchell, Grey and others saw villages of substantial permanent buildings capable of housing up to 1000 people how did our history curriculum manage to render this as Aborigines living under nothing more substantial than a piece of bark and a stick? How does the Victorian western district house where a settler attended a meeting of over fifty people get reworked as a temporary dwelling of no great significance?

Some argue, quite rightly, that Aboriginal people did not live in those houses every week of the year but how is that different from the modern holiday houses at Portsea, Tea Gardens and Albany? To deny our children knowledge of the observed fact of Aboriginal housing cannot be discounted as an oversight. Information of that kind should have been like gold to the curriculum designer and the legislator ... but perhaps it didn't fit the image of the nation they believed they were creating.

And if so many people were living together at the same time and in the one place what were they doing? Well, according to Charles

Sturt on the Warburton River, the centre of Sturt's Stony Desert, they were harvesting a grain crop to make flour and the most delicious cakes Sturt had ever eaten. Ernest Giles found siloed stores of this grain and flour weighing over a ton. And he stole it. Imagine the dent in the economy that would have made. And we wonder why Aborigines were fighting to repel the Europeans.

At Brewarrina in New South Wales Mitchell found the people harvesting fish within a system of fish traps so intricate and so cunningly constructed that scientists are still unsure what features of the design allowed them to withstand flood. Other scientists speculate that these traps are the oldest human construction on earth and, yes, you can see them from space. Would Australian engineering students find them fascinating? Only if they were told they existed. At Hutt River in Western Australia Aborigines were cultivating yam gardens so deeply you couldn't walk across them and so wide you couldn't see to the other side. These vast fields were divided by wide and heavily beaten roads and a system of wells for irrigating yam (*Dioscorea hastifolia*). Something was going on in Australia and we seem determined to ignore it.

And do these examples mean that every Aboriginal was contemplating the fusion between flour, water and heat or the miracle of the keystone? No, just as not every Briton worked out how to build Stonehenge or every Greek visualised the Acropolis or every Inuit perfected the recipe for rendering sea bird flesh. There was the normal range of endeavour in Aboriginal societies and the normal range of advancement, if we are prepared to call the shift from hunting and gathering to agriculture an advance, and it doesn't matter what we decide to call it but we do have to accept the fact that it was happening because the explorers' journals describe those processes.

And if we accept these things we have to wonder how they were achieved and sustained across the land without resort to war. The continuance of particular Australian languages in particular locations over a period greater than any other country in the world has managed, tells us of the stability of that peace. The world civilisations extolled in Australian history texts were done and dusted within a few hundred years. Some lasted a thousand but they were rare. Many were extinguished by the environment but, tellingly, most fell during war.

How and why did Australia manage a system of pan-continental government that resisted the propensity of humans to murder and steal in wars to conquer territory? I've never seen that question on any Australian exam paper but I would love to know the answer and we would be a fairer country if more of us wondered about this miracle of restraint.

The crucial difference perhaps was that that change was still rooted and moderated within the spiritual perception of the First Australians. The spirit creators, however, seemed not to be vengeful, indeed there seemed to be a spiritual coherence across the continent and a faith that never countenanced competing gods and power-jealous adherents.

Examination of the principle of this spiritual governance has all but escaped Australian scholarship. The exceptions are glorious but they are few and largely ignored for if they were esteemed their words would be the foundation of the country's history texts.

Shaun Micallef, Australian television comedian and host, goes to India to search for himself and record his progress on film. Thousands of Australians preceded him in search of their gurus and millions go to Bali to float a candle on a lily leaf. Further millions of us trudge around the Acropolis and Angkor Wat to find enlightenment but almost none go to Narooma in southern New South Wales to learn the story of the conversation between mountains.

What would another country do with the Brewarrina fish traps, a construction that is arguably older than any other human building? The Americans would have a hundred Greyhound buses visiting it every day and three airline flights for the rich. Any country would have it in the curriculum but in Australia no student knows about the fish traps at Brewarrina because the sole book discussing it was printed in 1976 and runs to just sixty pages.

Aboriginal people are constantly being advised not to be so angry. Even sympathisers of the Aboriginal cause tut-tut about Marcia Langton's stern demeanour and seething anger. But imagine that the culture so wilfully ignored was your own. Try and describe the magnitude of your anger, and don't hold back, because anger and sorrow of themselves are not criminal acts. Neither is deliberate ignorance, but it is both regrettable and repairable.

I am confident Australia has all the skills and the quality of mind and heart to close that gap but delays for whatever reason are not part of achieving the necessary success. It is easy to point at the horror of family violence as witnessed in Cairns in December 2014 and use it as a chance to walk away from Aboriginal achievement. But the poor, dispossessed and mentally ill have caused horrors like this in all countries and all ages, but when in full possession of their land and spirit Aboriginal people managed sophisticated governance. The positive for Australia is that elements of that management are still practised, the young are still inculcated with their history and culture and the opportunity to understand how that invention reflected the continent's nature is still available.

Something was happening in the spirit and intellect of Aboriginal Australians that may have been affected by isolation but that alone cannot account for its success. The determination to tolerate others, to generate harvests from the land without destroying the soil, the vision to include all in the bounty of both the food and the spirit is a rare commodity in world history. How was the management of economy and spirituality sold to the thousands of generations without someone wanting more and being prepared to kill for it?

This is not a Pollyanna question, it goes to the heart of human evolution because our world is showing all the signs that we cannot survive the current pervading principles of business and religion. Surely there is something to be learnt from a people who decided that sharing resources among all and resisting territorial greed was a useful human idea.

Once the true nature of the culture and governance of traditional Aboriginal Australia is understood we might begin a conversation, a conversation not based on the presumption that Aboriginal people are a problem to be solved.

The Intervention was meant to be the circuit breaker and problem solver but its failure was absolute. Take housing as an example; almost all the Intervention money was spent on housing for the builders and government operatives before a single house was built for Aboriginal people.

Aboriginal people need to be central to the design and delivery of remedial systems so that fly-in-fly-out non-Aboriginal workers do not absorb all the money set aside for the solution to a problem. It is too late to try and turn the long-term unemployed into builders at the eleventh hour and then throw up your hands when they fail; that process must begin when the students start school.

The teachers must be the best, the school must provide adequate resources and the aims must be high.

The Intervention was implemented from the assumption that the clients were feeble mendicants and that assumption prevails because Australia does not know the history of the country.

ALI COBBY ECKERMANN

Four Poems

INTERVENTION PAYBACK

I love my wife   she right skin for me   pretty one my wife   young one   found her at the
next community over   across the hills   little bit   long way   not far
and from there she give me good kids   funny kids mine   we always laughing
all together   and that wife   she real good mother   make our wali real nice   flowers and
grass patch and chickens   I like staying home with my kids

and from there I build cubby house   yard for the horse   see I make them things from left
overs   from the dump   all the left overs from fixing the houses
and all the left overs I build cubby house and chicken house

and in the house we teach the kids   don't make mess   go to school learn good so you can
work round here later   good job   good life   and the government will leave you alone

and from there tjamu and nana tell them the story   when the government was worse   rations
government make up all the rules   but don't know culture   can't sit in the sand   oh tjamu and
nana   they got the best story   we always laughing us mob

and from there night time when we all asleep   all together on the grass patch   dog and cat and
kids   my wife and me   them kids they ask really good questions about the olden days
about today   them real ninti them kids   they gunna be right

and from there come intervention   John Howard   he make new rules   he never even come to
see us   how good we was doing already   Mal Brough   he come with the army   we got real
frightened true   thought he was gonna take the kids away   just like tjamu and nana bin tell us
I run my kids in the sand hills   took my rifle up there and sat   but they was all just lying
changing their words all the time   wanting meeting today   and meeting tomorrow we was
getting sick of looking at them   so everyone put their eyes down   and some even shut their

ears   and from there I didn't care too much   just kept working fixing the housing   being happy working hard   kids go to school   wife working hard too   didn't care too much   we was right we always laughing us mob   all together

but then my wife she come home crying   says the money in quarantine but I didn't know why they do that   we was happy   not drinking and fighting   why they do that we ask the council to stop the drinking and protect the children   hey you know me ya bloody mongrel I don't drink and I look after my kids   I bloody fight ya you say that again   hey settle down   we not saying that   Mal Brough saying that   don't you watch the television   he making the rules for all the mobs   every place Northern Territory   he real cheeky whitefella   but he's the boss   we gotta do it

and from there I tell my wife she gets paid half   half in hand half in the store   her money in the store now   half and half   me too   all us building mob   but I can't buy tobacco   or work boots   you only get the meat and bread   just like the mission days   just like tjamu and nana tell us
and from there I went to the store to get meat for our supper   but the store run out   only tin food left   so I asked for some bullets   I'll go shoot my own meat   but sorry they said   you gotta buy food   that night I slept hungry   and I slept by myself
thinking about it

and from there the government told us our job was finish   the government bin give us the sack we couldn't believe it   we been working CDEP for years   slow way we park the truck at the shed just waiting for something   for someone with tobacco

the other men's reckon   fuck this   drive to town for the grog   but I stayed with my kids started watching the television   trying to laugh   not to worry   just to be like yesterday

and from there   the politician man says   I give you real job   tells me to work again   but different only half time   sixteen hours but I couldn't understand   it was the same job as before   but more little   less pay   and my kids can't understand   when they come home from school   why I can't buy the lolly for them like I used to before   I didn't want to tell them   I get less money for us now

Four Poems

and from there they say my wife earns too much money   I gonna miss out again   I'm getting sick of it   don't worry she says   I'll look after you   but I know that's not right way   I'm getting shame   my brother   he shame too   he goes to town drinking   leaves his wife behind   leaves his kids

and from there I drive round to see tjamu   he says his money in the store too   poor bloke   he can't even walk that far   and I don't smile   I look at the old man   he lost his smile too   but nana she cook the damper and roo tail   she trying to smile   she always like that

and from there when I get home   my wife gone to town with the sister in law   she gone look for my brother   he might be stupid on the grog   he not used to it   she gotta find him   might catch him with another woman   make him bleed   drag him home

and from there my wife   she come back   real quiet   tells me she went to casino   them others took her   taught her the machines   she lost all the money   she lost her laughing

and from there all the kids bin watching us   quiet way   not laughing around   so we all go swimming down the creek   all the families there together   we happy again
them boys   we take them shooting   chasing the malu in the car   we real careful with the gun   not gonna hurt my kids   no way

and from there my wife   she sorry she back working hard   save the money   kids gonna get new clothes   I gonna get my tobacco and them bullets   but she gone change again   getting her pay forgetting her family   forget yesterday   only thinking for town   with the sister in law

and my wife   she got real smart now   drive for miles all dressed up   going to the casino with them other kungkas   for the Wednesday night draw

I ready told you I love my kids   I only got five   two pass away already   and I not complaining bout looking after my kids   no way   but when my wife gets home   if she spent all the money not gonna share with me and the kids

I might hit her   first time

UNEARTH

let's dig up the soil and excavate our past
breathe life into the bodies of our ancestors
when movement stirs the bones
the boomerangs will rattle in unison

it is not the noise of the poinciana
stirred by the wind in its flaming limbs
the sound of the rising warriors echo
a people suppressed by dread

a hot wind whips up dust storms
we glimpse warriors in the mirage
in the future the petition is everlasting
even when the language is changed

boomerang bones will return to memory
excavation holes are dug in our minds
the constant loss of breath is the legacy
there is blood on the truth

A PARABLE

Interventionists are coming interventionists are coming
the cries echo through the dusty community
as the army arrive in their chariots.
Parents and children race for the sand hills
burying the tommy axes and the rifela
hiding in abandoned cars
along the fence line.
One woman ran to the waterhole
hiding her baby in the reeds
dusting her footprints with gumleaf.
Other children went and got their cousin
shouting mum you gone rama rama
you should see the clinic.
That night the woman went back to the waterhole
leaving her child in the reeds again
this time in a basket.
In the morning the children return
holding their cousin crying
mum you gone rama rama
you should see the doctor.
At the clinic I feel her pulse
check her blood pressure
test for diabetes.
Staring deeply in my eyes
until finally our heads bent
she whispers quietly in Luritja
this son him name Moses.

40-YEAR LEASES

high on compensation
they tell me right from wrong
say the old days are over
you gotta sign the paper
coming on the charter plane
all friendly sitting round
say we gonna fix this place
you gotta sign the paper
I sign the paper
charter planes fly away
no more sit down circle
I wait for the fixing
my wife says
what you waiting for
come fishing with us
just like the old days

JOHN LEEMANS
STRONGER FUTURES

11 June 2012

The Gurindji people at Daguragu and Kalkarindji are today calling on the government to get rid of the 'Stronger Futures' laws.

This Intervention must be abolished, not extended for another ten years. It is racist and has caused so much suffering in our community. We have lost everything and have no control.

We are supporting the statement of the Yolngu nations calling for an end to the Intervention, the shires and the policies which deny funding to Aboriginal Homelands. Like the Yolngu, we are strongly demanding self-determination and proper funding for our communities.

We cannot sign any leases with government over Daguragu. This is Aboriginal land, handed back by Gough Whitlam to Vincent Lingiari forever. Not to be taken away again by leases. We say no to the bribe being offered for a forty-year lease. We want control of our land. The Government Business Manager put in by the Intervention must leave Daguragu.

Since CDEP and the Daguragu Council were taken away from us, there are hardly any jobs. And so many of the jobs like Night Patrol are being done now by white people.

We do not want to work for the dole and BasicsCard.

We are the people who went on strike for equal wages and for land rights.

We are still fighting strongly. It's clear the government wants us to leave our lands in search of work but we will keep fighting until we get the message through – our land is our life and we will not leave.

We call on the unions who have helped us in the past and all supporters of Aboriginal rights around the country to keep fighting to get rid of the Stronger Futures laws and to win self-determination for our people.

BRENDA L. CROFT

SIGNS OF THE TIMES

'Aunty, you seen what I did to that sign?' my nephew John Leemans asked, a cheeky, purposeful grin on his face.

'No, where?' I replied, curious. 'Daguragu'.

'That sign' referred to John's customised version of one of the despised symbols erected outside Aboriginal communities throughout the Northern Territory at the commencement of the NT Emergency Response, aka the Intervention, in 2007. This one had been placed at the entrance into Daguragu, the place chosen by Gurindji Elders for their home settlement after they walked off Wave Hill Station in 1966.

This was the birthplace of the national land rights movement, an action that took two decades to be approved by the government of the time. Now, over two decades later still, this determined act and the hard-won approval had been declared of no consequence at all.

John, like everyone in the community, had been incensed at the placing of these signs, done with no discussion, a tainted gift that kept on giving; a reminder that traditional custodians had no power, no say in decisions made by distant bureaucrats. He decided to make his fury clear and attacked the representation of those faceless government men and women.

What once had stated, I say you are, therefore you are what I say, imposing itself on entry to a community, was now almost concealed by John's customisation under the colours of the Aboriginal ensign – red, black and yellow. The central orb had been punched through by a sharp implement, revealing angry jagged edges like bared teeth, but still evident were the words: 'Prohibited material'.

What if more Ngumpit* people and communities could mark 'Black spot' sites around the country, signifying the failure by western powers to engage justifiably with the First Peoples?

Whose territory is being (re)claimed, (re)marked, (re)scarified, declared null and void? De facto terra nullius or a return to the colonising days of missions and reserves, only slightly upgraded?

John wanted me to see his symbolic revision on the territorial marking of the NT Intervention. This was John's challenge to the nameless powers that were defining him and every other Ngumpit person in the community, with special attention to the men, as criminals. No fair go here.

At the time I was working in the remote parallel communities of Kalkarindji and Daguragu, coordinating the forty-fifth anniversary event, more generally known as Gurindji Freedom Day, on a mix of secondment and long service leave from the University of South Australia.

People come from nearby settlements such as Lajamanu, Yarralin, Pigeon Hole and further afield – Halls Creek, Kununurra, Yuendumu and Santa Teresa, as well as urban centres such as Alice Springs, Katherine, Tennant Creek and especially Darwin, where many descendants of Stolen Generation members taken from their traditional Homelands at Wave Hill and surrounds reside.

When the Gurindji Walk-off anniversary is held every fifth year it draws larger visitor numbers than during the smaller 'off' years, with a greater national focus on invited speakers and participants. These include Gurindji Walk-off supporters, politicians and activists from the period and the present day whose presence underpins the significance of the Gurindji Walk-off as the beginning of the national land rights movement.

It is widely acknowledged that the Gurindji Walk-off brought Indigenous land rights to national and international awareness.

---

* Ngumpit/Ngumpin – Gurindji word for man, Aboriginal

Elders in the communities of Daguragu and Kalkarindji remain fiercely proud of their longstanding action, determined to share their recollections with as many visitors as possible, ever enthusiastic to show people around the site of Jinparrak (Old Wave Hill station) where their fight began half a century ago.

However, with the advancement of each year their resolute ranks dwindle, as do those of equally staunch non-Indigenous supporters. The forty-fifth anniversary event was the final attendance of highly respected kardiya/whitefella activist Brian Manning, who dedicated his life to fighting for equal rights for Indigenous people in Darwin, Groote Eylandt, Wave Hill and later, for freedom in East Timor.

It was also the valediction for a number of senior Gurindji men and women, Walk-off Elders, including my family members. With the passing of each warrior, a direct link to a rapidly fading era vanishes. This seems even more so when sporting events appear to carry more importance than commemorating the distinguished actions of 200 plus men, women and children determined to live on their Homelands on their terms.

* * *

Since the NT Intervention was brought into force nine years ago I have found it increasingly difficult to call the Gurindji Walk-off commemoration Freedom Day as any concept of freedom appears severely curtailed, at least to my eyes. It did not always seem that way when I first started going back home to traditional country a quarter of a century ago but incrementally, things have deteriorated. Many Indigenous people are part of a shifting diaspora – living away from our traditional Homelands but fiercely proud of our heritage – and we want to make a positive contribution to our communities.

For those of us who have had the double-edged benefit of a comprehensive western education it is a means of giving back while also reconnecting with our people. The trade-off in gaining entry into a non-Indigenous worldview was – and remains – losing fluency in essential cultural capabilities of language, ceremony and kinship connections. We have to fulfil cultural responsibilities through different methods.

For me, cultural obligation was motivated by the words expressed by Uncle Mick 'Hoppy' Rangiari (c. 1926–2006) to me in a brief telephone call over two decades ago. I can easily recall the conversation and his softly spoken, Gurindji Kriol–inflected words. It was 1991 and I was sitting at my desk in Boomalli Aboriginal Artists Co-operative, an artist-run-initiative in Chippendale (Sydney) where I worked as Coordinator. I had just undertaken a family research trip up to the Northern Territory.

I had conducted interviews with family who were members of the Stolen Generations on an earlier trip in 1989 and again in 1991. Always fascinated with family history, I was trying to unravel where I fitted into an extensive family tree with myriad branches.

The journey from Darwin to Gurindji Homelands and the tiny communities of Kalkarindji and Daguragu was 800 kilometres and took a day. Accompanied by Gurindji Elder Aunty Daisy Ruddick (née Cusack) and our relation Sybil Fordham, who was the age of Aunty Daisy's daughters, our car contained three generations of Gurindji women.

Daisy had been removed from her family and placed in Kahlin Compound as an infant in the 1910s. Sybil had grown up on country with her family. My father had been taken from the Victoria River region in 1927 to Kahlin Compound where Daisy remembered him as a young child before he was sent away to other institutions. Daisy and Dad were considered cousins, both being Gurindji people associated with Limbunya to the west.

I was following in the footsteps of my father who had returned to Gurindji Homelands once, in 1989, on an earlier family research trip with the intention of writing his autobiography. His journey is another piece of the Gurindji diaspora jigsaw that is scattered across Australia.

Eleven years older than Dad, Daisy cared for the younger children, even after she had left the compound to work at Darwin Hospital. Always hungry, the children would hurt themselves so they could go to hospital for a check-up, knowing they would get a good feed from Daisy.

She lost touch with Dad's whereabouts in 1930 and they were not reunited until the early 1980s in Canberra where Daisy's daughter Josie worked with my father.

As we got closer to Kalkarindji, the years seemed to drop away from Aunty Daisy as she pointed out landmarks along the route. My time there – less than a week – had a profound impact on my psyche as a young person of Gurindji heritage.

On our first night a very dark – almost blue-black – tiny Elder, thin as a whip and hobbling with a distinctive limp, came to the door and introduced himself – Mick 'Hoppy' Rangiari. We were officially welcomed home.

This Walk-off leader was a key Elder of Kalkarindji and Daguragu and someone my father called 'brother'. Uncle Mick came into the kitchen of the standard-issue remote community house, sat down and had a cup of tea. I listened as he and Aunty Daisy yarned about her family, their voices giving comfort to each other, and to me.

After I had returned to Sydney Uncle Mick had rung me from the Kalkarindji Council office: 'We need you mob to come back and work up here.' 'We' – local community; 'you mob' – those of us who had learnt kardiya/whitefella ways, as a result of our parents or grandparents being removed from their communities. It would take me twenty years to take up Uncle Mick's invitation.

* * *

One of the outcomes of the NT Intervention not mentioned in any government report is that there are no longer any culturally safe havens for the custodians, cultural managers and educators of Indigenous knowledges. How can there be when communities feel they have been

Above Lazy Late Boys playing at the 45th Gurindji Freedom Day concert, Kalkarindji, 28 August 2011, with lead singer John Leemans second from left. Photograph copyright/courtesy Brenda L. Croft.

Below Hetti Perkins, Jenny Kitching, John Leemans, Mia Christophersen and Brenda L. Croft at Kalkarindji the day afte rhte 45the Gurindji Freedom Day weekend, 29 August 2011. Photograph copyright/courtesy Brenda L. Croft.

Left Vincent Lingiari, Victoria River, 1966–67. Photograph copyright Brian T. Manning, courtesy of the Manning family.

Below Aboriginal strikers, Gurindji Walkoff from Wave Hill Station, Victoria River, 1966–67. Photograph copyright Brian T. Manning, courtesy of the Manning family.

stripped of basic human dignity and the hard-won rights that Elders spent so much energy securing for their people over many decades?

Vincent Lingiari and his compatriots would be devastated to see the undoing of Gurindji determination to live on their lands, untroubled and free to determine their own futures. Various government authorities have inflicted death by a thousand cuts in the slow unmaking, directly or by default, of any small success achieved.

Muramulla Gurindji Mining Lease Cattle Station,** established in March 1971 by Walk-off Elders to provide a business foundation for future generations, struggled to operate. Their stock were killed in the TB and Brucellosis eradication program of the 1980s. The company had folded by 1987, as noted in Brian Manning's Vincent Lingiari Memorial Lecture at the Northern Territory University in 2002 (Manning 2002).

Although the land claim was initiated in 1966 and the handback ceremony was held in 1975, the claim was not formally ratified until 1986, by which time Vincent was very frail. He died in January 1988 with a number of local land claims still outstanding. Politicians, activists and supporters from across Australia attended his funeral.

The veneration of one of this country's true leaders was held days before Australia celebrated its bicentennial. Thousands of years' custodianship vs. two centuries of contested 'ownership'; the colonial project continues today – a nation founded on multiple white lies.

* * *

My father never returned to Kalkarindji and Daguragu. He did not finish his autobiography, nor live his life as he anticipated. In 1994 the sudden death of my brother Lindsay affected him badly. Less than two years later in July 1996 the cumulative effects of grief and ill-health cut short his life.

**   *Muramulla* is incorrect spelling of *Ngurramala – Ngurra – country; Mala – owner.* The combined meaning is 'traditional owner, boss(es) of the country', according to the patriline – Dr Felicity Meakins, linguist, University of Queensland and Erika Charola, pers. corr. 6 February 2015.

My brother Tim and I undertook our first adult journey together, flying to Darwin with our father's ashes in a small box, we collected Dad's younger sister, Aunty Nancy with another relative Robbie Mills, before heading down to Kalkarindji just before the thirtieth anniversary of Gurindji Freedom Day.

It was my second and Tim's first trip home. I reflected how difficult it must have been for my youngest brother who was only twenty-five years old and had lost his older brother and his father in less than two years.

We left Darwin at midday and were then delayed further in Katherine, not getting onto the Buchanan Highway until after dusk, with at least six hours ahead of us. Our passengers fell asleep, leaving my brother and me to talk through the hours on the road still ahead. We arrived at Kalkarindji after midnight, no lights on in the small settlement but we managed to work out the residence of the local policeman. Unfortunately, nobody answered our desperate knocks on the door so we camped in our swags under a bough shelter in front of the community store. We awoke to community members reservedly watching us as they arrived at the shop.

We relocated to the local church minister's house where my aunt and I later shared a room while Tim slept on the verandah. That first day an elderly couple arrived on foot. They walked through the gate and sat down opposite us on the verandah. Senior community representatives Peanut Bernard Puntiyarri and Ida Malyik Nampin asked about our father and his Gurindji connections.

As Elders, they had to approve the service being held and burial in the local cemetery. I told a brief version of Dad's removal from community in the 1920s, his time in children's homes, his trip home in 1989 and the family names Dad had passed on to me after his return.

One name in particular brought a beaming smile to both Elders' faces. They then embraced us, saying they were our grandparents – kaku and ngapuju.† We were then introduced to other family

---

† Gurindji kinship words: *Kaku* – father's father (and his siblings); *Ngapuju* – father's mother, from *Gurindji to English Dictionary*, Batchelor Press, 2013.

members in both communities and reunited with Uncle Mick in Daguragu.

Dad's memorial service coincided with the thirtieth Gurindji Freedom Day events that were being held the day after. Many of our Darwin relatives were in community for both events. A major Freedom Day anniversary meant that the community was hosting some heavy hitters from 1970s federal politics including Gough Whitlam and Tom Uren.

At the culmination of Dad's service the funeral procession headed to Kalkarindji cemetery a kilometre away at the end of a rough dirt track. Dad's ashes were placed in the ground, finally laid to rest in his Homelands, alongside his compatriots.

My father wanted kardiya people to try and comprehend the impact of colonisation on our people, not only throughout their lives, but also the ongoing deleterious effect on their descendants, whether we live in remote communities or in far-flung towns and cities.

Every time one of our people was taken away a connection was broken, and although attempts were made to repair those fractures, those connections will always be weakened. This continent remains a contested site of colonisation.

After Dad's funeral my brother and I did not return to Kalkarindji and Daguragu until the fortieth Gurindji Freedom Day event. The preceding years were etched deeply into the faces and bodies of the remaining Walk-off Elders. Uncle Mick was exceedingly frail, wheelchair-bound, his voice barely a whisper when uttering a few words into the microphone during speeches at Victoria River.

I knelt beside him and asked him if he remembered me. Hunched over, his eyes hidden behind dark sunglasses and the shadow cast by his stockman's hat, he nodded and whispered, 'Yes.' I knew that he was not long for this world.

In December 2006 I returned for his funeral, which hundreds of people attended – Aboriginal and kardiya. Brian Manning gave the main eulogy in the open-air service under the bough shelter in front of the council offices. When I arrived, ngapuju Ida gestured for me to sit beside her, cross-legged in the dirt, holding my hand throughout the service.

The procession then travelled to the cemetery and while everyone was gathered around Uncle Mick's grave I made my way to the opposite corner of the grounds looking for Dad's grave.

I stood in front of my father's grave looking towards Wave Hill, the namesake of the original cattle station in the late afternoon light, aware this day was the true end of an era as Hoppy Mick, the last of the Gurindji Walk-off leaders, was laid to rest in his beloved country.

***

Five years on I was coordinating the forty-fifth anniversary event, which felt akin to unsuccessfully wrestling a handful of mercury that kept splitting and slipping this way and that, always just out of reach.

Funds sought from the Aboriginals Benefit Account were approved in April 2011 but not released until less than three weeks before the event was scheduled to start in late August. Not knowing if or when funds would be available made it difficult to contract people to provide services or confirm participation; promote the event; place orders for goods, food, supplies for the expected influx of visitors – just about everything. Needless to say, with funds released so late – for reasons never explained – there was a mad scramble just before and during the three-day event, which greatly stressed and drained everyone involved in its organisation.

Once funding was released, the level of frustration in dealing with varying local, regional and federal bureaucracies intensified each day in the short time available and I wondered what I was trying to prove and to whom. Why had I offered to undertake what seemed increasingly impossible? Who did I think I was and why did I think I had anything to offer anyone? It did not take long to realise this was only a microcosm of the frustrations and obstacles experienced by people living in community every day, month in, year out. The lack of duty and care by many in power seemed deliberate, or at the very least wilfully obstructive – were they keen for the event to fail, or worse, for the community to implode and cease to exist?

I went from feeling rage and despair at the compounding indignities the entire community had forced upon them, to completely useless, to conflicting elation at being home on country and reunited with family. I had project managed major events over three decades but this time it was very personal and I did not want to let anyone down.

The difficulties for those living in remote communities are complex and demanding. Once you leave the nearest urban centre the cost of basic living requirements – fuel, general foodstuffs, clothing, small household goods, toiletries, electrical goods, electricity, and pretty much everything – leaps exponentially. Most urbanites on an average wage would struggle to make ends meet. I was hard pressed to work out how my family survived fortnight to fortnight.

Try making do on the basic fortnightly allowance from Centrelink, living in an overcrowded house that has little concept of the nuclear family, having access only to a vehicle that would be deemed unroadworthy in any town or city, let alone having to meet emergencies that might be associated with health issues. Often there is no vehicle at all, a situation that can have severe cultural repercussions. This occurred recently when family members living in Kalkarindji and Daguragu could not access a working vehicle, or the fuel money needed to travel 100 kilometres down the road to Yarralin near Victoria River Downs, to attend an Elder's funeral.

It is often impossible for family members living outside community to attend funerals as months can pass before a burial decision is made, or relevant close family members are available, or anybody seems to know when or where a funeral will be held. The first you know is after the burial has been and gone, sometimes even catching community members unaware.

Facebook has become a de facto medium for family gatherings: at least it provides a means of keeping in touch with the many nieces, nephews, cousins, brothers, sisters, aunties and uncles of my particular Gurindji diaspora – some of whom I am yet to meet face to face.

My particular freedom to come and go, even though it has been for research work with family and community members, is not a possibility for many in the community, but that situation can change when mining royalty payments to individual traditional owners come into play.

The exponential cash flow associated with such payments can be highly problematic for communities and individuals: creating a false economy for an intense, gruelling period when alcohol consumption soars, along with domestic violence and financial pressures on Elders and family members. During these times an almost corporeal tension descends on the community, like an enervating fog sapping reason out of the atmosphere.

When the flow of alcohol and money dries up – as it swiftly can, like a flash flood – a collective exhalation of relief is expressed by community members who do not drink, the situation returns to 'normal', or as normal as it can be in such circumstances, where everybody is either related or knows each other. Privacy is a luxury. I understand why people turn to grog as a means of self-medication. When there is often little to look forward to each day, in terms of meaningful existence on country, those gaps are filled with substitutes.

People dearly want to be able to access sites and care for country but if there is no access to a suitable vehicle with able-bodied people to do the arduous driving over rough country, then people have little choice but to 'sit down', either at the art centre, outside the shop or at an overcrowded home. What choices are available when there are seemingly minimal capacities for people to contribute to the advancement of a community that has repeatedly seen previous advancements in past decades invalidated by the current government of the time's on-trend policies?

When outsiders – kardiya or other Ngumpit from elsewhere – hold the few employment opportunities often interstate, then disinterest and antipathy understandably become the default setting.

Why not drink and run amok or do 'nothing', that is, offer passive resistance?

However, when positive options are provided you can see the difference and benefits for all involved. This is clearly manifest in inter-connected partnership ventures between community organisations (Karungkarni Art and Culture Centre, Kalkarindji Educational Centre and School), regional statutory bodies (Central Land Council and the Mungaru Mungaru Gurindji Rangers), and tertiary institutions (University of Queensland, University of Melbourne, University of New South Wales, etc.).

Ngumpit, kardiya and Gurindji diaspora working in community-approved consultation with Elders, community members and school children on stimulating projects such as Gurindji and associated languages and knowledge books, CDs, posters, websites and exhibitions generate visibly positive outcomes, if feedback from participants and outside observers is any indication. This is the case when compared with the punitive quarantine policy on welfare payments – a futile effort to force parents to make children attend school. Kardiya teachers do not speak the local languages so a widening gulf grows between parents, students and educators, in tandem with a general lack of engagement with the compulsory western curriculum. The loss of two-way language teaching is still felt within the community and was further undermined by the cessation of Diwurruwurru-Jaru (Katherine Regional Language Centre) in 2010. The revival of the language centre as part of Mimi Ngurrdalingi Aboriginal Corporation is underway, which will be really positive for the region.

What work could be undertaken by high school or university success stories in the community upon graduation when there are so few positions available? Most people want to live on their customary Homelands, not in cities and towns where problems multiply and are compounded by homelessness and being on other peoples' country.

Arts/cultural centres can only be a haven for a finite number of community members, mainly Elders. Funding restrictions often mean operating on a shoestring budget, dependent on the energy of the incumbent arts centre coordinator and no matter how robust an individual is – or if you are lucky, a couple are – there is only so much that can be achieved. The burnout rate for arts and cultural workers is extremely high.

* * *

The means of fighting back against the inequities are extremely limited. One way is to fight your own, to inflict damage upon yourself and/or your own mob, to contest the crumbs that are scattered as appeasements while the wellspring of anger and fury builds up and finally explodes/implodes. Another is to literally attack the symbols of the oppressor, the hated signage that has been installed as a means of keeping people in their place, locked up, locked down, the ultimate insult, a final solution keeps playing on an endless loop.

At the entrance to the authorised Gurindji settlement, Kalkarindji – site of the Police Station, the school, the health centre, the community store and social club, the art centre, the community council offices, the Central Land Council office and the mechanics' workshop – stood another customised NT Intervention sign.

This one had been attacked by more than a sharp implement. It had been driven into – hard – by a road grader or equally heavy vehicle. Knocked off its centre and split apart, it looked like it was fighting to stay upright. FIGHT RACISM had been spray-painted in hard black scrawl across the bottom of the demeaning text, which pronounced the declarations NO LIQUOR/NO PORNOGRAPHY. Both those redesigned signs made me laugh out loud, a way of shouting you reckon we can't do a damn thing, maybe you're right, but we can sure as hell show you we won't just lie down and take it. Nearly five years later both symbols are long gone, torn down by unknown community members, only the steel posts a shadow-sign of what once stood.

I have asked what happened to them as they are artefacts of a people still under siege, incrementally undermined and surrounded, enclosed, and I feel they should be kept as a record of what was done. Nobody seemed to know who had taken them down, or where the remnants are. Once it became clear that there was no legal reason for their presence they did not last long. If only it was as easy to remove other impositions on people trying to live as they wish on their own lands.

Sometimes I imagine what it would be like to have a different type of sign barring entrance to unwanted visitors. I realise that the permit system, rescinded as a result of the NT Intervention, was supposed to do this in the past.

How does a community deny entry to unwelcome guests who are authorities – apparently omnipotent – attempting to force-feed Indigenous communities and individuals the twenty-first century format of assimilation?

Wrong Way Go Back/Trespassers Keep Out

Ngurnalu pina karrinyana kutitij, Ngurnalu kutij karrinyana, ngantipany-ja yumi-ngka/We know where we stand, we stand in our law.††

---

†† From the author's perspective these signs would read as follows: *Wrong Way Go Back* with the standard road sign colours of red background and white text replaced by the colours of the Aboriginal flag; *Trespassers Keep Out* by Quandamooka artist Avril Quaill's 1982 screen-print poster where the image *could* be cheekily read as an Aboriginal Elder standing guard outside his property; and *Ngurnalu pina karrinyana kutitij, Ngurnalu kutij karrinyana, ngantipany-ja yumi-ngka/We know where we stand, we stand in our law* – design by Chips Mackinolty for the forty-fifth Gurindji Freedom Day, including detail of an image by Brian Manning, c. 1966 and text based on lyrics from Kev Carmody and Paul Kelly's anthem 'From little things, big things grow', 1990.

RODNEY HALL
THE CONSTITUTIONAL CONNECTION

Of all the challenges facing Australia none is more deep-rooted or intractable than the unresolved suffering caused by the dispossession of the Indigenous peoples. Until we address this openly we will continue to make inappropriate and patronising policies: regulating, intervening, punishing. We will continue to be baffled by alcohol abuse, infant mortality rates and a grossly disproportionate number of Aboriginal people in jail (many for minor offences such as disorderly behaviour or non-payment of fines).

How do we deal with this? Not by sending in the army, that's for sure. We ought to be seeking the source rather than reacting to the symptoms. This will take us straight back to 1788 and the need to correct our self-image as a nation to acknowledge prior ownership. An opportunity to do so is predicted within the life of the next parliament because a constitutional referendum has been promised with support on both sides of politics.

But it is my fear that the wording of the referendum question will deliver little more than window dressing – a brief preamble at best. It might be said that this will be better than nothing, but what we need is a whole new document that includes, at every stage, the first inhabitants. The problem, then, is how to address this larger issue. How can the public be brought to agree to a new constitution?

Firstly by exposing them to information about the old.

Most Australians would be surprised to learn that we, the Australian people, are not even mentioned in the present constitution, the bedrock of our laws. None of us: neither black nor white. The constitution assumes that sovereignty rests with Queen Victoria, her heirs and successors. Only by redressing this colonial anomaly can we finally define ourselves (as including the original inhabitants) and take full responsibility as a nation.

The common objection is that the 1788 invasion happened too long ago to be relevant. This does not hold water. Most countries in the world have been taken over by force at one time or another within the scope of written history – a fact which is generally acknowledged in their self-image. What is unique here is our denial, disguised by the euphemism 'settlement'.

It is as if the evidence of 60,000 years of prior human habitation is somehow theoretical and not real, as if the dispossession of the Aboriginal peoples never happened, and as if the accumulated infrastructure of the past 227 years has come down to us, miraculously complete, without cost to anyone.

In reality the production of wool, beef, wheat and gold during the nineteenth and twentieth centuries paid for building the towns, cities, roads, railways and ports we still take for granted as ours to live in and use. Wool and beef production, so essential to this prosperity, depended on vast grasslands. These grasslands were created by the Indigenous clans over countless generations for husbanding their own wild game (anyone seeking more information will find it in *The Biggest Estate on Earth* by Bill Gammage).

In the battle between the trees and the grass – as Aboriginal wisdom has it – fire is principally the ally of grass. This cleared land was seized by the invading colonists as ideal for pastures (the explorer Thomas Mitchell aptly called parts of Victoria 'Australia Felix') and for agriculture. Wool was the heart of the colony's wealth and wheat soon became the biggest cash crop. As for gold, the gold was taken when the land was taken. Together with gold came copper, coal, iron ore and the rest.

While such bounty made the colonies rich, it left the original owners poor. And they still bear the legacy of dispossession.

The Constitutional Connection

So let's get the story straight. European immigrants did not 'settle' the land, they took it by force – as if it was vacant and just waiting to be occupied. In their ignorance they could not recognise the proof of hunter–gatherer intervention, nor assess what others had achieved or created here. They were looking for the wrong signs of ownership.

The cultural depth of Aboriginal ceremonies combining all artforms was dismissed as only fit for anthropological catalogues.

And the vast native languages were ignored as irrelevant. What completely passed without notice was that some of them were as large as English. What's even more remarkable is that they were kept alive by being committed to memory. Just imagine knowing all of the 400,000 words in the twenty-seven volume *Oxford English Dictionary* ... that is to say, knowing the meaning of each and every word, plus its use – without the aid of writing or reading! An astonishing feat of memory.

Such were people our ancestors dismissed as primitive.

Even today the national malaise of wilful ignorance goes largely unaddressed, leaving the former owners of the land in limbo. I'm inclined to think it is a failure of the imagination rather than intentional hypocrisy. But, whatever the cause, there is an urgent need to have the truth out in the open. It's time for the guilt to be exposed and dealt with. The question arises: How can the general public ever be brought to understand?

Well, let's suppose for a moment that the Japanese had won the war in the Pacific in 1945 (as they nearly did). Let's suppose a huge migration of people arrived from Japan, many times outnumbering us, imposing their language and enforcing their laws. Wouldn't we, as Australians, rebel? Wouldn't we hate living under the invaders' heel? Wouldn't we resent their institutions and defy their police? Wouldn't we keep this grievance alive? And, if our rebellion failed, wouldn't we, too, face despair and hopelessness? Perhaps we would even take to drink ... while making sure to pass our rebellious frustration down from generation to generation.

In fact, such an invasion actually did happen: it's just that we were the invaders. And we still don't admit any injury to the wounded spirit of those whose land was taken from them. The tragic history of dispossession, stolen children, the introduction of diseases and alcohol has led to a succession of Band-Aid measures, apologies, alcohol bans, withheld wages and enforced intervention … as if the health and social problems of Aboriginal communities are self-generated.

We created the problem.

And it cannot be healed by force of law any more than it can be healed by budgetary allocations. All political argument these days tends to be based on economics, which puts the cart before the horse. Economics is a by-product of society, not the other way around.

To begin at the beginning, the power of any culture centres on its language.

For all of us, whatever our race or background, language is the most important thing we ever learn. Without language there is no law, no science, no religion, no sport, no education. Nothing. So, let's begin with the right choice of words. Let's name what happened and face up to the facts of history. Maybe then reconciliation can make real progress.

Every nation shapes itself by stories selected from a vast pool of historical facts.

In the days when we told ourselves Australia was a white Anglo-Celtic society isolated in the Asia–Pacific region we behaved accordingly and, rather than communicate with our neighbours in Indonesia, Timor or New Guinea, for example, we preferred to deal with their colonial masters, the Dutch, the Portuguese and the British. Only when we began telling ourselves the multicultural story, embracing variety, the emphasis on being flexible, did we acknowledge our neighbours directly. Just in time, too, because in 1973 Britain dropped us from the economically privileged status we'd had under the empire (this was one of the conditions the UK had to meet in order to be accepted into the European Union).

But, despite changing again since then, our national story seems somehow stuck.

In recent years anyone who was mystified or distressed by Australia's shameful special pleading on the issue of an international agreement on greenhouse emissions, or by our attempts to avoid sharing the impact of the vast hordes of refugees displaced around the world – in many cases as a spinoff from western commercial intervention and the global greed for resources – should look at our self-image: the story we tell about who we are and how we came to be here. The problem begins there.

If we are ever to begin putting this to rights then acknowledging prior ownership is the key.

The weird thing is that opponents of this view are so often eager to embrace their own personal family history and convict legacy. Ancestry websites enjoy immense popularity. So, it's not true that the general populace doesn't care about the past … they just don't care about other people's past.

The fact of the matter is that when the British colonists arrived the two races were at opposite poles of cultural development: energetic and ruthlessly courageous Europeans – driven by the clock and notions of progress, whose chief pursuit was acquisition – in conflict with a ceremonial metaphysical culture derived from the prevalence of spirits in a timeless continuum and enshrined in words and laws entirely committed to memory.

No two peoples could have been further removed or more incomprehensible to each other.

Finally, the invasion succeeded, driven by the supreme adaptability characteristic of Europeans. Indigenous systems of knowledge were, by contrast, comparatively static and place-specific. Of course, the people knew about inter-tribal fighting, but they had no idea of combining with neighbouring tribes (often age-old enemies and rivals) to form a united army. And they had no idea what an invasion from the sea might be. It had never happened before.

The radical idea of total foreigners seizing the land was completely new.

During the public hysteria whipped up over Mabo and then Wik, as became quite clear, suburban Australians feared that their backyards could be taken from them – despite all legal evidence to the contrary. Well, there was a reason. And their strident opposition gave them away. Beneath this fear lay a national guilt. True, the great mass of the population may not have heard about the Myall Creek Massacre or the Waterloo Creek Massacre, or the Cape Grim Massacre in Tasmania or the countless other massacres and murders, but the inheritance of guilt emerged across the entire country.

The dark secret that haunts the Australian heart is knowing that we took what we have. We waged war. Not with an army, but with armed bands of citizen militia, backed by troops from the garrison. We fenced the land without permission. We drove off the original owners. We poisoned their waterholes. But the Indigenous nations never gave in. They were not passive. There has never been a peace sought or an official recognition of the invasion. They are still resisting by one means or another.

Acknowledgment is crucial to identity.

The perennial question, 'Who am I?' engrosses every thinking human being. This is basic. Our behaviour depends on the answer we find. And the search to uncover truth is a lifelong quest. We all feel it. This is no less than a search for the story at the heart of experience, at the heart of our self-knowledge, the story of our loves and disappointments, our grief and our happiness. It governs whom we trust, how we behave, and what we do with our lives.

So it is with a nation, too, and the nation's collective future. Nations also seek the story of who they are, where they are and how they became like this … simply because of the need to know. If we do not include Indigenous Australians as equals in our story we are unlikely to cease discriminating against them with interventions and prohibitions. The very idea of sending troops in to impose law and order within one's own country should be shocking to everybody. Yet it happened without significant opposition.

For all these reasons the promise of a referendum is welcome. But in my view the change must go further than a preamble.

Prior ownership by the Indigenous population needs to be embedded in the definition of sovereignty. The best chance of achieving this is to rewrite the whole thing (as so many other nations, including South Africa, have done). What have we got to lose? The point is that none of us has more than four specified citizen rights in the present document: the right to trial by jury, freedom of religion, compensation if our property is resumed by the state, and the right not to be discriminated against on the basis of the state we choose to live in.

In 1999 things could have changed forever with the momentum of a new millennium, but the opportunity was wasted. Opinion polls showed a substantial majority of Australians supported the idea of a republic. The task was to convert the raw figures into a majority of votes in a majority of states. At the first constitutional convention held in the South Australian Parliament in 1997 there was a chance. Some of us there argued for a whole new constitution to include Indigenous people and the environment to address the needs of a modern state.

But by the time the Canberra convention came round two years later this had already been bombed out of the water by the Australian Republican Movement (ARM) – Malcolm Turnbull, the journalist Paul Kelly and others – who used their numbers to insist on a 'minimal' republic.

Instead of a visionary future to include the Aboriginal nations, they succumbed to John Howard's manipulative tactics ... and then squabbled among themselves over the lesser issue of whether the proposed President should be elected or appointed by parliament. Compared to the broad sweep of the Adelaide discussions, the 1999 constitutional convention was a sorry affair with no dynamic, no debate, simply a string of individuals filing up to the microphone and having their say. Any debate over what kind of republic we should have was suppressed. Timidity led to a resounding defeat at the polls. This the ARM has never apologised for.

The head of state is secondary to defining sovereignty (though, sadly, Bill Shorten in an ABC interview on 1 February 2015 seems still hung up on the issue). My own view is that we don't need a President at all. The Prime Minister can be head of state. Instead, let's adapt the Aboriginal social model: a council of Elders. Rather like the German constitutional court, this council of Elders would have only two functions – to open parliament or to dismiss it. They would guarantee stability far more effectively than an individual, whether elected or appointed (remember Sir John Kerr?).

Sovereignty is the issue that links the call for a republic with the promise of inclusion for the Indigenous peoples. A new constitution would shape the future. We need to speak as the nation we wish to be … and rid ourselves of the old Victorian document written by British lawyers. If we get it right we can greatly improve our chances of resolving racial issues at home – without the use of troops or prohibitions – as well as relations internationally.

As it is we're stuck with governments so frustrated by their own failures that they resort to enforcement.

The Intervention in the Northern Territory was yet another case of getting it wrong. Policing, in this sense, is always going to be a failure because it disempowers communities. Re-empowering them is what is required. Claims of child sex abuse are, of course, extremely serious and must be immediately addressed. But in that case it would have been far better to work through the kinship system to help build self-respect and find a solution from within. This was a glaring example of 'we know best'. Just how patronising it was can be measured by imagining what an outcry there would be if the government sent the same army personnel to intervene after accusations against the Roman Catholic Church.

Society, by its nature, is a shared pool of strength, resources and support systems. Inclusion involves the right to a just share of this collective security. Nothing less will do.

In these globalised times the international community is watching (the very community which we, as an exporting–importing nation, depend upon for our survival). In the new environment of the twenty-first century, in which information, business and social networks are expanding to create a global state without borders, the old stories have begun to fail. A new story is overdue.

It is time for the truth about who we are and who was here first.

YOLNGU STATEMENT

24 June 2012

1 The Yolngu Nation rejects the Stronger Futures Bill (and those associated) and calls on the Senate to discard these Bills in full.

We have clearly informed you that we do not support the legislation.

The Australian Federal Government can achieve all its aims through partnership in our communities. They have no need to grant themselves the continuing and new powers contained within these Bills.

2 Until the Stronger Futures Bill (and those associated) are thrown out of the Australian Federal Parliament the Yolngu Nation call on all traditional owners across the Northern Territory to refuse:

A) participation in land lease negotiations with the Australian Federal Government and

B) approval for any exploratory licences.

3 The traditional owners of prescribed community lands have been placed under extreme pressure by the Australian Federal Government to grant them head leases over these communities. Traditional owners want independently facilitated negotiations that can result in enhancing interests of both the traditional owners and the Australian Federal Government.

4   The Land Councils are increasingly being pressured by the government to act outside their roles and become agencies of government. We want our Land Councils to advocate for our needs and not have their independence curtailed by government funding arrangements and political interference.

   The Yolngu Nations call on the Australian Federal Government to ask the Auditor General for a review of the relationship between the Australian Federal Government and the Land Councils of the Northern Territory.

5   The Yolngu Nations call on both the Australian Federal and Northern Territory governments to end their interventionist policies and agendas and return to a mindset of partnership based on the principles of self-determination.

Appendix 1 to the Yolngu Statement

DJUNADJUNA YUNUPINU, DALKARRAMIRR
for the Gumatj Nation
Spoken in English and Yolŋu Matha

Intervention when it first came in we thought it was good to help our people ... But now our experience is that it has not been beneficial. It has turned our young people against their Elders because it has undermined our ability to determine things for ourselves.

Schools – our bilingual program is not being supported, courts – [it's a new] stolen generations – police [are taking over and not acting in appropriate cultural ways].

[The Intervention] takes us back to the 1920s, '30s – to the early mission days, the Stolen Generations. Our memories have been taken back to the time when the Welfare people stepped into our land.

We thought that [the Intervention] was manymak (good), but experience showed us a different picture. We see the experience of other black people across the world (their struggles) and we see that here.

Where is all that self-determination, where has all that yäku (name) gone?

You can change names [to Stronger Futures] to convince [us that things are better] but you are still following the same [track].

Our Homelands … People are moving in [to communities]. Homelands have bäyŋu (no) road fixing, bäyŋu (no) help for airstrips, all houses are built in town [attracting people in].

If we are citizens together in this country, lifting up the one flag, each calling Australia our home, then we must work with respect. Respect for ourselves, our land, our law, and our language. These words 'self-determination' and 'self-management' they have been taken out of the [government's] dictionary. When our Elders first heard these words they were happy. Now later forty years (gone.)

SAMUEL WAGAN WATSON

INTERVENTION ROUGE

A Poem

*A red, dusty garnish that carries both authentic sweet and sour flavours of the Top End. Has the capacity to enliven the palette and also leave a bad taste ...

Like a cyclone, you didn't realise the insidious destruction it was capable of perpetuating/ condemning a people and country that had looked a dark cloud in the face too many times before/ everyone knew this kind of storm already by its burning, branding, retina signature/ the ageless folds in the landscape were a perfect canvas for the myths and legends about to land and dance toxic songlines/ meticulously woven lies and facades of one-horse-town-film-sets that can be used over and over again/ staged tumbleweeds rolling when prime-movers and prime ministers blow through and only run you down/ bureaucratic road kill and necessary victims who stood too long in the way of development/ flash-blinded in the eye of yet another fatal storm/ wet season, dry season and from here to eternity/ a police state that brands a kiss of death upon your future/ a cataclysmic smear of Intervention rouge ...

Instructions: When cooking with Intervention rouge you can use as much direct flame as you want, but the truth will always respond as a viscous-kind of soup. The plot thickens … the plot thickens … eventually.

- If you require a heavier taste of deceit embellish this recipe of disaster with a spicy pinch of pornography or nuclear waste.
- Pour into a sink-hole-sized dish bored by a mining magnate and let it sit. Have plenty of salt in your Mise-en-place to rub into gaping wounds.

DJINIYINI GONDARRA
Spokesperson for the Yolngu National Assembly

ROSALIE KUNOTH-MONKS
Spokesperson for the Alyawaar Nation

MEDIA RELEASE

Yolngu Nations Assembly and the Alyawaar Nation,
27 June 2012

Should this Stronger Futures legislation pass through the Senate and become law, it will be a day of mourning for all Aboriginal peoples. This legislation will be the cause of great suffering in our hearts.

For those of us living in the Northern Territory the anguish of the past five years of Intervention has been almost unbearable. Many have simply given up hope. We have been burying people who can no longer live with the pain and despair.

We had believed that we were moving to a time of security, where we would no longer live from day to day in a state of fear but would be supported to find our own destiny in the security of our law and our culture.

We little expected to be thrown into such turmoil by a government determined to remove from us control over everything that we most value.

Money alone can never be the answer. Government has never

understood and still fails to understand that badly needed funds must be accompanied by the willingness to allow us to determine the direction of our lives.

There must be respect and genuine partnership, not the top-down approach which undermines and devalues us as a people.

How is it that so many from across Australia – from small organisations, from churches and national institutions – understand the value and importance of our people determining their own futures, whereas government does not?

If this legislation should pass the Senate, one thing that government needs to know is that Aboriginal people will fight. We will never accept this racist legislation that separates us from other Australians and creates its own apartheid in our country.

Furthermore those thousands of people who have given us their statements of support will be with us. We will fight together for real justice!

Aboriginal peoples of the Northern Territory will never give up their rights – their right to live in true safety with the certainty that their culture and their language and their law will be protected and respected, as it is under international law under conventions to which Australia is a signatory.

We put the government on notice. Do not pass this racist legislation.

EVA COX

THE INTERVENTION: BAD POLICY AND BAD POLITICS

It is instructive to document the effects of decisions taken over the last seven years by three separate federal governments, under two different governing parties, involving four Prime Ministers and four ministers in charge of Indigenous issues.

All these players displayed bipartisanship in devising policies and delivering processes that over-rode presumed political differences, and this continues despite acerbic divergence in other areas. This agreement is odd, given that there were no data supporting the effectiveness of the initial Intervention; nor have the expanded programs been proved effective by Government-funded evaluations.

These evaluations have found neither evidence of benefits nor that most policies have met their stated objectives. The release of the second official evaluation of the NT income management program in December 2014 again failed to offer any clear evidence of improvements in wellbeing or value for money.

Interestingly, this latest report did not generate any official acknowledgment of failure to show significant benefits. As we will see, the NT Emergency Response (NTER) has generally failed to improve the lives of the people specifically targeted. The data below show clearly that the NTER and its sequel programs (Stronger Futures and New Income Management) are expensive failures.

Yet, despite the evidence that many Indigenous NT communities and individuals are now worse off than before the 2007 Intervention, some of these failed programs are being considered for expansion as part of implementing the McClure recommendations on social security payments and the Forrest employment report.

This lack of official recognition of the failure of these poorly designed initiatives may further 'widen the gap', however defined. Good policy-making to improve the lives of people in the NT requires governments to learn from their mistakes – not only about what needs to be done but also, most importantly, about how to do it. Learning from the errors made in creating the current mess should be the basis for designing effective programs that will remedy the many difficulties facing Indigenous communities across the nation.

Background to the Intervention

In 2007, the soon-to-be-gone Howard government decided to look tough, and so introduced the NTER program devised by Vietnam veteran Mal Brough, Minister for Aboriginal Affairs. The military-style Intervention was claimed to be necessary to deal with a 'sexual abuse emergency' identified in a report to the NT Government by Pat Anderson, an Indigenous Elder, and Rex Wild QC, 'Little Children are Sacred' (Anderson and Wild 2007).

A series of controls was imposed on seventy-three named communities which curtailed the freedoms of individuals and communities to make their own decisions about property, shopping, certain local activities and Commonwealth income support. These sudden changes, made with no consultation or advance notice, shocked the affected communities. In addition, the program seemed to have little connection with the issues raised in the original Anderson and Wild report. This report had identified the need to address possible sexual abuse and other serious needs of children, but made it very clear these problems could only be solved if first the governments engaged in consultation and collaborative action with local communities. Its first recommendation was:

That Aboriginal child sexual abuse in the Northern Territory be designated as an issue of urgent national significance by both the Australian and Northern Territory Governments, and both governments immediately establish a collaborative partnership with a Memorandum of Understanding to specifically address the protection of Aboriginal children from sexual abuse. It is critical that both governments commit to genuine consultation with Aboriginal people in designing initiatives for Aboriginal communities.

We commend the report not only to the government and the people of the Northern Territory but to the government and people of Australia. Our hope is that the nation will work together for the sake of all its children. (Anderson and Wild 2007.)

This crucial recommendation was totally ignored when the Federal Government created the NTER in June 2007. The lack of consultation was the program's first major failure, as the goodwill of local communities was undermined by the arrival of troops and other control staff. The Commonwealth damaged any potential good outcomes from the start by ignoring the above recommendation for a well-planned collaborative strategy which built on local strengths and cultural values.

The initial design of many parts of the Intervention demonstrated obvious prejudice and gross generalisations about some Aboriginal people, communities and traditional lifestyles. Controlling people's money infantilises them and reduces their agency in deciding how to spend their time and money. The loss of control over some services, abolition of the Community Development Employment Projects (CDEP), and control over community land and housing are other examples. The top-down designs by Canberra also undermined existing services and unfairly imposed controls over people who were managing their lives quite effectively.

The initial Intervention was clearly defined as racially discriminating, necessitating suspension of the *Racial Discrimination Act* in 2007, so the government could quarantine half of income support benefits paid in the seventy-three targeted Aboriginal communities. However, this was only a starting point. The Howard government had broader ambitions to use its targeting of black benefit recipients as a cover for expanding these types of changes to other welfare recipients. By using some named Aboriginal communities as both guinea pigs and stalking horses, the rest of Australia, including the welfare sector, were less likely to object or recognise the potential unfair threats to wider welfare policies and make a fuss.

Some of the push for the program came from long-held conservative assumptions, bureaucratic and political, that 'self-determination' had failed. The same assumptions had led to the abolition of the Aboriginal and Torres Strait Islander Commission and the desire to 'mainstream' programs to correct assumed Indigenous deficits by controlling the delivery of services centrally, thereby returning to what is effectively an assimilation model. The idea that Canberra could solve NT problems without local input is very much a product of these assumptions.

Back in 2007, some of us protested the NTER and raised questions publicly on the loss of rights and modes of intervention that were being imposed. However, in the throes of an election campaign, the plight of a few black communities in the NT was not seen as important by politicians or the media. We then hoped the incoming ALP government would rectify the previous government's errors: remove this authoritarian set of programs and collaboratively address the issues identified in the Anderson and Wild report.

However, the change of government did not change the crass setting-up of the NTER. The failure of the incoming ALP government that November to reverse the initiatives confirmed a level of bipartisanship that was surprising, given Howard's and Rudd's stated differing views on the Apology. The ongoing history of these so-called reforms over the last seven years suggests that both major parties' policies, in this portfolio at least, are equally contaminated by deeply prejudiced assumptions about Indigenous people and their communities.

This bipartisan deficit in official understanding has resulted in failed programs, wasteful spending and deteriorating wellbeing, not only in the original targeted communities, but also in the wider NT population and spilling over into other vulnerable welfare groups. This has left the Greens as the only political party in power to offer a very vocal, but minor, critique of the programs.

The Processes Over the Last Seven Years

The initial NTER was an invasive, irrational example of overkill. It was absurd to think that the imposition of control programs devised in Canberra would fix a supposed epidemic of child abuse, as well as health deficits and education failures. However, no attention was paid to what was working, what could work and what certainly did not work. Therefore, the modifications made during the course of seven years often compounded, rather than improved, early errors.

Shortly after its election, the Rudd government commissioned a review of the NTER, led by Western Australian Indigenous leader Peter Yu. The final Yu report was not very supportive of the NTER but was ignored. There were rumours that the original draft had been 'improved', to be less critical of the program, as is outlined in the email below from a member of one affected community.

> When Kevin 007 ousted the instigators of the Northern Territory Emergency Response we waited for the roll-back of the Intervention. The pre-election promise of the roll-back morphed into a review of the NTER after one year. The thorough Peter Yu review cost a few million dollars – another bargain we thought. In October 2008, Paul Toohey reported in an article in *The Australian* that the official version of the report dramatically differed from the leaked draft report. The highly

critical draft had morphed into a bland report that supported the Intervention.

'Too frequently, often at a subliminal level, Indigenous culture is regarded by policy makers as an impediment to the future development of remote communities, rather than an essential resource for their development' appears in the leaked draft, but is not to be found in the final report. Pourquoi pas?' [Why not?] (Brull 2011).

The programs in 2015 continue to undermine existing community strengths and structures. Problems are blamed on the communities and individual resistance. The two major parties share paternalistic welfare assumptions and a wider set of economic biases against all those seen as economically non-productive. These shared viewpoints provide both parties with excuses for attacking traditional social and cultural aspects of some Indigenous communities and, by extension, for attacking non-Indigenous and unemployed people in general.

While this approach may have been expected of conservative parties, the ALP's failure to take the criticisms and negative evidence seriously remains a serious blot on its party policies. Rudd's Indigenous Affairs Minister, Jenny Macklin, could have halted the process early by taking on board the poor results. The slow roll-out meant that only 1400 people were on Income Management by late 2007 when they took over. Instead, Macklin chose to continue the roll-out so by 2010, the number reached 17,000, when the ALP introduced some limited changes. Had Labor taken note of the early evidence or even the original doubts expressed in the draft Yu report, the complex problems now rife in the NT could have been addressed in ways that worked effectively. The money could have been spent on programs that were jointly planned and needed – but bad bipartisanship won out over evidence, despite the rights of those affected.

This bad bipartisanship showed when Tony Abbott's opposition supported the Intervention's extensions in April 2011, when he also praised the original Coalition's initiatives:

> It took courage back in 2007 for then Prime Minister John Howard and Indigenous Minister Mal Brough to announce what was known as the Intervention in Aboriginal communities across the Northern Territory. It was a rapid response to the Little Children are Sacred report, which revealed the terrifying reality of child abuse, health and social degradation within remote Indigenous communities.
>
> The Intervention was necessarily swift, as large numbers of police and army personnel moved in to communities in crisis. Alcohol restrictions were put in place, medical examinations were carried out on Indigenous children and school attendance was enforced, while 50 per cent of individuals' financial welfare payments were quarantined for food and life essentials. While controversial at the time, the Intervention had dramatic results, improving the health and welfare of children and reduced alcohol abuse in many Indigenous (sic) communities.

The above view again ignored the lack of evidence that the programs, that were part of the original NTER, were effective. He clearly illustrates the attitudes of both major parties involved seeing themselves as saviours of individual locals from the depredations of their communities and the 'Aboriginal industry'. There is no recognition of, or respect for local leaders or of the need to work collaboratively with Indigenous communities, despite occasional rhetoric to the contrary. Both sides tend to justify their views by naming some Indigenous people, who were either known supporters of paternalistic change, or groups hoping that short-term protection would fix some current issues, despite the lack of evidence. These 'supporters' offered their opinions rather than evidence, and these were not supported by any other data.

Data on Seven Years of the Intervention and Income Management

It needs repeating that the whole Intervention episode is a serious example of bad policy-making, as both major parties' support for the NTER and its sequels goes against the evidence, including their own commissioned recent evaluation report by the Social Policy Research Centre (SPRC 2014). The details of this report show that even the Government's own contracted evaluators have not been able to find positive outcomes either in the NT generally, or in specific programs such as Income Management. This data has to be accepted as unbiased.

The above report starts with a summary of general recent data from the NT, summarised in the extracts below, which show most of the Territory's wellbeing statistics have deteriorated over the last few years, post Intervention.

Overall statistics for the NT offer little evidence of serious improvements. To quote:

- School achievement shows that while there are some gains in the early years of school these are not reflected in the data for later years. The pattern of changes for Indigenous children in the Northern Territory are generally similar to those found for Indigenous children nationally.
- School attendance has improved at the provincial level, but has either remained stable or fallen in remote and non-remote locations, suggesting no generalised trend.
- Across a wide range of child health indicators there is no evidence of any consistent positive change.
- There has been a substantial decrease in per capita alcohol consumption from the mid-2000s. However, this decrease started well before the NTER and is almost certainly driven by factors other than income management.
- The number of alcohol-related presentations to emergency

departments and admissions to public hospitals by Indigenous people in the Northern Territory has increased dramatically since the mid-2000s.
- Imprisonment rates of the Indigenous population have increased in the Northern Territory since 2002 at a faster rate than among the Indigenous population Australia-wide.

When the data are taken as a whole, not only does it suggest that there has been very little progress in addressing many of the substantial disadvantages faced by many people in the Northern Territory, but it also suggests that there is no evidence of changes in aggregate outcomes that can plausibly be linked to income management (Bray and others, page 235).

From a more partisan side, the anti-Intervention group STICS (Stop the Intervention Collective Sydney) summed up their critique in a flyer for a 2014 Human Rights Day forum:

> Over seven years have passed since the Howard Intervention in Aboriginal lives and communities brought new and shocking levels of disruption and degradation to First Nation communities around Australia. The housing crisis has not been resolved. The Intervention was implemented in the name of the children, yet child removals have reached unprecedented levels and are still rising. A child removal epidemic is gripping Aboriginal communities across Australia, with 14,000 Aboriginal children currently in 'out of home care', more than were removed at the height of the Stolen Generations.

The SPRC evaluation data and other official data summed up above clearly show the general failure to improve lives by the programs introduced by Howard, and added to by the ALP government. Yet these are currently being continued and may be about to be expanded by the Abbott government. Income management is one of these areas being discussed and is therefore discussed in some detail below.

Income Management

The evidence collated here shows that the overall strategy is not working, as is clearly illustrated by new detailed data on income management. Income management is based on many problematic assumptions about the needs and capacities of Indigenous people and communities. The program, in most of its versions, makes the clearest statements on perceived deficits of Indigenous people, by equating their managing their lives to their presumed lack of capacity for individual money management.

The first assumption is that dependency on government payments indicates potential weaknesses, and that therefore the money would likely be misspent. Income quarantining therefore reduces the autonomy of income recipients by assuming that they obviously cannot manage their lives. The further assumption is that removing at least half their income from their control would somehow order recipients' lives and encourage their commitment to self-interested money management. These neo-liberal assumptions emphasise 'rational' individual self-interest as the appropriate driver of financial decision making.

Looking in more detail at the Income Management (IM) program, the flaws of both process and content of the policies and program become clearer. The original 2007 program covered all income support recipients in the seventy-three communities, including age and veteran pensioners. It quarantined 50 per cent of the income by putting this under the control of Centrelink staff, making it available via a BasicsCard that could only be used at approved retailers and could not be used to buy alcohol, porn and cigarettes. The target population was obviously Aboriginal people, so the *Racial Discrimination Act* was suspended.

In 2010 the Labor government introduced some changes that were designed to make it more generally acceptable, they thought. They removed all pensioner recipients from the compulsory category, targeting IM to working-age welfare recipients. Labor's newer version of income management also was formally de-racialised but still overtly targeted mostly Indigenous people. While now NT recipients potentially include all NT people on long-term working-age payments, it offered both a voluntary version and possible exemptions to those compelled to be part of it. However, the data show that appeals for being exempted were granted to most non-Indigenous recipients who applied, but few Indigenous ones.

The following Labor government media release announced the wider roll-out of the program beyond the initial communities:

> Legislation currently before the Parliament will strengthen the NTER to provide the foundations for real and lasting change in Northern Territory Indigenous communities. The legislation repeals all NTER laws that suspend the operation of the Racial Discrimination Act and introduces a non-discriminatory income management scheme. The new income management scheme will commence across the Northern Territory – in urban, regional and remote areas – as a first step in a national roll out of income management in disadvantaged regions.
>
> This represents a significant step forward in the Government's continuing welfare reform agenda. The Government's welfare reforms will increase parental responsibility, fight passive welfare and protect vulnerable people including women and children.

There was a Senate Inquiry set up in 2011 by which time there was lots of data and these were contained in many expert submissions to the Inquiry on the proposed changes. I read most of these and about 90 per cent of those looking at the effect of income management, claimed it showed little evidence of benefits even then, and there were considerable doubts about the efficacy of such financial controls. The paucity of evidence to support the extension was documented in an issue I prepared for the *Journal of Indigenous Policy* (Cox 2011).

This publication collated evidence and expert opinion that was massively against the expansion of the programs. Despite the opposition of some seriously well informed groups, the legislation for extending income management went ahead and many additional groups were added. These included non-NT areas, child protection families, vulnerable people, as seen by Centrelink, and in 2013, those under eighteen years who cannot live at home.

The data reproduced below are taken from the latest Government-commissioned evaluation and show that Income Management has failed to achieve its goals (SPRC 2014). In their words:

Summarising the Impact

'The overall conclusion is that there is no evidence of any consistent positive impacts on problematic behaviours related to alcohol, drugs, gambling, and financial harassment. Nor have there been improvements in the extent to which financial hardships and stresses are experienced – for example, running out of food, not being able to pay bills, or on community level outcomes such as children not being looked after properly, school attendance, drinking and financial harassment.

'Despite the magnitude of the program, the evaluation does not find any consistent evidence of income management having a significant systematic positive impact. Some 35,000 people have been on the program at some point, and there were 18,000 people on it at the end of December 2013, many of whom have been on it for extended periods.

'The key findings are:

- Data on spending point to continued major problems of diet and poor levels of fruit and vegetable consumption, in particular for Indigenous people living in remote communities. There is no evidence of income management having resulted

in changes in spending or consumption, including on alcohol, tobacco, fresh fruit and vegetables.
- At the household level across a wide range of measures there has been no aggregate improvement in financial wellbeing; although some groups report an improvement in the level of financial harassment they experience, they also report more frequently having to ask others for money, and there has been no reported reduction in harassment at the community level.
- At the family level individuals report there has been a decline in the overall incidence of any difficulties related to alcohol, drugs and gambling, but no change in the incidence of severe problems from these.
- In fact, all groups show a worsening of these severe problems, although this is only statistically significant for Indigenous people on Voluntary Income Management. This group also reports specific improvement in problems from alcohol, but worsening for gambling. At the community level no significant improvement has been reported, and looking at broader measures across the Northern Territory, there is little evidence of change in alcohol-related harm. If anything, these outcomes have worsened, although there is no evidence that this is in any way related to income management.

'There is no evidence of changes in school enrolments or learning outcomes that can be attributed to income management, and in many locations there are stagnant or falling rates of school attendance. Those on income management report no significant change across a range of child wellbeing outcomes in their communities over the past two years (SPRC 2014, page 340).'

This set of poor results should be clear enough, yet, despite the lack of evidence of benefits that support Income Management programs, the signs are that the current Coalition government will continue to expand them. As there is no opposition from the Opposition, the major parties will have the Senate numbers for continuing the inequities and damage that these programs create. Even the prospect of finding savings in this portfolio, does not attract the government bean counters to cut the program because of high administrative costs of up to $100 plus per week per recipient in remote areas.

Conclusion – Bad Programs, Appallingly Delivered

The data show that governments of both persuasions have made a right mess of the Intervention by both introducing and adding to badly designed, inappropriately delivered programs at great expense. It is important to reiterate and reinforce the failures of process that underpin all these initiatives. Starting with the advice from Pat Anderson and Rex Wild to do things collaboratively, reiterated by many others since, the evidence is clear that Indigenous policies won't work unless they have been developed appropriately in partnership with those they affect and those who may deliver them.

This conclusion is similar to those clearly stated in the most recent report on 'Overcoming Indigenous Disadvantage' (2014), chaired by the Productivity Commission. This report again stresses that it is not just what the policies offer, but how they are developed and delivered, that matters. These process factors are closely aligned to the success predictors identified in previous reports, by the Australian Institute of Health and Welfare, on what works. These recommendations stress cooperative approaches between Aboriginal and Torres Strait Islander Australians and governments. They support the need for 'bottom-up' rather than 'top-down' approaches, as well as culturally appropriate programs. The NTER and its subsequent versions met none of these criteria: they were imposed top down and were neither appropriate nor accepted. Apart from their incorporating crass racist assumptions about what was needed, both major parties failed dismally to use the criteria for what works developed by their own fairly conservative advisors, the Productivity Commission and the Australian Institute of Health and Welfare, who offer evidence-based advice that cannot be claimed to be based on prejudices.

The problems are continuing under the current regime's proposals under the Indigenous Advancement Strategy. The most recent issue, No. 16, of the *Journal of Indigenous Policy* (see website address on page 253 – 'What Works – and Why the Budget Measures Don't') collects the evidence of what works and doesn't work, and how these criteria are being ignored in the current changes.

There is now no excuse for the lack of broader analysis and critical questioning by policy makers from both major parties. However, part of the problem is that the wider population is now used to failures, so widespread low expectations lead to the tendency to assume that lack of progress stems from recipients' failures to make the effort, not bad processes by policy makers. That viewpoint explains the frequent 'nothing works' responses from politicians and ill-informed pundits, who point out that the programs have cost $25 billion for limited benefits but accept no blame (Mundine 2013).

Mick Gooda's call to 'work with us, not for us' in his 2014 report for the Human Rights Commission again raises the reason for continued failures and limited successes as being because of lack of appropriate meaningful engagement. His call recognises the 'secret' of what works and what does not is in the governance processes: the repeated failure to engage appropriately with Indigenous communities to devise and deliver policies and programs.

So far, all these suggested criteria of what works, plus the data in official reports and websites, have had little influence on policy makers despite the period 2007–2014 being littered with examples of bad policy-making and outcomes. The consequence is the failure of the Intervention (Biddle 2012) and its Stronger Futures replacement, as, despite their high costs, neither program can claim any significant positive results.

On the political front, only the Greens have continued to be critical in their views, but have also been ignored because the bipartisanship of the major parties is a serious problem. Neither has mentioned, let alone acknowledged, the findings of the latest evaluation, which suggests the problems will continue and be expanded. The questions we need to ask are:

> What can we do to reduce the damage being done now and in the future?

and

> How can we create more civil societies where Indigenous policy agendas are driven by principles and rights, not prejudice?

DENI LANGMAN
TRADITIONAL OWNER OF ULURU

*A Letter to the Politicians of Australia Who Will
Debate the Stronger Futures Legislation, June 2012*

Palya Everyone,

I never thought I would be so affected by this statement from Rosalie and Djiniyini. It is like having everything I dreamed of disappearing from my sight. (See their media release on page 179.) I am so upset at this happening to us and after all the hard work we have put into trying to stop the Stolen Futures legislation getting passed in parliament and becoming law.

I don't know yet if it has been voted on in the Senate, but when I think of politicians in Canberra, who never bothered to get to know First Nations People or understand our culture and simply don't care that we are human beings as they are, it makes me very sad and my heart aches for all those who have never known freedom in their lives and the deaths of the children who saw nothing but despair in their future lives and ended it with a rope or other form of suicide, I can only cry from the pain they felt and the hopelessness they looked forward to.

I can only ask those politicians who don't care for their fellow human beings: 'Do you feel good about what you are doing to the First Nations People today?' 'Does this power you have over our lives make you a better person?' But most importantly, 'Will you tell your grandchildren what you did to the First Nations People this day and how you destroyed the lives of so many First Nations People and caused their deaths prematurely?' 'Will you have the guts to admit what you have done, to your grandchildren, or will you hide this truth from them when they ask you, that question of curiosity?'

'Who were the First Australians in this Land?' 'Will you feel the shame of Generations of First Nations People being trampled underfoot by your political policy of racism and discrimination and greed and how you used your power to keep them forcibly shackled to a yard or fenced in an area away from their country and communities, all because you wanted their wealth in their land ownership?'

That wealth you will never know!

I wonder how you will tell your grandchildren these atrocities you did to the First Nations People.

If you will tell the truth to them.

If you will finally say you are sorry for what you did and mean it.

If you will shed a tear for the people who only wanted to live their old age in freedom on their traditional lands and teach THEIR grandchildren the wealth of knowledge they had.

These beautiful people are no longer with us now. They died of broken hearts and stolen dreams by politicians who never cared to treat us like human beings.

You will have to look into your grandchild's eyes and see the emptiness they feel of losing such a wonderful heritage and culture forever, for your greed.

ARNOLD ZABLE

HERE IS WHERE WE MEET

Been enough intervening, not enough listening. Not enough sitting. Sitting in the dirt, sitting on the verandah. Sitting in the shade beneath the house. The earth, as far as the eye can see, clad in greens, ochres and reds. The sky so blue it hurts. The air so dry it sucks in the breath. Yet cool enough in the shade to converse. And time enough to take in the silence, to notice that far-distant cloud.

'It's going to rain', the old man says.

'Give it six hours, but believe me it's going to rain. Best place to be is here. Sitting in the shade beneath the house.'

* * *

This is a tale of maps: The first could be any one of many Indigenous communities where the people have regrouped. Or never left: Country that the people have lived on upwards of 60,000 years. Could be in the Kimberley, in the red centre, or somewhere up north. The place will remain unnamed. I have not spent enough time here. I am a guest. Learning to see what I have never seen, listening to stories I have never heard … I am here to listen, not to intervene. Here to converse, exchange tales. To find that place where we truly meet.

* * *

The kitchen is where my parents sat, late night, in a single-fronted terrace: built against the sky, ironclad in stucco and brick. Cool enough to induce ugly patches of damp. Rat-infested when the family moved in. The landlord didn't give a damn. My parents got rid of the rats, repaired the roof, plastered the cracks and got on with their lives. And late at night they sat in the kitchen with old world friends.

I strained to hear them as I lay in bed. Their voices, as in a lullaby, sang the names of places on a distant map, towns and villages, a city: Bialystok. Bransk, Orly, Grodek, Bielsk. Border country, disputed territory, tales of a time just one generation ago when dark clouds were beginning to swell.

It ended badly. The lucky ones got out. They sailed to the New World in flight from the Old. Settled in Melbourne, a city at the ends of the earth.

I lived in a house of absences, ghosts. Gazed at albums of photos.

'Who are these people?' I asked.

'Three of my six sisters, one of my three brothers, your uncle Joshua, your cousins Chaimke, eleven, and Freda, six years old,' mother replied. Of nine siblings and her extended family only three survived. On my father's side, it appeared, there was no one left.

In time I did the journey, travelling alone, months on end, rucksack on my back. I set out mid-1986. Walked the streets of towns, villages and cities, places whose names I first heard as I drifted asleep on the other side of the world. I returned with the maps of my parents' youth, sat anew in the kitchen of that single-fronted house. I had the triggers now, the means to invoke ghosts: 'Saw birch trees the length of the empire,' I tell mother, 'ghostly white. Standing alone, standing in packs. The beryose,' she says, as if in a trance and she sings, in Yiddish, the mother tongue: 'Oh come quiet evening, and rock the fields to sleep/ we sing you a song of praise, oh quiet evening glow/ How still it has become, the night has come to stay/ the white beryose, remains standing in the forest alone.'

Mother tells stories through song. She finds it too painful to tell them in words.

***

With my father I sat on a bench in Curtain Square, the neighbourhood park. Beneath the Moreton Bay figs, lined up, six abreast, on either side of a dirt path: the square, the epicentre of my childhood now the quiet retreat where we drift, father and son, between silence and words. The silences are broken by a gust of breeze, the bark of a dog, and our intermittent conversation triggered by maps, the names of thoroughfares I have now walked.

'Sienkiewicza Avenue,' I say.

'Ah, that's where we played billiards and chess and where Kondruchik the White Russian sold ice-cream on a summer night. Where in the Macedonian quarters we ate Turkish delight, and where we went to movies on a Saturday night.'

The stories flow quickly now that I know the maps: tales of a distant country, of love and comradeship, of community and resistance; and of the genocide that brought it to an end.

***

I am standing in front of a map, circa 1995, an exhibit produced by the Koorie Heritage Trust on display in the state museum. I know instantly where I have seen such a map before: Nine years earlier, in a pavilion located in a forest of birches and pines, within a clearing where Treblinka death camp once stood. The map details places of massacre. They range hundreds of kilometres west, and east to the Soviet border, a vast swathe of ancestral lands.

In the clearing there is a gathering of stones. Each stone bears the name of a town, city or hamlet from which those who died there were transported one generation ago. I search among the stones for the names I first heard in that distant kitchen: Bielsk. Orly. Grodek. Bransk. I light a candle in front of the stone marked Bialystok: the Polish city where father was born, where mother's family moved when she was a child. The city where they lived the first third of their long lives: The city where they met. And left. Just in time.

***

Now I am standing in front of a map of the state of Victoria as seen through Aboriginal eyes. Dated 1836 till 1853, titled The Massacre Map, it marks over sixty sites of known killings of Indigenous people. A caption adds: 'Many thousands more died beyond prying eyes.'

I am contemplating a vast mystery: Why is it that after so many years of living in the city my family settled in soon after I was born, why is it that in all that time, not once did I hear the words Wurundjeri? Woiwurrung? Kulin?

I played on the banks of the Yarra River as a boy, launched myself on ropes into its ochre waters and propelled myself down into its opaque depths. Why did I not know its ancient name: Birrarung, River of Mists? Why did I not know of the clans who fished it, swam it and gathered on its banks?

Why did I have no knowledge of the Kulin moiety ancestors: Bunjil the eagle and Waa the crow? Why was it that after so many tram journeys from my neighbourhood to the beaches that rimmed the bay, I had not heard of the Boonwurrung, the coastal people? Why did I have no inkling of the ancient map?

* * *

Been too much intervening, redrawing of boundaries. Land grabs. I ask Jim Berg, Gunditjmara man, founder of the Koorie Heritage Trust: 'Where can I find out more?' 'Go see Auntie Joy,' he says. 'She knows.'

* * *

Weeks later I break free of the city, drive sixty kilometres northeast, and pull up in the drive of a weatherboard house. There is grandeur here at the feet of the ranges of the Great Divide, a clarity that comes after days of rain. Clouds drift from the upper slopes. Peaks disappear and reappear as the mists rise. The greens of the valley are deep and lush. Magpies and kookaburras hover by the verandah in anticipation of their daily feed. Wurundjeri Elder Joy Wandin-Murphy opens the door and ushers me into forty millennia of history.

Here is where we meet. A line comes to mind: They came from the old world to the new, only to discover it was far more ancient than the old.

* * *

We sit in the lounge room and converse. On the wall there is a black and white photo taken in the early years of the twentieth century. There are nine people in all, grouped in two rows. In the centre, in the back row, stands Joy's grandfather, Robert Wandin, Wandoon, as he was known. White haired, wearing a jacket, waistcoat and suit, he stands beside his wife, Jemima, dressed in a high-necked formal white blouse and long black skirt. Robert and Jemima are flanked by six of their ten children, and a family friend. The youngest child, an infant, is Joy's father, James Wandin. The photo emanates dignity and pride.

Robert was the nephew of William Barak, says Joy, the traditional Ngurungaeta, leader of the Wurundjeri clan. In June 1835, as a young boy, Barak was said to have been present when John Batman signed the so-called treaty with Elders of the Kulin. Treaty or no treaty, within decades, the lands were taken, the ancient map erased, the Woiwurrung language driven underground. The first intervention was all but complete.

* * *

Joy knows the ancient maps well. In 1987 as a project officer for Aboriginal Affairs Victoria, she set out with anthropologist Alistair Brooks on a twenty-month journey to retrace the boundaries of Aboriginal Victoria. Joy and Alistair consulted Aboriginal Elders, and examined maps drawn up by anthropologists, who in turn had gathered their information from Indigenous people at a time when they were being dispossessed.

The Wurundjeri was a clan of the Woiwurrung language group, Joy says. The two names have in recent times become synonymous. Theirs was a vast territory ranging from the mountains of the Great Divide, east to Mt Baw Baw, west to the Werribee River, south to Mordialloc Creek, and deep into the heart of Melbourne, to the boundaries of the Boonwurrung, people of the coast. The Woiwurrung and the Boonwurrung are two of five peoples who form a confederacy known as the Kulin.

Again that mystery: I went through sixteen years of schooling in Melbourne: primary, secondary, tertiary. Studied European histories, Asian histories, versions of Australian history, but not once did I hear these names. So complete was the first intervention that the very names were driven underground.

* * *

Been too much intervening. Ancient maps discarded. Boundaries whittled away. Knowledge ignored. Yet the stories were passed on. Ancestries reclaimed. Back in the 1980s, the Wandins commissioned anthropologist Diane Barwick to work with them to draw up a family tree.

Joy spreads the documents on the living room table. There are five generations delineated tracing the Wandins back to the eve of the European invasion. There are names of renowned Ngurungaeta: Ningulabul, the songman, whose people lived in the Macedon area; Bebejan, whose kin lived on the banks of the Yarra in the area where the inner city now stands; his wife, Tooterie, a woman of knowledge, and William Barak, witness to the desecration of his people and the confiscation of their lands.

Barak saw the invaders assume control. He saw his people driven onto reserves and mission stations. He saw them whittled away by imported diseases and sporadic killings; saw their spirits all but broken. Barak was with them, in 1863, on the Acheron Station, near present day Buxton, when yet again the encroaching settlers intervened. They were ordered off the station and it fell to Barak and his cousin Simon Wonga to lead their dispossessed peoples in search of refuge, an enduring home.

Many times in the two decades since Joy first pointed the way I have imagined that trek: the Wurundjeri and Boonwurrung, and the remnants of other Victorian tribes making their way through the rugged terrain of Black Spur country to the outskirts of Healesville, two years before the township was formed. They settled on the banks of Badger's Creek, on a traditional camping site they named Coranderrk, after the mauve and white flowering Indigenous bush that graced the area: a place within their once vast territory that they hoped would finally be safe from intervention, an enclave they could call home.

* * *

Joy guides me over the site of Coranderrk Station, a sweeping vista of undulating countryside, originally 12,000 hectares. The people seized the opportunity to work the land. They engaged in enterprise and became self-sufficient. They tilled the soil, dug irrigation channels, planted wheat and hops, built a school, a bake house, a church, timber houses and a brick homestead. Played by the rules of the new game.

Station superintendent, John Green, sat with them, worked with them, listened, recognised their adaptive skills and knowledge. Witnessed their loving bond to the land. Became their ally. Of Green it can be said: He came from the old world to the new, only to discover it was far more ancient than the old.

* * *

Been too much intervening, tearing communities apart: Yet again, local settlers and government authorities feasted their eyes upon the land. It was seen as too valuable to remain in Indigenous hands.

The people took a stand. After the death of Simon Wonga in 1874, William Barak became the Ngurungaeta of the Wurundjeri. He was, says Joy, a man of many parts: Leader of his people, a diplomat and negotiator, an artist who depicted Woiwurrung life and its ceremonies, a singer, a dancer and craftsman, a man who led his people in their darkest times.

In the 1870s and 1880s Barak led three marches, walking the sixty or so kilometres from Coranderrk to Parliament House to protest against plans to close down the station and distribute the land to farmers who coveted its fertile soils. His people filed petitions, penned letters. Sent deputations, formed allies, spoke up at hearings. They fought for their last portion of land, and for the reinstatement of John Green, the man who had sat with them on equal ground.

Despite the protests, the interventions continued. A body blow was dealt to the community with the passing of state government legislation in 1886, the 'Half-caste Act', requiring people of 'mixed descent' under the age of thirty-four to forsake the station. In its wake sixty residents were ordered off, ripping apart families and depleting Coranderrk of its labour force, destroying its soul.

The last haven of the Wurundjeri and other peoples was whittled away. When Joy's father, James Wandin, born and raised on Coranderrk, returned from the European battlefields, wounded after active service in the First World War, he was ordered off the station, says Joy, after being defined as half-caste. By 1924, the station was closed down and the remaining peoples transferred hundreds of kilometres east to Lake Tyers.

'Why do you keep taking away things from us?' Aunty Joy quotes Barak as saying. 'We are dying away by degrees.'

* * *

Been too much intervening: yet where there is intervention, there will be resistance. The resistance of the Wurundjeri has been constant. When Coranderrk was closed, five older people refused to be moved. They remained living there until they died. In 1933, Joy's brother, the late James Wandin was the last Indigenous person born at Coranderrk Station, in the home of Jemima Wandin, his grandmother. Granny Jemima passed away in 1944. She was the last Indigenous person to die on Coranderrk.

Yet the culture endured. The stories, the memories, fragments of language were passed down in families who continued to see themselves as Wurundjeri. The Wandin family, and other Wurundjeri descendants, continued living in Healesville and the Upper Yarra region, maintaining their close ties to Coranderrk.

When Joy's father, James Henry Wandin, died in 1957, Joy, fourteen years old at the time, tried to fulfil his final wish to be buried in the old Coranderrk Cemetery, the very last half acre of remaining Wurundjeri land.

The struggle continued. Joy Wandin-Murphy notes key dates of the re-emergence of her people. 1985 marked the creation of the Wurundjeri Tribe Land Compensation and Cultural Heritage Council. In September 1991, the Coranderrk Aboriginal Cemetery was handed back to the Wurundjeri. The following year the Wurundjeri acquired the former army school of health, a thirty-eight-hectare portion of the Coranderrk Station. In 1998, a pocket of the station was returned to the council after the Indigenous Land Corporation purchased a minute portion of land.

The rebirth continues. New generations of Wurundjeri are reclaiming language, retelling and passing on stories, cultivating knowledge, practising culture, partnering in the protection of significant places: From Coranderrk to Mt William, the site of a green stone quarry, once the epicentre of a trading system that extended for distances of up to 600 kilometres. From traditional camping grounds along the length of the Birrarung, to countless sites within the metropolitan area: ancient burial grounds, meeting places. The invisible is being made visible, the ancient map restored.

* * *

Here is where we meet.

There is a Yiddish term, Luftmensch. Literally, 'man of air'. It is a term I adapt from the original concept where it was used in depicting people who, due to economic restrictions, resorted to making a living out of nothing, people forced to live by their wits, on shifting ground, feet ungrounded, heads in the air.

I have re-interpreted the term to embody the state of displacement, of the refugee, the migrant: the seekers of asylum, uprooted from their Homelands. Those who have been running from one place to the next for so long, they no longer feel the ground beneath their feet.

In 2002, Indigenous writer Kim Scott published his epic novel *Benang*. The Indigenous narrator, Harley, has a profound sense of up-rootedness. At one point he begins to literally lift from the earth. He no longer feels the ground beneath his feet. He becomes a flying narrator. He is anchored only when tethered to his typewriter, his writing desk. He is grounded only when recounting his tales.

Here is where we meet: The refugee, the emigrant, the seekers of asylum, experience a sense of deracination because of their enforced journeys; while the Wurundjeri, the people of the Kulin, Indigenous peoples Australia-wide, were uprooted because the earth the people had walked for millennia was virtually cut from beneath their feet.

***

It can be seen from above, the island-continent, observed from the windows of aeroplanes, breaking free of the rigid gridlines of cities, paddocks and homesteads, to the unfenced vastness of untamed terrain; from orderly settlements to anarchic wilderness; from isolated coastlines to ash-white saltpans and serrated ridges, flatlands, jagged escarpments.

I've been flying to the interior: inland to the red centre, up north to the Territory, out west to the Kimberley. With a bird's-eye view of vast estuaries, tributaries fanning out like multiple leaf-veins, of streams bursting through gaps within mountain ranges, carving out ravines and canyons. Looking down upon swirls of pale blues and violet, ochres and purples, broken by arrow-straight tracks and highways, working counterpoint to the asymmetrical contours.

I have begun to walk country walked for millennia, begun to know the ancient map writ large, its vast quilt of Indigenous communities. To walk in the wake of rains: dry river beds-cum-raging waterways, long dormant seeds bursting into flower. Been circling rocky monoliths glowing at dusk like red-clad phantoms.

Begun to walk with those who have a name for each feature, a sharp eye for obscure waterholes, the code for sacred places. Have begun to sit, with men and women of knowledge, receiving the gift of their ancient knowing. Begun to tune in to the lilt of a multiplicity of languages.

I have begun to learn of other interventions, tales of how the Elders have taken a stand for Country, of the cultural movements that have risen as a way to maintain and pass on knowledge, to provide meaning to wayward youngsters. And as a means of making a living where jobs have been scarce since, in yet another intervention, back in the 1970s, Indigenous peoples were evicted from pastoral ranches with the coming of full wages. Made to leave stations they had worked on for a pittance, cattlemen and domestic servants, pawns in an economy based on virtual slave labour. Big story this. I am only at the very beginning.

Getting to know also, of the latest intervention: the first intervention of a new millennium. Beginning to know its fundamental flaw, that in its essence it was designed without consultation: a repeat of the festering flaw that has lain at the heart of previous interventions.

Beginning to learn that it took place without that simple act of sitting. Side by side, on equal ground. Working it out. Sitting with the community, sitting with the Elders. Attuned to the interplay between silence and words.

Yes, big story this, and we are only at the beginning.

And an old story too: Where there is intervention, there will be resistance.

That is how it is.

'It's going to rain,' the old man says.

'Give it six hours, but believe me it's going to rain. Best place to be is here. Sitting in the shade beneath the house.'

* * *

Every year I make the pilgrimage: I break free of the city and drive northeast, sixty kilometres. I turn off the highway into Barak Lane and pull up a couple of kilometres in, by the gate of the Coranderrk Cemetery.

A herd of sheep grazes on the slopes rising from the valleys. Goats descend to drink from the dam waters. A black bull moves by, lowing. The winds are rising. All is movement: the branches of the eucalypts shading the cemetery, the seedlings and saplings, the clumps of daisies and shed bark, the reeds bending low over the dam waters.

Among the scattering of stones stands an inscribed headstone marking the grave of Winnie Narrandjeri Quagliotti, Wurundjeri Elder, a leader in the fight for recognition. When she died, in August 1988, she became the first Wurundjeri buried on this site in over four decades. Nearby stands a granite stone dedicated to the memory of William Barak. On a moss-encrusted cairn, a steel plaque records the story of the epic trek across the Black Spur and the history of Coranderrk Station.

The leeside of the plaque records the names of the people who found their final resting place here, beginning in 1863, the first year the people regathered. There are many Wurundjeri names, grouped in families, and names listed under the heading of tribes whose territories extended throughout the state: Survivors who found refuge on Coranderrk Station at a time when their people were being decimated.

These are names rescued from oblivion. Below them are engraved the words of Aboriginal poet Oodgeroo Noonuccal, Kath Walker: 'We belong here, we are of the old ways.'

* * *

A station wagon pulls up at the cemetery gates. A young Aboriginal man makes his way to the cairn. He stops in front of the plaque and searches among the names. His eyes linger on one name. He stands for a long while, head bowed; makes his way to the cemetery boundary. And sits, knees folded. Looks out upon the valley.

And I know. I know without having to ask. He too is on a pilgrimage in search of his forebears. I know he has located the name of an ancestor. Know that he is feeling something of what I felt as I made my way, in 1986, through Jewish cemeteries on the outskirts of the towns whose names I first heard sung in the distant kitchen: Bransk, Bialystok, Bielsk, Grodek, Orly. Seeking ancestral names among the decaying gravestones: scattered over fields, hidden within forests. Untended. Awaiting restoration.

We sit within the same half-acre. We sit as the evening closes in. We sit as the mists begin descending. There is no need to talk. A chorus of frogs rises from the dam. The shrill cry of cicadas reverberates in the valley. We sit as the land gives way to nightfall. Here is where we meet.

YALMAY YUNUPINGU

HUMAN RIGHTS AND SOCIAL JUSTICE AWARD

Excerpts from her Keynote Speech
24 June 2014

We are exhausted by the routine attacks that undermine and destabilise the community, educators and systems in place. We are frustrated with naïve people coming into our communities, unfamiliar with cultural differences, making decisions and recommendations for us.

* * *

Teachers, parents, communities, principals and governments need to work together to work through these issues and stop blaming each other. Maybe consultation is not being delivered in a proper manner and talking face to face with right people.

* * *

There should be fundamental human rights and freedom given to every human race or communities related to education in Australia. It is about self-determination. We are not brainless or crippled.

* * *

We can manage our own communities. In the documentary, *Utopia*, in Roeburne in the mineral-rich Pilbara 80 per cent of children suffer from an ear infection called otitis media that causes partial deafness and they are going blind from trachoma. What is government going to do about this? Wait until they are all dead one by one and then rush for emergency response?

* * *

Sometimes it is very exhausting to keep fighting but still we have the right to get our human and social justice back.

* * *

We are still living in pain and trauma. We are in pain already and more and more pain is falling on top of us. It makes us feel weaker and weaker. People are getting sick, tired and stressed.

* * *

We want our governments and politicians to believe in us and develop mutual understanding and mutual respect. Please don't treat us as though we walking around invisible or even we don't exist or make decisions on our behalf.

Sometimes we feel that we are being punished, undermined, manipulated and assimilated in our own country called Australia. Why do we sing 'Advance Australia Fair?'

* * *

When governments attempt to manipulate and dictate our lives, such as threatening to send all our teenagers away from our communities or telling us that we can't teach our children how to read and write in their own language, we feel like a knife has gone through our body and the knife keeps going deeper and deeper. When these political statements are put out in the media it becomes like a tsunami that sweeps through our village. They don't turn around and look behind us. They don't see that there are people in pain calling for help, reconciliation and for human rights.

I feel reconciliation is an empty word, consultation and negotiation are empty words, freedom is an empty word, and promise is also an empty word. These words are often being used in speeches, newspapers and TV. This government today needs to be realistic using these words.

* * *

I come from a balanced world, Yirritja and Dhuwa. It is like the yin and yang philosophy. Everything that exists in our Yolŋu world are either Dhuwa or Yirritja – every land, song and dance, people, language, wind, trees, plants, birds, sky, animals, snakes, sea creatures, native foods and fruit and everything in our environment are either Yirritja or Dhuwa where balance is in place by nature.

Metaphors have a significant place in Yolngu culture and life. They provide a foundation to work from, offering a way to work together effectively. We talk about the ngathu metaphor for education.

Ngathu is the cycad palm nut that contains cyanide. The cycad nut can be made into a sacred bread but must go through the correct process otherwise it is poisonous and if consumed can lead to death. However, if the correct process is followed, it can sustain life.

I am using the metaphor of the cycad nut here in an attempt to illustrate the importance of following the correct process. For genuine partnerships between governments and communities to be established, the correct process must be followed including authentic and transparent dialogue. Don't expect us to work with governments towards approaches that we believe won't work and may not lead to greater outcomes. The history of those experiments doesn't lead to great social outcomes. We are disheartened and frustrated by the social challenges we face daily in our communities.

ALEXIS WRIGHT

BE CAREFUL ABOUT PLAYING WITH THE PATH OF LEAST RESISTANCE

Article 17: *Everyone has the right to own property alone as well as in association with others; no one shall be arbitrarily deprived of his property.*

When his grandfather spoke on his traditional country, the boy knew he was listening to the voice of Aboriginal Government.

There are many, many paths in your country, good boys and girls. Good stories. Good life. Go take the right one. Plenty of good ones. People here, all of your family can tell you which one. Play wherever around here all right, but never go anywhere near one bad story. Try to be right story.

He already knew that many people in his community were calling him *'naughty boy'*, but he goes *nice way*, 'Yes. Oh! Hello Aunty. Hello Uncle.' So on and so forth, *styling up* – he greets them all accordingly. He knew how to be respectful, as he was supposed to be, to each and every one of dozens of relatives stopping to look, and muttering, *'the house of smart aleck'*, seeing him sitting outside in the front yard of his parents house, *'watching television like some lazy whatnot'*.

Watching his relatives filing into the house to talk to his parents about his behaviour, he felt as though his brain had been transformed into a savage dog. His head was on fire and the dog was locked behind clenched teeth. He was bursting at the seams to break out and scream at the world that nobody's words would bother him.

Yeah! Well! *You got to love him*, the relatives say, after trailing in and out of the house to see if he was still there, once they had finished warning his parents about what the Government would do to them. His ears pricked up, and he turned down the TV a notch or two, to hear the heated conversation inside the house.

The loudest voices were saying, 'Don't you people here have ears? Haven't you heard what the Government in Canberra is talking about on the radio and the TV and all that?

'Well! The Government, you know, has gone mad – more mad – madder than before – when it comes to Aboriginal people. It is all on the news. They are sending the army in to all of the Aboriginal communities to take control of your kids if they don't go to school. It will be the army who will be telling parents what to do. Didn't you hear about that?

'This Government in Canberra mob – never happy that we got land rights, now wants to break up Aboriginal land again, that's what they want to do, and they are going to do it too, because it looks like the whole country is big *note-ing* itself – mouthing off about things they know nothing about, and telling the Government what to do by making a *blackfella* story into a white story. You want to get that television set off of your son once in a while and listen to a bit of news once in a while, because the Government said that they will be giving us orders from now on about how we spend our own money.' His eardrums burn – he really was on fire, and he hones in, listening more closely to the conversation inside the house. 'The army are already on the way.' His parents were warned that the Government was sending the army in to storm into all of their homes.

'Just like you have seen armies pushing around all of those other poor people on the earth, like in the war on terror over in Iraq and Afghanistan.'

And there it was, you could bet on it every time – a plague of fearfulness in the atmosphere flaring up, and simply by osmosis he is hit by a silent twang, and his spirit slapped back inside his parents. He thought it was a trick, that their fear was joined to him by invisible elastic that could be pulled by either of them in an instant, to make him feel what it was like inside of their skin. He knew that they were frightened of the police, frightened of the government and frightened of officials, which meant they were frightened of any white person in the vicinity, and any others in a proximity that radiated outwards and onwards until it encompassed the entire continent. A shiver disconnected him. He did not want their fear.

'They will be searching you to see if you are abusing your kids.' He strained to hear the whispering stuff and muffled voices talking about the news of how Aboriginal men were sexually abusing all the children.

'No, nobody knew which men, but it looked like all Aboriginal men were doing it, even here and everywhere, according to what was being said on the radio and on the TV too. *We are just finding out about it now.*'

He heard his parents being told that all of the children would be forced to have medical checks to see what was wrong with them. The army will be arresting all of the children and taking them to see a doctor to see which ones are being abused, and they might find out something else too, why they are not going to school. The voices become shrill, saying, 'You got to make him.' He should be flogged and flogged solid, until he went to school.

He heard them say that everyone in the whole community will starve more now, because parents will lose all of their welfare money if he does not go to school. *You can't make me!* The voices shout so he can hear what they are saying, even from where he is sitting outside of the house.

'Tell him that the Government's intervention into the Aboriginal communities in the Northern Territory will make him go to school every day, or else they will clear the lot of us away from our traditional land again. We won't be able to live here any more. Tell him they are going to take him away, along with everyone else's children too. Parents will all be separated again from their children, just like the Stolen Generation days.'

He knows that many of his relatives have too many people living in their homes just like his place, which was called overcrowding, and most of their children were not going to school either. Why were they trying to force him to go to school?

'No! Don't tell him, just flog him and make him sit at school, or everyone will starve to death in this place.'

'You tell him all this is the Government's law now, and we are telling you that the Government's law wants you to flog him until you kill him if he doesn't go, otherwise they will close this place down.'

He thought all the talking about the army coming into his home had to be some kind of joke, but he could tell by the way that his parents were screaming that they were pretty shaken up and the fear in their voices really confirmed in his mind once and for all that this was no joke. They were responding in the only way that they knew, by telling everyone to get out and leave them alone. The country's ghosts only knew how he wanted the whole community to explode when they heard him say exactly what he thought about the Government to their face when they turned up with the army.

He punched himself for bravery, commanding himself that he was not frightened of any Government. If they wanted to make war – *Well, go for it!* He would give them war. He imagined himself falling from the sky like a high-speed missile, which he would steal from the army – *Whoa!* His hands were joined high above his head, and he dived straight through the air, and down, *BANG!* He had set up the television in the front yard by running a thirty-metre-long yellow extension cord out through a window of the house from a broken plug in the wall that he had played around with until he made it work. He wanted to show everyone how he looked after himself. He felt that smart about fixing the broken plug, he thought if he ever got an education the first thing he would do would be to make the biggest missile in the world to protect his grandfather's traditional country so nobody could take it away again.

All of his relatives have now come by, even the ones who were

Be Careful About Playing With the Path of Least Resistance

visiting and camping at his parents place in the backyard, and he thought by now they would have exhausted themselves after spending all morning just talking about how the Federal Government Intervention Policy would work, and he reckoned that, altogether, they had not missed one single thing that they wanted to say to his parents for the final time that day. You know how they looked when they left? *You could see their tongues hanging out for water.*

Their message had been made clear: *We fought for our land rights for years before we got it back.* If *smart aleck* decides not to go to school, they said, he will be forcing the whole community to leave their country forever, and they will all have to go and live like dogs, fighting with all the drunks on the fringes of the town, which was about 400 kilometres away from their traditional land. He could still hear their voices fading into a settled place in his brain that lived, just to keep reminding him: *Who will be left to look after the country? No one ... will know the songs. We will not be allowed. We will not be able to come back. It will be too hard. Everyone will forget. The Government will be the winner. They have always wanted to take our land rights back. It will just take one smart aleck going about doing the wrong thing.*

The school was a brand new showcase building the Government built to help a politician win votes in his electorate. It was the only building that had been replaced in his community for years. The lime-green colour of the school was very nice – an achievement so rare, so everyone claimed, and had started calling the building 'rapid-quick time' – compared to anything else that they had tried to work for with the Government. The community was proud of the school, but not him. He thought the school was an eyesore amid the few dozen houses in the community that were so old the wind had blended the colour of the walls with the red earth, and this was the predominant colour he had grown up with since his birth, twelve years ago.

He wished the school could teach him something radical and brand new – something that would be useful for a boy living here to know, like how to fix up his mum's stove. Or, just imagine if they taught other miracles. He would like to know how to fiddle with the broken fridge and fix it up because nobody had seen a repairs and maintenance man in years. He contemplated how he might be able to go down to the rubbish tip and find some electrical bits, but he reckoned he still needed to know how to do the job. What else did he need? Tools! Money! Dream on! His mind travelled through a litany of malfunctioning plumbing and electrical wiring until he was exhausted from the thought, and he disentangled himself from suffocating wires and pipes that invaded the consciousness of the entire community.

The schoolteachers loomed large in his mind and now, after what he had heard from all of the relatives bothering his parents, they had become the centrepiece of his contempt. 'You know,' he snapped at a children's presenter on TV, 'if they are so smart, how come those losers don't teach anything useful?' He did not know what was worse – the boring television presenter or the teachers who talked about nothing all day and were to blame for making him feel mad.

He imagined the teachers flying above him in flights of white-winged unreachable clouds that ploughed on regardless in words that were just clouds, moving in the opposite direction to where he was sitting down below. His head felt hot under his mop of hair sticking out like a nest of straw. He could not get these teachers out of his mind.

Well! Take a look at him. There he was in the classroom day after day until he could not stand another moment of not understanding one single thing they were supposed to be teaching him. He felt his day had turned into a pile of rubbish like yesterday, and the day before that, and he reached further back in time until he could not remember feeling demented like mad, drunken people.

There was nothing worthwhile to watch on kids' TV that stopped the secret moving in the pit of his stomach. It was the secret he had not been able to tell anyone. It was about what was happening to him at school. In his loneliness, he brought the bundle up to his throat, where it became blocked, and he sent it back down. Once this ball started bouncing up and down it would make him feel sick. He would not allow himself to think about what he knew and did not want to know, that he had failed before even reaching the years ahead to finish his schooling in the ugly, slimy-green school, where he felt as though he was a toad, sitting in vomit.

Nah! He would not do that. He was not going to waste his time. *I want to stay feeling clean.* He could not think of any teacher giving him a clue about what he would do with their education. *Why waste having a good shower on them?* He flicked the TV flicker around for the sake of flicking. He shoved his bad thoughts out from the classroom and into the schoolyard. He cast his mind over the little trees that clung to life in the heat of the day, or the winds of winter, and had never grown at all, having remained like little sticks with a few half-dead-looking leaves. Schoolteachers were not smart about that, making a garden on his country, *were they?* He looked around at his country's landscape of red, browns, grey and yellow, olive and blue, and thought it looked good just the way it was already. It was full enough with too many plants like the spinifex grasses, eucalyptus trees and all the scrubs with their own spiritual stories. The flicker was working overtime, pushing the bad thoughts between the images of cartoons on two TV channels. He left the TV on full static and walked down the road, dreaming about the hunting dog he wanted to own. He decided to visit his grandfather because he had dogs. 'Give me one of your dogs.' He had asked his grandfather the same question every time he saw him. There were plenty of dogs living with the old man, but his grandfather loved all of them. He waited for the same answer while wondering which one he would choose between the biggest or even the littlest, but he would not take the *ugliest* one, even if old grandfather changed his mind and gave it to him.

'Maybe I will give you a dog one day when you grow up a bit.'

'I know how to look after a dog and I need one now because I am leaving here to live in the bush before the army gets here.' The old man laughed.

'I don't know what is going on in that young mind of yours about the army and all that stuff, but I will give you my best dog one of these days, but not now.'

A few of the younger dogs played with the boy, teasing them with sticks while he was deciding what to do next, and what occurred to him was the little game he kept playing with himself, and he thought of everyone talking about him once they had heard what he had done.

'This boy, skinny one with rubbish head,' his grandfather would say, 'already knew that he was not supposed to take that one old overgrown path at the back of the community, but you know, from plenty of tracks he could have chosen – all of them with big stories of the epics he belonged to from the beginning of time, he did what? *Why did he go and do that for?*' Then he thought of his parents, his mother and father crying that they have been *perplexing themselves silly* to understand what mystery sickness he had that had drawn him like a magnet to that one overgrown track – *the one over there*, lying beneath a covering of dry grasses. He even knew it would be impossible to count the number of times he had been told not to go near that track.

He felt the bad story about the track stirring him inside, which kept him noticing the way the grass grew like a door at the entrance to where this story began, and this was the reason why he kept going back to watch the phenomenon, of how the grass had almost concealed the path. Soon, he thought, the path would disappear altogether if nobody walked on it, and if he had not been any the wiser, even he would never have known that it ever existed. The memory would be gone forever and he would have forgotten the reasons for the country taking over the footprints that had been made from children who had gone there to commit suicide. All of it will be gone when the grass covered the stories his people had condemned to die, to never be spoken of.

Hey! Itchy! Titchy! Feet so Itchy! In the game of daring the children played, teasing each other to find out which one of them would be game enough to go to paradise, and he let their words float while they grew larger in his mind, to energise him until he was under the spell. The thought of travelling had always been locked inside of him like a colossal force, and now it pulled him through a pathway created from children's rumours that had been embellished from whatever may have once been true. The idea of being dangerous, of leaving, made him feel strong. It was even better than thinking he could steal a missile. A volcano in his lungs spilt lava and its heat was driving him crazy with wishing, and he felt like this each time he went near to the barely visible, abandoned opening between the dry grasses. He liked playing this game that kept singing him to a wild volcanic dance in his imagination, pulling his eyes further in to where the track ended some distance away to a sunlit opening among a circle of ghost gums with white trunks and a canopy that was held in an embrace – a glen he should never go to at the end of this path, in fear that his life might disappear forever, because no child who went there had ever come back.

This game had become something special to him, and he was beginning to feel ambivalent, and he did not care, because his attraction to what he ought to avoid was growing lovable through a fiery argument that he controlled and owned. His wishing was becoming his soulmate; a strange friend to run to from the secret he knew about himself of a learning, a knowledge of his future, that he had lost his way already in the classroom while the voices of teachers reverberated through the air as sounds that told him that he would not succeed in life without an education.

He slipped from the knowledge of failure, unable to capture a picture of himself in the future that he could love, nor could he retreat back to the past and begin again like a little child, and he slipped further into this special relationship with the path that stood apart from anything else that he knew, and let it fuel him with the power of destiny. He felt stronger, like he was once, before he could no longer understand the lessons of school. He was thinking alone with his own fiery secret, which was as precious as the one other abandoned dream of owning hunting dogs.

This was the game of a conqueror, the way he casually walked in a roundabout way towards the path, so he would not be noticed, and stood at the entrance of the track, kicking the grass aside with his bare feet. He felt the warming blood of a warrior, a soldier, or a rich man at the wheel of a new car. He saw himself inside a television, hunting for a future inside a boy, and racing towards invincibility among the spirits. The call came to him through the wind rattling the leaves, or it came through birds beating on the hardwood of a tree trunk, or from among the branches scraping against each other. All called of knowing him. He felt the need growing stronger, and it was as if he already knew that just to exercise his own willpower would change his life, for the better, to make him rich, who only knew what would happen then? He did not care.

The thought occurred to him that he would go through the path in a flash, and he believed he would be back in a minute. This short journey to the glen among the trees where for no other mysterious reason at all he just wanted to stand in the lovely shade among the ghost gums. Nobody would ever know if he went there, if he took one, or two, steps further along the path. One time, when he was about to try after making a decision he could go forever, a cloud of yellow butterflies crossed in front of him, stopping him in his tracks. Then an owl swooped at the idea one night. Another time, when he had made up his mind that he did not care whether he came back, an eagle had arrived in front of him, landing among the branches, as though warning him to stop.

He wanted to run headfirst into the place where children he had known had asked for invincibility in their death, and had their spirit freed, only leaving the memory of a child who had taken his own life behind for the families to mourn. He stood in front of the path ready to go as quickly as if he was at the starting line of a race, so that he could run to the rest of his life. Suddenly, instead of the loud shrill of the whistle, he heard his grandfather's voice quietly speaking behind him.

'You are going to our Aboriginal Land Council meeting today

to learn about all the important business of looking after our human rights, our culture and our ancestral land. It is time you learn to make sure nobody takes that one away from us.'

He ran off quickly, surprised that his grandfather was not worrying about the Government or the army, and even dispelling his own thoughts, nagging: *Path! Path! What about the path?* Forget that path. Nobody questioned his grandfather. When his grandfather spoke, he knew that he was talking for the spiritual ancestors that had created their country. He was not going to be left behind. He would have to pack the swag, to go with his grandfather, who said that they would travel for many, many hours, maybe even two days.

'Now, don't muck me around. I am going to show you plenty of stories for the country along the way. You will remember all of them.'

He knew he would now be one of the people who came home telling stories of travelling through their country in all the seasons of scorching heat, or extreme cold, or maybe big starry nights, moving over very rough roads, and what happened on the way when the car broke down. He would talk about the big meeting of Elders that took place in another community – a place on an open plain close to the sky dreaming, or another place that was resting against a rocky range that was the body of an ancestor laying in the spinifex grassland of the vast Aboriginal-owned land governed and cared for by the tribal nations and language groups of his own people.

'You are old enough to start learning about the big responsibility of looking after the stories for the country now, and maybe if you listen and learn something you might even become responsible for looking after country one day.'

The boy sat between his grandfather and his best dog on the long journey of stories, and his grandfather showed him their big argument, which was where the miners were digging up and breaking the spiritual resting places on their traditional land.

'This is why I want you to be strong and to get a good education. So you can fight all of that one for me with a proper pen-and-paper job.'

The boy nodded truthfully, because he would walk over hot coals for his grandfather.

When they arrived home after several months of travelling with the other senior Indigenous law people for some of the important religious ceremonies to honour the country, he found that his parents had left the community. Many of his aunties and uncles had gone away, too. He was told that they had gone to live in town because they were scared of the Government and the army.

The government in Canberra had changed again, and now the intervention laws affecting his people were called *Closing the Gap*. It still meant that if you were an Aboriginal person living in a remote community on your traditional land, then you had less rights than other people in the country, and were forced to live under special laws that ruled over your life. The only choice his parents had was to either stay on their land and live under these laws, with very little control over their lives any more, or leave.

Over at his grandparents' place it was really chock-a-block with all of the children who had been left behind so somebody else could try to force them to go to the slimy-green school that still looked the same, and still meant nothing in the lives of any of these children. He thought of the silent grandmothers, and grandfathers, and old aunties and uncles anyway worrying for some money for tucker, with nowhere else to go and all they wanted to do was to stay with their country to look after it, and now looking after all of the children, including the ones they were already caring for, like the ones whose parents were handicapped, or a long way away sick in hospital, or had passed away, or were serving time in some distant jail, or had gone now for any of a hundred reasons that call people away for ceremony and looking after country because that was their responsibility.

He thought there had to be somewhere where he would find some money to buy his grandparents food when the Government and the army came and took all of their welfare money away for three months, like they said they would do, because they could make

Be Careful About Playing With the Path of Least Resistance

a law to starve them all if the kids were not going to school. He would not let them starve. He would rob someone, and he pushed the thought away that kept occurring to him that he would go somewhere ...

DJINIYINI GONDARRA
Yolŋuw Makarr Dhuni Spokesperson

MARK YINGIYA
Guyula Yolŋuw Makarr Dhuni Spokesperson

HELEN NYOMBA GANDANGU
Yolŋuw Makarr Dhuni

CONVENER MATTHEW DHULUMBURRK GAYKAMANGU
Yolŋuw Makarr Dhuni

STRONGER FUTURES

The Yolŋuw Makarr Dhuni, October 2013

We want self-determination. We want democracy. We want the power of the people in Arnhem Land and in all Aboriginal communities to be recognised and our rights respected.

We want the Intervention to be thrown out, and we want the Northern Territory Government to lobby the Federal Government on our behalf.

The Federal Government must start to listen to the voices on the ground. No more deception, no more lies, we want the Intervention out now and self-determination to be taken seriously.

We never consented to this law, and we were never asked if we wanted the continuation and extension of these laws under the deceptively named 'Stronger Futures' Act.

We will not tolerate this bullying and it is no way to treat human beings. We are being led around like dogs on a lead with the BasicCard, compulsory acquisition of our land, police coming into our houses without a warrant, and having our law disqualified from recognition or consideration in court.

All this was done and continues to be done under the lie that we are hiding paedophiles and that child abuse comes from our culture. This is disrespectful, slanderous and fundamentally untrue. It is undermining our law, our culture and our whole identity.

All this so Government can get legitimacy for taking over our communities.

We demand an apology from the Federal Government.

We have our own system of law to prevent disagreements from escalating. We keep peace and order through good governance and we have very serious and consistent ways of teaching respect and discipline to all our young people. We have ways of dealing with people who have broken the law that means they are not a threat to the community while they are taught responsibility and maturity. These processes are being eroded through community disempowerment and government attacks on our legitimacy as leaders and our society as a whole.

* * *

Since the Intervention and the ban on bilingual education, school attendance has dropped because Yolngu children don't have a familiar school environment, and they don't see the point in going when all the jobs have gone.

CONTRIBUTORS

Debra Adelaide

Debra Adelaide is the author or editor of more than a dozen books, including the best-selling *Motherlove* series (1996–98) and *Acts of Dog* (2003). She is also an Associate Professor teaching creative writing at the University of Technology, Sydney. Her novels include *The Hotel Albatross* (1995), *Serpent Dust* (1998) and *The Household Guide to Dying* (2008), which was published in over a dozen countries including France, Germany, Spain, the USA and the UK. In 2013 she published a collection of short stories, *Letter to George Clooney*, which was shortlisted for several literary awards. Her latest books are the edited collection, *The Simple Act of Reading* (2015), and a novel, *The Women's Pages* (2015).

Pat Anderson

Ms Pat Anderson is an Alyawarre woman known nationally and internationally as a powerful advocate for disadvantaged people, with a particular focus on the health of Australia's First Peoples. She has extensive experience in all aspects of Aboriginal health, including community development, advocacy, policy formation and research ethics.

Ms Anderson has spoken before the United Nations Working Group on Indigenous People, and currently serves as the Chairperson of the Lowitja Institute, Australia's National Institute for Aboriginal and Torres Strait Islander health research. The Institute is an innovative research body that brings together Aboriginal and

Torres Strait Islander organisations, academic institutions and government agencies to facilitate collaborative, evidence-based research into Aboriginal and Torres Strait Islander health.

She has also been the CEO of Danila Dilba Health Service in Darwin, Chair of the National Aboriginal Community Controlled Health Organisation, Executive Officer of the Aboriginal Medical Services Alliance Northern Territory (AMSANT), and was the Chair of the CRC for Aboriginal Health from 2003 to 2009. Ms Anderson has had many essays, papers and articles published. She was a co-author with Rex Wild QC of 'Little Children are Sacred', a report on the abuse of Aboriginal children in the Northern Territory. In 2007 she was awarded the Public Health Association of Australia's Sidney Sax Public Health Medal in recognition of her achievements and she was awarded Human Rights Community Award (Tony Fitzgerald Memorial Community Award) in 2012 and an honorary doctorate from Flinders University in 2013. She is based in Canberra.

In June 2014, Ms Anderson was appointed Officer of the Order of Australia (AO) for distinguished service to the Indigenous community as a social justice advocate, particularly through promoting improved health, educational and protection outcomes for children.

Larissa Behrendt

Professor Larissa Behrendt is the Chair of Indigenous Research at the Jumbunna Indigenous House of Learning at the University of Technology, Sydney. She has published numerous textbooks on Indigenous legal issues. Larissa won the 2002 David Uniapon Award and a 2005 Commonwealth Writer's Prize for her novel *Home*. Her second novel, *Legacy*, won a Victorian Premiers Literary Award. She is also the author of *Indigenous Australia for Dummies*. Her most recent book is *Finding Eliza: Power and Colonial Storytelling* (2016, UQP). Larissa wrote and directed the Walkley nominated feature documentary, *Innocence Betrayed* and has written and produced several short films. Larissa was awarded the 2009 NAIDOC Person of the Year award and 2011 NSW Australian of the Year. She is the host of 'Speaking Out' on the ABC Local Radio network.

Eva Cox

Eva Cox was born Eva Hauser in Vienna in 1938, and was soon declared stateless by Hitler so grew up as a refugee in England, until 1946, Italy and then Australia from age ten. She remembers being cross in Kindergarten that boys were offered drums, and girls the tambourine or triangle. All these early experiences primed her political activism and made her an irrepressible advocate for making societies fairer. She is an unabashed feminist and passionately promotes inclusive, diverse and equitable ways of living together. She was the ABC Boyer Lecturer (1995) on making societies more civil. Her 1996 book *Leading Women* explained why women who made a difference were usually labelled as difficult, a label she wears as a change necessity. She has been an academic, political advisor, public servant, and runs a small research and policy consultancy. A sociologist by profession, she promotes ideas widely and eclectically in books, online, in journals and through other media. Eva has been recognised in various ways: Australian Humanist of the Year, a Distinguished Alumnus at UNSW and an Edna Grand Stirrer award. She also stirs through being a Fellow of the Centre for Policy Development and as a Professorial Fellow at Jumbunna Indigenous House of Learning (UTS).

Brenda L. Croft

Brenda L. Croft is from the Gurindji/Malngin/Mudpurra peoples of the Northern Territory and Anglo–Australian/German/Irish heritage. Involved in the contemporary arts and cultural sectors for over three decades as an artist, arts administrator, curator, educator, researcher and consultant, Brenda has worked at local, regional, national and international levels. Her work is represented in major public and private collections in Australia and overseas.

In 2016 Brenda received an Artistic Associate Fellowship (Photography) from Barangaroo Authority/Lendlease. In 2015 she received the Berndt Foundation Post-graduate Award, and a National Indigenous Art Award Fellowship from the Australia Council for the Arts. In 2013 Brenda received the Visual Artist of the Year, Deadlys National Aboriginal and Torres Strait Islander Music, Sport, Entertainment and Community Awards.

For her academic work Brenda was awarded a Master of Art Administration from the University of New South Wales in 1995 and received a UNSW Alumni Award in 2001. In 2009 she was awarded an Honorary Doctorate (Vis Arts) from the University of Sydney. She was the recipient of an Australian Research Council Discovery Indigenous Award from 2012–15 and is undertaking her PhD at the National Institute for Experimental Arts, UNSW Art & Design, where she is an honorary Research Fellow.

Ali Cobby Eckermann

Her first collection *little bit long time* was written in the desert and launched her literary career in 2009. Her works have been published in various languages, and she has travelled widely to showcase Aboriginal poetry overseas.

In 2013 she toured Ireland as Australian Poetry Ambassador and won the Kenneth Slessor Prize for Poetry (NSW) for *Ruby Moonlight*, a massacre verse novel. She was the inaugural recipient of the Tungkunungka Pintyanthi Fellowship, and invited to attend the International Writing Program at the University of Iowa in 2014. Her memoir *Too Afraid to Cry* was launched in New Delhi, India in 2015, on her way to the Jaipur Literature Festival.

Ali retains her dream for an Aboriginal Writers Retreat, to promote the volume of Aboriginal grassroots voices, and for healing.

Lionel Fogarty

Lionel Fogarty is a poet and Indigenous rights activist. Lionel's first poetry collection, *Yoogum Yoogum*, was published by Penguin in 1982, and he is the author of numerous poetry collections including most recently, *Dha'lan Djani Mitti: Collected Poems*. Lionel is involved in The Red Room Company, a progressive poetry organisation and Unlocked, a not-for-profit poetry program for inmates of NSW Correctional Facilities.

Djiniyini Gondarra

Born in Milingimbi, eastern Arnhem Land in 1945. In 1969 he trained as a minister under the Uniting Church and worked with his own people at the Galiwin'ku parish, Arnhem Land from 1976 to 1982. He was a lecturer in Theology at Nungalinya College, Darwin and received a Diploma of Theology (Honorary) from there in 1984, and in 1991 received a Cultural Doctorate in Literature (Honorary) from the World University, Roundtable, Arizona, USA. He was awarded the Order of Australia Medal (OAM) in 1995.

As well as being the Chairman of ALPA since 1993, Rev. Djiniyini is currently the Director of Duduy'ngu Pty Ltd, which provides consultancy and cross-cultural services. He is also Director of Yirrkala Business Enterprises. Over the years, Rev Djiniyini has served on many committees and councils including: Member of the Steering Committee of the Australian Indigenous Cultural Network (1998–2001), CEO of Aboriginal Resource and Development Services Inc. (1998–2001), CEO of the Northern Regional Council of the Uniting Aboriginal and Islander Christian Congress (1998–2001), Director of Reconciliation Australia (2000–2001), Member of Council for Aboriginal Reconciliation (1998–2000), Chairman of Uniting Aboriginal and Islander Christian Congress (1990–1993 and 1995–2000), Member of Central Committee of the World Council of Churches (1991–1994), Moderator of Northern Synod, Uniting Church in Australia (1985–1987), Secretary of newly formed Aboriginal Presbytery, Northern Synod, Uniting Church in Australia (1985), and Vice-President of Uniting Aboriginal and Islander Christian Congress Uniting Church in Australia (1983–1987).

He has been described as one of the most influential Aboriginal leaders of our time and one of the most qualified lawmen.

Yinjiya Mark Guyula

Yiṉiya Mark Guyula is a Liya-dhälinymirr Djambarrpuyŋu man whose traditional lands include Badaypaday. His ancestral language and connections are Dhuwal Djambarrpuyŋu. He has been the senior lecturer in the Yolŋu Studies program at Charles Darwin University for some years. He has worked as an aircraft mechanic and trained as a pilot. His work includes research on intellectual property, gambling and gambling-related harm, water conservation, sustainable housing, gifted and talented children, and financial literacy programs.

Rodney Hall

Rodney Hall is a writer with an international reputation. Many of his books have been translated into other languages (French, German, Danish, Swedish, Portuguese, Spanish and Korean). He has twice won the Miles Franklin Award and twice been awarded the gold medal of the Australian Literature Society. He was a foundation member of the Queensland Council for the Advancement of Aborigines and Torres Strait Islanders and a member of their campaign committee for the 1967 referendum.

Natalie Harkin

Natalie Harkin is a Narungga woman from South Australia. She has written poetry for many years and her current PhD research is an archival poetic response to her family's Aboriginal records, informed by blood-memory and haunting. She is a member of her local Aboriginal writers group and the First Nations Australia Writers' Network, and was invited to conduct a poetics masterclass at the 2014 International Writers Festival, Ottawa. She is part of the Unbound collective at Yunggorendi, Flinders University, a group of Aboriginal women academics, experimental writers and artists creatively interrogating the State's archives and colonial history.

Rosalie Kunoth-Monks

Rosalie Kunoth-Monks is an Arrente, Alyawarra Elder who lives in the Utopian Homeland where she was born. When she was sixteen she starred in the lead role of the Australian classic film *Jedda* directed by Charles Chauvel. After being an Anglican nun for a decade she became involved in social work and politics. Since then, she has been a prominent and respected advocate and spokeswoman for the Aboriginal people – a government advisor, an interpreter, an environmental campaigner, a Shire president and has chaired or contributed to many boards and councils devoted to Indigenous issues. She stood for the Senate for the First Nations political party.

Her awards include the Dr Yunupingu Award for Human Rights, 'recognising her work of over half a century as a community leader in Utopia, Northern Territory, and as a stateswoman leading all First People's and others towards greater justice and equality,' the Order of Australia Medal and the Northern Territory's Tribute to Territory Women Award.

In 2015 she was awarded the Northern Territory Australian of the Year.

Deni Langman

Deni Langman is a traditional Uluru owner and Elder.

John Leemans

John Leemans is a translator, activist and member of the Gurindji people. He speaks Kriol, Gurindji and Warlpiri, is a spokesperson for the Kalkaringi community which is 470 km south-west of Katherine, NT. John organised the Gurindji Protest against the Intervention in 2010 and currently works as an Aboriginal Interpreter Service team member in Katherine, NT.

Melissa Lucashenko

Melissa Lucashenko is an award-winning novelist who lives between Brisbane and the Bundjalung nation. Her writing explores the stories and passions of Aboriginal people and others living around the margins of the First World. Melissa's most recent novel, *Mullumbimby*, was awarded the 2013 Deloitte Queensland Literary Award for Fiction, won the 2014 Victorian Premier's Literary Award for Indigenous Writing, was shortlisted for the Nita B. Kibble Award and longlisted for both the Stella and Miles Franklin awards. *Mullumbimby* is also longlisted for the IMPAC Dublin Literary Award 2015.

Melissa is a Walkley Award winner for her non-fiction, as well as a founding member of Sisters Inside. Her website is at www.melissalucashenko.com.au.

Jeff McMullen

Journalist, author and filmmaker for five decades, Jeff McMullen AM has been a foreign correspondent for the Australian Broadcasting Corporation, reporter for *Four Corners* and *Sixty Minutes*, anchor of the 33-part series on ABC Television, *Difference of Opinion* and host of forums on National Indigenous Television.

Recent documentaries have focused on the human rights of the First Peoples and the chronic illness taking many lives. His short film, *East Coast Encounter*, is travelling Australia as part of an exhibition by leading artists, poets and historians who explore James Cook's 1770 contact with Aboriginal people and the impact of terra nullius.

He is a director of the Australian Indigenous Mentoring Experience and has helped develop early learning and the Literacy Backpack Program in twenty-two remote communities.

In 'Dispossession: Neo-Liberalism and the Struggle for Aboriginal Land and Rights in the 21st Century' (in *Black & White* published by Connor Court 2013) McMullen analyses the market fundamentalism shaping Indigenous policy.

A Life of Extremes: Journeys and Encounters (HarperCollins Australia) is his memoir, examining the global pattern of conflict, environmental degradation and species extinction, as well as sharing ideas from some of the world's bravest individuals on a brighter future for the human family.

P.M. Newton

After thirteen years in the NSW Police P.M. Newton went to Mali to write about travel and music, then to India to study Buddhist philosophy. Her first novel, *The Old School*, was shortlisted for the Indie Awards and the Ned Kelly Award for First Fiction and won the Sisters in Crime Davitt Award and the Asher Literary Award. Her second novel, *Beams Falling*, was shortlisted for the 2014 Ned Kelly Awards. Her short fiction and essays have appeared in *Seizure*, *Review of Australian Fiction*, *Anne Summers Reports* and *The Drum*, www.pmnewton.com.

Christine Olsen

Writer, producer and director Christine Olsen is the writer and co-producer of the film *Rabbit-Proof Fence*. Her other film credits include the three part political/historical series on Indonesia, *Riding the Tiger* (AFI nominated for Best Television Documentary and the ATOM Award for Best Television Series) and *Invitation to a Wedding*, an Islamic road movie.

In 1996 she was awarded a Distinctly Australian Producer Fellowship. She co-produced the short film *At Sea* (1996) and co-produced and co-directed *My One-Legged Dream Lover* (1998). She was executive producer of *Hephzibah*, which won the AFI Award for Best Documentary Film in 1999 and produced *High Noon in Jakarta* (2001), wrote, directed and produced the award-winning short film, *The Big Day* (2004) and was executive producer of *The President Versus David Hicks* (AFI Award for Best Documentary, Logie Award for Best Documentary Series). In 2007 she produced the feature-length documentary, *The Siege*, Sydney Film Festival, Sundance.

Bruce Pascoe

Bruce Pascoe has Bunurong and Tasmanian family and is a Yuin man. He published and edited *Australian Short Stories* magazine from 1982 to 1999. He has won multiple awards including the Australian Literature Award 1999, the Radio National Short Story 1998, FAW Short Story 2010 and the Prime Minister's Award for Literature (Young Adult) 2013. His books include *Night Animals, Fox, Ruby-Eyed Coucal, Shark, Ocean, Earth, Bloke, Cape Otway, Convincing Ground, The Little Red Yellow Black Book* and *Fog a Dox*. He is a board member of the Victorian Aboriginal Corporation for Languages and First Languages Australia. He was Secretary of the Bidwell-Maap Aboriginal Corporation. His most recent book, *Dark Emu*, was published by Magabala and was shortlisted for the Victorian Premier's Indigenous Award 2014 and shared the Indigenous

Writers' Prize, and won Book of the Year at the NSW Premier's Literary Awards 2016. *Fog a Dox* won the 2013 Prime Minister's Award and was shortlisted for the Western Australian Premier's Book Award and the Deadly Award. Bruce lives in Gipsy Point in Far East Gippsland with his wife, Lyn Harwood. He has two children and three grandchildren.

Nicole Watson

Nicole Watson is a member of the Birri-Gubba people of Central Queensland, and the Mullenjarli people of Beaudesert. She is a former lawyer and is currently employed as a senior lecturer in the Faculty of Arts and Social Sciences, University of Technology, Sydney.

Samuel Wagan Watson

Hailing from honourable ancestors of the Birri-Gubba, Mununjali, Germanic and Gaelic peoples, Samuel Wagan Watson grew up in a family of accomplished authors, political players, entrepreneurs, academics, artists and raconteurs. He was born 'illegally' in Brisbane in 1972, and survived his teenage years on the Sunshine Coast.

Collected works of Samuel's poetry have achieved prodigious accolades and have been translated into seven languages, various musical compositions, the subject of film and television productions and public/visual art projects.

Samuel has been commissioned to write for a number of government and corporate entities, ranging from Brisbane City Council to the Japan Aerospace Exploration Agency.

He is currently a freelance writer working on selected commissions and has just released his fourth collection of poetry with the University of Queensland Press, entitled *Love Poems and Death Threats*.

Samuel is an active ambassador for the Indigenous Literacy Foundation, rogue_poet@outlook.com.

Rachel Willika

Rachel Willika, a Jaowyn Elder from the remote Aboriginal community of Manyallaluk in the Northern Territory, was the first Jaowyn community person to attend university after successfully completing the Flinders University Foundation Studies Program. She has expressed opposition to the Intervention in media and speeches throughout Australia. Her successful techniques in educating community children have made her a role model. A submission by Professor Claire Smith called 'Jaowyn teaching Jaowyn' for the Indigenous Jobs and Training Review on Improving Employment and Training Outcomes in Remote Regions is a pilot study based on Ms Willika's work in educating her children and grandchildren.

Alexis Wright

Wright is a member of the Waanyi nation of the southern highlands of the Gulf of Carpentaria. Her books include *Grog War*, a study of alcohol abuse in Tennant Creek, and the novels *Plains of Promise*, *Carpentaria* and *The Swan Book*. She is a Distinguished Fellow in Western Sydney University's Writing and Society Research Centre.

Yalmay Yunupingu

Yalmay Yunupingu is a linguist and teacher with a 1996 Graduate Diploma of Teaching. In 2004, she was appointed senior teacher at the Yirrkala Bilingual Program where she is currently employed.

During her long career as an educationalist, Yalmay has been a strong advocate of bilingual or 'two-way' teaching.

In 2005, she was awarded the Northern Territory Government's Teaching Excellence Award in the Remote Primary category for her work at Yirrkala Community Education Centre (CEC) and, in 2006, was awarded the Australia Day Local Government Award, Citizen of the Year, for the Yirrkala community.

Yalmay started painting later in life. She also made pandanus mats and etchings in 2003 and woodblock prints in 2004 at the Garma Festival.Her work has featured in the 13th *National Aboriginal and Torres Strait Islander Art Awards*, 1996, at the Museum and Art Gallery of the Northern Territory; *Painters of the Wagilag Sisters Story*, 1997, at the National Gallery of Australia; and *Painted Places*, 1998, at the Bayly Art Museum, University of Virginia, USA.

She is the daughter of artist Mathaman Marika from the celebrated Marika family of Yirrkala and wife of the late Yothu Yindi frontman Mandawuy Yunupingu.

Arnold Zable

Arnold Zable is a writer, novelist and human rights advocate. His books include *Jewels and Ashes*, *The Fig Tree*, *Café Scheherazade*, *Scraps of Heaven*, *Sea of Many Returns* and *Violin Lessons*, a book of stories spanning the globe. He is the author of numerous columns, features and essays, and is a co-author of *Kan Yama Kan*, a play in which asylum seekers tell their stories. His first account of his journeys with Aboriginal Elders was published in 1995. He has worked in many cross-cultural projects and conducted workshops for a range of groups including asylum seekers, refugees, the deaf, problem gamblers and survivors of the Black Saturday bushfires using story as a means of self-understanding. In recent years he has conducted annual workshops for Cambodian writers. Born in New Zealand, Zable grew up in Melbourne and has lived and worked in New York, India, China, South-East Asia, Papua New Guinea and throughout Europe. Zable is the immediate past president of PEN International Melbourne, an ambassador of the Asylum Seeker Resource Centre, and has a doctorate from the school of creative arts, Melbourne University where he was appointed a Vice Chancellor's Fellow. He was recently awarded the Voltaire prize for human rights advocacy and the advancement of freedom of expression.

ACKNOWLEDGMENTS FOR THE FIRST EDITION

This book has had a unique provenance. Being unable to find a publisher became a positive factor – once the tide of support from the community and individuals rolled in. We have had practical, committed support and guidance from all over Australia, experts have donated their time, money and expertise and come together to ensure that this book happens.

First of all we'd like to thank and honour the Elders and other community members who have allowed their quotes and speeches to be published and for their unremitting struggle for their people. Thank you Rosalie Kunoth-Monks of Utopia, Rev Dr Djiniyini Gondarra of Galiwin'ku, Harry Nelson of Yuendumu, Djapirri Mununggirritj from Yirrkala, Yananymul Mununggurr from the Laynhapuy Homelands, Diane Stokes at Muckatty Station, Maurie Ryan and John Leemans at Kalkarindji, Reggie Wurridjal and Helen Williams at Manigrida, Barbara and Walter Shaw in the Alice Springs Town Camps, Harry Nelson at Yuendumu, Dhanggal Gurruwiwi from Wallaby Beach and Matthew Dhulumburrk Gaykambayu from Ramingining, Deni Langman, Miriam Rose Ungunmerr-Baumann of Nauiyu and George Gaymarani Pascoe of Milingimbi, Yingiya Mark Guyula, Yalmay Yunupingu and Rachel Willika of Eva Valley.

Because we could not find a publisher, obtaining funding was vital for the success of this anthology, so a heartfelt thank you to Zoe Rodriguez and the staff at Copyright Agency Limited who generously funded a significant part of this project as well as giving us valuable affirmation about the value of this book.

Warm thanks to

WITA (Women Inspired to Action) Marie Milne, Ann Long and Janice Haworth who generously raised funds for us through crowd-funding. Their support was crucial and heartened us at a difficult time.

Graeme Jones and Tracey Kirby of the typesetting firm Kirby Jones for their extraordinarily generous offer to do our typesetting and design free – a crucial help for us financially.

Michele Harris and 'concerned Australians' who immediately and enthusiastically gave us support. Michele's expertise and insight into this area has been at all times essential and we are indebted to her and 'concerned Australians' for her excellent imprint on this book.

Tara Wynne whose expertise, support and encouragement have been invaluable at all times – she has been a tower of strength throughout the process.

Jeff McMullen for his advice, enthusiasm and help as well as his great essay.

Debra Adelaide for her help in getting together the grant as well as her beautiful story.

Pamela Hewitt who donated her superb editing skills to work with us in the edit.

Brenda L. Croft for donating the powerful photos used for the cover and elsewhere in the book and her moving story. Brenda would also like to thank Avril Quaill, Chips Mackinolty and Brian Manning's family for the generous inclusion of their respective works, particularly as they have waived any reproduction fees.

Danny Vendramini who donated his great expertise in designing the cover.

Acknowledgments for the First Edition

We are very grateful for their superb technical skills which we could not have otherwise afforded.

Laura Dunn and Sophie for helping us to set up the Facebook page.

Raimond Gaita, Tara June Winch, Kris Olsson, Susan Johnson and Gail Jones who all agreed to contribute at the outset but for various reasons had to regretfully withdraw. They remained very supportive of the project.

Claire Smith for her help.

And warm thanks to Hanne Birk of Bonn, Germany for her donation and support and to Bonn University for their forthcoming conference on the Intervention.

And a very warm thanks to the following donors all over Australia and one from New Zealand who responded so generously to our crowdfunding request. Thank you for making this book possible.

Kathryn Matthews, Helen Loughlin, Janice Haworth, Marie Milne, Rebecca Lee, Christa Schoebel, Leith Maddock, Michael Jonge, Jean Bedford, Deborah Green, Rob McCormack, Robyn Maher, Haydyn Broley, Angela Savage, Anthony Messenger, Monika Trauth, Pamela Hewitt, Naomi Jacobs, Patricia O'Gorman, Karen Chisholm, Sue Stucky, Janet Grevillea, Wendy Carter, Elizabeth Mackie, Anna Russell, Lucy Abbott, Ann Long, Airdrie Long, Xavier, Alison and Henryk Dekkers, Marie Milne, Matt Hilton, Janet Giles, Helen Coles, Jennifer Strauss, Cathy Gill, Ross Hamilton, Shona Fleming, Jesse Blackadder, Judy Frazer, Suzanne Franzway, Carol Kenchington, Davinia Thornley, Patricia Hobbs, Isobel Bishop, Robyn O'Brien, Sara Bennett, Llynda Nairn, Judy Tonkin, Janet Galos, Patricia Saunders, Alison Smith, Caroline Davis, Philip Constable, John Goodwin.

In particular we would also like to thank Sue Gilbey, a disability pensioner and the first Australian ever to receive the Bremen Peace Award, a prestigious international peace prize, who generously donated a very large sum of money and wrote, 'I have been giving some thought to all of this and I truly believe what you are doing is vital to getting the word out about the racism that was and continues to be the NT Intervention. I have a little money from fundraising that was loosely about the Intervention and after consulting with others believe this would be the best place to put it.' And above all we would like to thank all the writers who contributed to this anthology with grace, eloquence, power and passion. Their great insight and knowledge have ensured that this book will be read and studied and we hope used as a resource in the opposition to the Intervention.

Another version of 'Be Careful about Playing with the Path of Least Resistance' by Alexis Wright was published in *Freedom: Short Stories Celebrating the Universal Declaration of Human Rights* by Amnesty International, 2009.

'Intervention a poem' by Natalie Harkin was first published in Harkin, N., *Dirty Words*, Cordite Books, Melbourne, 2015.

'Intervention Payback' was first published in *Little Bit Long Time* by the Australian Poetry Centre as part of the New Poets Series (2009) and subsequently reprinted by Picaro Press and in *The Best Australian Poems* edited by Robert Adamson in the same year.

'Parable' and '40 Year Leases' by Ali Cobby Eckermann were published in *Kami* by Vagabond Press (2010) and *Love Dreaming & Other Poems* by Vagabond Press (2012).

'From the Northern Territory Emergency Response to Stronger Futures – Where is the Evidence that Aboriginal women are leading self-determining lives?' by Nicole Watson. This article was published in its entirety in the *Australian Feminist Law Journal*, no 35, in 2011 pages 147–163.

NOTES AND SOURCES

ANITA HEISS & GEORGINA GARTLAND *Preface to new edition*
1   'The Little Children are Sacred report appeared to be leading towards community empowerment, which is a long way from current government thinking', from Walk with Us: Aboriginal Elders call out to Australian people to walk with them in their quest for justice, Concerned Australians, Melbourne, 2011, p. 7, <www.concernedaustralians.com.au/media/Walk_With_Us.pdf>.
   97 recommendations at <www.inquirysaac.nt.gov.au/pdf/report_by_sections/bipacsa_final_report-recommendations.pdf>.
2   Walk with Us, Concerned Australians, pp.4–8, <www.concernedaustralians.com.au/media/Walk_With_Us.pdf>.
3   Loss of Rights: The despair of Aboriginal communities in the Northern Territory, Concerned Australians, Melbourne, 2010, pp 40, 63–65, <www.concernedaustralians.com.au/media/Loss-of-Rights-Rept-2010_v2.pdf>.
4   The permit system was removed and five-year leases compulsorily imposed. As the first phase of the Intervention ceased longer leases were expected in some areas – many say coerced – in exchange for the provision of basic services.
5   To bring them under a single system of quarantining and further depoliticise robust Indigenous organisations, as discussed by Jon Altman in 'Scrapping CDEP is Just Plain Dumb', ABC *The Drum*, 2007, <www.abc.net.au/news/2007-07-26/scrapping-cdep-is-just-plain-dumb/2513782>. Jon Altman has written extensively on the increasing failings of the NT Intervention, <http://apo.org.au/resource/journal-indigenous-policy-issue-14-jon-altman-arguing-intervention>.
6   For a summary of this see: S Cooper, The Northern Territory Emergency Response Report by the Review Board, *Indigenous Law Bulletin*, vol. 31, 2008, <www.austlii.edu.au/au/journals/ILB/2008/31.html#fnB34>.
7   Walk with Us, Concerned Australians, p. 59, <www.concernedaustralians.com.au/media/Walk_With_Us.pdf>.
8   'Protecting the rights of Aboriginal children, women and the elderly are the most important human rights, Indigenous Affairs Minister Jenny Macklin has declared, brushing aside criticism of the Northern Territory intervention by a UN special delegate on indigenous rights ... Ms Macklin said she would not be swayed by the criticism', <www.missionandjustice.org/jenny-macklin-defends-northern-territory-intervention/comment-page-1>.
9   Loss of Rights, Concerned Australians, p. 64, <www.concernedaustralians.com.au/media/Loss-of-Rights-Rept-2010_v2.pdf>.
10 General Recommendation, p. 32. Walk with Us, Concerned Australians, pp. 13–18, <www.concernedaustralians.com.au/media/Walk_With_Us.pdf>.
11 'Concluding observations of the Committee on the Elimination of Racial Discrimination', United Nations: *International Convention on the Elimination of*

All Forms of Racial Discrimination, 2010, <www.concernedaustralians.com.au/media/CERD.pdf>.

12 The reinstatement did not include a 'not withstanding' clause, hence did not ensure full consistency with the RDA. See 'Inquiry into the Welfare Reform and Reinstatement of Racial Discrimination Act Bill 2009 and other Bills', Australian Human Rights Commission Submission to the Senate Community Affairs Committee, 2010, <https://www.humanrights.gov.au/inquiry-welfare-reform-and-reinstatement-racial-discrimination-act-bill-2009-and-other-bills>.

13 Walk with Us, Concerned Australians, p. 10, <www.concernedaustralians.com.au/media/Walk_With_Us.pdf>.

14 UN Committee on the Elimination of Racial Discrimination (CERD), General Recommendation no. 32, 'The meaning and scope of special measures in the International Convention on the Elimination of All Forms [of] Racial Discrimination', 24 September 2009, CERD/C/GC/32, <www.refworld.org/docid/4adc30382.html>.

15 For a list of measures and what people had to say, refer to 'Stronger Futures Legislation (and Associated Bills) Chart', Concerned Australians, <www.concernedaustralians.com.au/media/Stronger_Futures-Chart.pdf>.

16 For example, read *A Decision to Discriminate, Concerned Australians*, 2012, <www.concernedaustralians.com.au/media/A_Decision_to_Discriminate.pdf>.

17 *The Intervention: An Anthology*, pp. 212–213.

18 'Review of Stronger Futures in the Northern Territory Act 2012 and related legislation, Chapter 4: Income Management', <www.aph.gov.au/Parliamentary_Business/Committees/Joint/Human_Rights/Committee_Inquiries/strongerfutures2//Final_report/c04>.

19 Review of Stronger Futures in the Northern Territory Act 2012 and related legislation, Chapter 4: Income Management, [4.99], [4.101], [4.102], [4.104], <www.aph.gov.au/Parliamentary_Business/Committees/Joint/Human_Rights/Committee_Inquiries/strongerfutures2/Final_report/c04>.

20 Review of Stronger Futures in the Northern Territory Act 2012 and related legislation, Chapter 5: School Enrolment and Attendance through Welfare Reform Measure, [5.108], <www.aph.gov.au/Parliamentary_Business/Committees/Joint/Human_Rights/Committee_Inquiries/strongerfutures2/Final_report/c04>.

21 Ibid. [5.108; 6; 7.]

22 Loss of Rights, concerned Australians, pp. 62–64, <www.concernedaustralians.com.au/media/Loss-of-Rights-Rept-2010_v2.pdf>.

23 'Chris Graham rates Mal Brough and Jenny Macklin poorly on Indigenous Affairs', ABC Brisbane, available at: <http://blogs.abc.net.au/queensland/2013/08/chris-graham-rates-mal-brough-and-jenny-macklin-poorly-on-indigenous-affairs.html>. [Listen from 8.30 minutes onward.]

24 <www.theguardian.com/australia-news/2016/feb/08/northern-territory-intervention-fails-on-human-rights-and-closing-the-gap>.

25 <http://apo.org.au/resource/journal-indigenous-policy-issue-14-jon-altman-arguing-intervention>.

26 'Northern Territory Intervention fails to close to gap', Monash University media release, 2016, <http://monash.edu/news/releases/show/castan-centre>. 'Northern

Territory intervention 'fails on human rights' and closing the gap', <www.theguardian.com/australia-news/2016/feb/08/northern-territory-intervention-fails-on-human-rights-and-closing-the-gap>.

27 <www.abc.net.au/news/2014-12-04/number-of-indigenous-australians-in-prison-a-'catastrophe'/5945504; http://www.sbs.com.au/news/article/2016/02/09/nt-intervention-fails-key-reforms-report>.

28 2016 Stronger Futures review showed up massive failures of government. It was not effective, nor a proportionate measure. For example, see Review of Stronger Futures in the Northern Territory Act 2012 and related legislation, Chapter 3: Measures to address alcohol abuse, [3.56]. <www.aph.gov.au/Parliamentary_Business/Committees/Joint/Human_Rights/Committee_Inquiries/strongerfutures2/Final_report/c04>.

29 Loss of Rights, Concerned Australians, pp. 62–65. <www.concernedaustralians.com.au/media/Loss-of-Rights-Rept-2010_v2.pdf>.

30 On the increasing abuse of women, see for example: In the Absence of Treaty, compiled by Concerned Australians, Melbourne, 2013, pp. 33–34. <www.concernedaustralians.com.au/media/In_The_Absence_of_Treaty.pdf>.

31 Helen Davidson, Coalition Moves to Abandon Review of Northern Territory Intervention Policy, Guardian Australia, 26 February 2016, <www.theguardian.com/australia-news/2016/feb/26/coalition-moves-to-abandon-review-of-northern-territory-intervention-policy>.

32 In the Absence of Treaty, Concerned Australians, pp. 44–45. <www.concernedaustralians.com.au/media/In_The_Absence_of_Treaty.pdf>.

33 In the Absence of Treaty, Concerned Australians, pp. 24–28, 30–33, 53–59. (However, suggest reading entire book), <www.concernedaustralians.com.au/media/In_The_Absence_of_Treaty.pdf>.

34 Review of Stronger Futures in the Northern Territory Act 2012 and related legislation, Chapter 2: Matters not dealt with by the committee's 2013 report, <www.aph.gov.au/Parliamentary_Business/Committees/Joint/Human_Rights/Committee_Inquiries/strongerfutures2//Final_report/c02.>.

35 'Quotes by Rosalie Kunoth-Monks', Respect and Listen, <www.respectandlisten.org/miscellaneous/rosalie-kunoth-monks/media.html>.

36 Review of Stronger Futures in the Northern Territory Act 2012 and related legislation, Chapter 1: Government senator's additional comments, <www.aph.gov.au/Parliamentary_Business/Committees/Senate/Finance_and_Public_Administration/Commonwealth_Indigenous/Report/d01.>.

37 Submissions closed 15 May 2016 and report due to be tabled in December 2016, see: <www.anao.gov.au/work/performance-audit/indigenous-advancement-stragegy>.

38 Jon Altman -research professor at the Alfred Deakin Institute for Citizenship and Globalisation, Deakin University, Melbourne, <www.989fm.com.au/podcasts/lets-talk/prof-jon-altman-2/>.

39 <www.abc.net.au/news/2016-02-09/closing-the-gap-doomed-to-fail-without-more-indigenous-input/7149442>.

40 Why is it so hard to Close the Gap? Dr. Jackie Huggins, <www.abc.net.au/7.30/content/2015/s4403428.htm>.

PAT ANDERSON *The Intervention: Personal Reflections*

> The history of disruption, intervention and institutionalisation to which Aboriginal and Torres Strait Islander families and children have been subject has left many of those families confronting severe difficulties in securing the adequate care and control of their children ... it is apparent that many Aboriginal families are in crisis. (Vol 2, part C. ft 93)

After Rex and I had finished the consultations, we sat down to write the Inquiry report for the Northern Territory Government. We called it 'Little Children are Sacred' because this reflected what some of those communities told us, from Arrernte people in Central Australia to the Yolngu of Arnhem Land. Our main finding was consistent with what many Aboriginal people had been saying for a long time, namely that:

> There is a significant problem in Northern Territory communities in relation to sexual abuse of children. Indeed, it would be remarkable if there was not, given the similar and significant problems that exist elsewhere in Australia and abroad.
>
> We put forward almost one hundred recommendations to address the issue. These recommendations covered a whole range of areas – child protection services, health services, policing, rehabilitation, prevention, family support, education, housing, alcohol, employment, and more. Page 6

But for me the very first recommendation was the most significant. It said:

> It is critical that both [the Northern Territory and Federal] governments commit to genuine consultation with Aboriginal people in designing initiatives for Aboriginal communities [to address child sexual abuse and neglect]. Page 7

Notes and sources

NICOLE WATSON *From the Northern Territory Emergency Response to Stronger Futures – Where is the Evidence that Aboriginal Women are Leading Self-Determining Lives?*

1. S Gordon, Australian Broadcasting Corporation, 'Intervention Bills to pass, despite inquiry', *PM Monday to Friday*, 10 August 2007.
2. L Behrendt, 'Consent in a (Neo) Colonial Society: Aboriginal Women as Sexual and Legal "Other"', *Australian Feminist Studies*, vol. 15, no. 33, 2000, p. 353.
3. Senate Standing Committee on Legal and Constitutional Affairs, Legal and Constitutional Affairs Committee, Senate, *Unfinished Business: Indigenous stolen wages*, 2006.
4. R Wild & P Anderson, *Ampe Akelyernemane Meke Mekarle 'Little Children are Sacred'*, Report of the NT Board of Inquiry into the Protection of Aboriginal Children from Sexual Abuse, 2007.
5. *Stronger Futures in the Northern Territory: Discussion Paper*, Australian Government, 2011.
6. M Langton, 'The end of "big men" politics', *Griffith Review*, vol. 22, 2008, p. 158.
7. M Langton, 'Trapped in the Aboriginal Reality Show', *Griffin Review*, vol. 19, 2007, p. 13.
8. R Kunoth-Monks, *This is what we said*, Concerned Australians, 2010.
9. M Brough, *Parliamentary Debates*, House of Representatives, Commonwealth, 7 August 2007.
10. Equality Rights Alliance, 'Women's Experience of Income Management in the Northern Territory', Canberra, Equality Rights Alliance, 2011.
11. A Nicholson, M Harris & G Gartland, *Loss of Rights: The Despair of Aboriginal Communities in the Northern Territory*, A submission to the UN Committee on the Elimination of Racial Discrimination, Concerned Australians, 2010.
12. *Health Impact Assessment of the Northern Territory Emergency Response*, Australian Indigenous Doctors' Association and Centre for Health Equity Training, Research and Evaluation, University of New South Wales, 2010.

JEFF McMULLEN *Rolling Thunder: Voices Against Oppression*

1. N McKenzie, 'Pedophile Ring Claims Unfounded', *The Age*, 5 July 2009.
2. P Turner, AAP News, 27 June 2007.
3. N Bryant, 'Mal Brough Crashes Through', *The Monthly Essay*, September 2013.
4. R Wild & P Anderson, *Ampe Akelyernemane Meke Mekarle 'Little Children are Sacred'*, Report of the NT Board of Inquiry into the Protection of Aboriginal Children from Sexual Abuse, 2007.
5. Australian Institute of Family Studies, Australian Government.
6. Y Zhao, et al, 'Decomposing Indigenous Life Expectancy Gap by Risk Factors', *Population Health Metrics*, 2013.
7. J McMullen, 'Syndrome X: The Silent Plague Threatening the World's Oldest Cultures', *Balayi, Culture Law and Colonialism*, UTS Sydney, May 2005, <www.jeffmcmullen.com.au>.
8. Royal Commission into Institutional Responses to Child Sexual Abuse, <www.childabuseroyalcommission.gov.au>.

9 M Kirby, Constitutional Law & Indigenous Australians: Challenge for a Parched Continent, Law Council of Australia Forum, 22 July 2011, Canberra.
10 J Howard, *ABC News*, report in *Our Generation*.
11 J McMullen, Children of the Sunrise, Speech to Australian Catholic University, 25 June 2007, <www.jeffmcmullen.com.au>.
12 C Graham, 'Bad Aunty: The truth about the NT Intervention and the case for an independent media', Chris Graham at Large website, 30 July 2012.
13 N Robinson, citing Patrick Dodson in the *Australian*, 12 December 2008.
14 D Gondarra, interview by Jeff McMullen, Darwin 2009, and in film *Our Generation* (2010) directed by Sinem Saban and Damien Curtis. Associate Producers Dr Djiniyini Gondarra, Jeff McMullen and John Butler, 2010, <www.ourgeneration.org.au>.
15 J McMullen, *In Black & White: Australians all at the Cross Roads*, R Craven, A Dillon & N Parbury (eds), Connor Court, 2013, pp. 105–126.
16 R Trudgeon, *Why Warriors Lie Down and Die*, Aboriginal Resources & Development Service Inc., Darwin, 2000.
17 E Wensing, Land Justice for Indigenous Australians, CASS-CAEPR Conference, ANU, Canberra, 4–5 September 2014.
18 D Harvey, *A Brief History of Neoliberalism*, Oxford University Press, 2005, pp. 159–164.
19 Harvey 2005, p. 16.
20 H Hughes & J Warin, *A New Deal for Aborigines and Torres Strait Islanders in Remote Communities, Issue Analysis*, Number 54, The Centre for Independent Studies, March 2005, p. 2.
21 S Cornell & J Kalt (eds), *What Can Tribes Do? Strategies and Institutions in American Indian Economic Development*, American Indian Studies Center, UCLA, Los Angeles, 1992.
22 Hughes & Warin 2005, pp. 1 and 4.
23 Hughes & Warin 2005, pp 11–12.
24 N Scullion, featured in *Our Generation* (2010) directed by Sinem Saban and Damien Curtis. Associate Producers Dr Djiniyini Gondarra, Jeff McMullen and John Butler, 2010, <www.ourgeneration.org.au>.
25 M Kirby, *Wurridjal v Commonwealth* (2009) 237 CLR 309 at 394 [213].
26 J Anaya, Canberra News Conference, SBS News, 27 August 2009.
27 R Kunoth-Monks, Interview with Jeff McMullen, 6 December 2014.

BRUCE PASCOE *Bread*

Bruce Pascoe's most recent book, *Dark Emu: black seeds agriculture or accident?*, Magabala, 2014 discusses the ideas in this essay.

BRENDA L.CROFT *Signs of the Times*

Manning, B. 2002, 'A blast from the past: an activist's account of the Wave Hill Walkoff', 6th Vincent Lingiari Memorial Lecture, Mal Nairn Auditorium, Northern Territory University, 23 August 2002.

Notes and sources

EVA COX *The Intervention: Bad Policy and Bad Politics*
Pat Anderson and Rex Wild 2007, 'Little Children are Sacred', Northern Territory Government Inquiry into the Protection of Aboriginal Children from Sexual Abuse, <www.inquirysaac.nt.gov. au/pdf/bipacsa_final_report.pdf>.
Biddle, N. 2012, 'Northern Territory Intervention extended ... but is it working?' The Conversation, <https://theconversation.com/northern-territory-intervention-extended-but-is-it-working-8005>.
Bray, J.R., Gray, M., Hand, K. & Katz, I. 2014, 'Evaluation of New Income Management in the Northern Territory project', Social Policy Research Centre Report 25 <http://apo.org.au/files/Resource/sprc_newincomemanagementevaluationfinalfull_2014.pdf>.
Brull, M. 2011, 'Destroying Indigenous community and culture', ABC, *The Drum*, <www.abc.net.au/news/2011-12-01/brull-destroying-Indigenous-communities-and-cultures/3704796>.
Cox, E. 2011, 'Evidence-free policy making? The case of Income Management', *Journal of Indigenous Policy* 13, <www.jumbunna.uts.edu.au/researchareas/newmedia/JIP12online2011.pdf>.
Cox, E. 2015, 'What Works – and Why the Budget Measures Don't' *JIP* 16 <www.uts.edu.au/sites/default/files/article/downloads/JIP_16_2014.pdf>.
Gooda, M. 2014, '"Work with us not for us", Commissioner tells Parliament', Australian Human Rights Commission, <www. humanrights.gov.au/news/media-releases/work-us-not-us-commissioner-tells-parliament>.
Social Policy Research Centre (SPRC) 2014, 'Evaluating New Income Management in the Northern Territory: Final Evaluation Report', <www.sprc.unsw.edu.au/media/SPRCFile/Evaluation_of_ New_Income_Management_in_the_Northern_Territory_full_report.pdf>.
Mundine, W. 2013, 'Warren Mundine responds to "$25.4 billion lie"', *The Stringer*, <http://thestringer.com.au/warren-mundine-responds-to-25-4-billion-lie-5330#.VLcgH8v9nmR>.

Further references and sources
We would like to thank 'concerned Australians' and STICS for their invaluable websites from which many of these statements were sourced including speeches and releases published in their entirety.
<http://concernedaustralians.com.au> See below for a list of concerned Australians' publications.
<www.stoptheintervention.org>
Other useful sites are:
<https://rollbacktheintervention.wordpress.com>
<www.aboriginal.sydneycatholic.org/index.php/programs-a-resources/social-justice/nt-intervention>
<www.creativespirits.info/aboriginalculture/politics/northern-territory-emergency-response-intervention>
<www.ncca.org.au/departments/natsiec/advocacy/issues/172-northern-territory-intervention>

ROSALIE KUNOTH-MONKS *Reflections on the Intervention*
For more information, sources and complete speeches see <www.humanrights.gov.au/news/podrights/pod-rights-2011-episode-13-intervention-northern-territory-0>
<http://arena.org.au/nt-intervention-forum-rosalie-kunoth-monks/>
<www.cpa.org.au/guardian/2012/1577/04-nt-aboriginal-elder.html>
<www.respectandlisten.org/miscellaneous/rosalie-kunoth-monks.html>

RACHEL WILLIKA *Statement*
<www.smh.com.au/news/opinion/go-back-you-are-intruding-on-our-lives-and-our-safety/2007/10/01/1191091029279.html?page=fullpage>
A history of the Gurindji struggle can be seen in this short video <www.youtube.com/watch?v=guge6MI6cTA>
Our own facebook page is <www.facebook.com/pages/Intervention-Anthology/748973198484069?f ref=ts>

DJINIYINI GONDARRA *Quotes from Speeches on the Intervention*
<https://natsiec.wordpress.com/2010/08/16/report-written-by-rev-dr-djiniyini-gondarra-oam-on-visit-to-cerd/>

YINGIYA MARK GUYULA *Statement*
<http://stoptheintervention.org/facts/your-voice/yingiya-guyula-liya-dhalinymirr-clan-djambarrpuynu-people>

BOOKS AND REPORTS BY 'CONCERNED AUSTRALIANS'
See website for further details and downloading <www.concernedaustralians.com.au/publications.html>
In the Absence of Treaty (2013)
A Decision To Discriminate (2012)
Walk With Us (2011)
Cuts to Welfare payments for School Non-Attendance, Requested or Imposed? (2011)
NT Consultations Report (2011)
Children of the Intervention (2011)
Opinion: NTER Evaluation (2011)
This is What We Said (2010)
Loss of Rights (2010)

www.ingramcontent.com/pod-product-compliance
Ingram Content Group UK Ltd.
Pitfield, Milton Keynes, MK11 3LW, UK
UKHW041259180426
11947UKWH00008B/571